TEN GREAT LIES THREATEN WESTERN CIVILIZATION

TEN GREAT LIES

THREATEN WESTERN

CIVILIZATION

BARRY HOWARD MINKIN

INSIGHT PRESS * USA

IN-SIGHT PRESS
A Minkin Affiliates imprint
1840 Schooldale Drive
San Jose, CA 95124

This publication is designed to give the author's personal opinion, supplemented by supporting evidence collected by the author's best attempt to compile accurate and authoritative information in regard to the wide variety of subject matter covered. However, it is sold with the clear understanding that most of the research material presented is based on published secondary sources of unknown reliability. Therefore, the author strongly recommends all readers use particular caution before they accept or reject the author's personal opinions or secondary source comments and conclusions about specific people and organizations mentioned in this book.

The author and publisher specifically disclaim any liability, loss, or risk, personal or otherwise, which is incurred as a consequence, directly or indirectly, of the use of any of the contents of this work.

Minkin, Barry Howard.
Ten Great Lies Threaten Western Civilization / Barry Howard Minkin
p.   cm.
Includes index

ISBN 978-0-9792904-0-4
Library of Congress Control Number 2007901341
Catalog suggestions:
1.   Future trends-Belief systems-subtle, false, dangerous.   2.   Western values-Decline of.   3.   Diversity-Problems with-United States.   4.   Left Wing-US.   5.   Right Wing-US.   6.   Israel-Palestinian myths.   7.   Illegal immigration-United States.   8.   Legal abuse-United States.   9. Government waste-Failure of US.   10. United Nations-Bias.   11.   Media bias-Global.   12.   Environmental concerns-global.   13.   Independent voters-United States.   14.   University-Brain washing.   15.   Race relations. I.   Title.

FOR MISS REBA, JAN, BRETT, MELISSA, KIRK, KYLE, AND ASHLEIGH
Also in loving memory of Isadore (Joe) Minkin and Uncle Tony

ACKNOWLEDGEMENTS

As I look up from my computer screen after having put over 115,000 words into print, I feel a sense of relief. I have finished a project that was emotionally difficult and has consumed my attention for too many years. I could not have reached the finish line without the love, support, motivation, valuable contributions, and criticism of family, friends, and colleagues. I want to acknowledge a few of the many caring people in my life.

Thanks to Brett Jordan Minkin, Don Wolfe, Geraldo Jaffe, and the FAIR organization, who were major contributors to specific chapters in this book, and to Arthur T. Heist, Mitchell Levy, webmaster Victor Eydus, Shawn from Digipod, and Natalie from Lightning Source for their assistance.

Very special thanks to Carrie White and Rachel Minkin for editing this work. Thanks also to Jan for all her help, insights, and love. I feel so blessed to cruise through life with such a special woman.

Finally, thanks to Carl, Peter, Judy, David, Michael, Nancy, Abe, DJ, Joel, Larry, Jim, Dom, Brenda, and Charlotte, and the very special Weiss, Minkin, Turk, Lewis, and Eydus families, whose support and love sustain me, and to all those who have fought and those who continue to fight to protect the values that make our country great.

CONTENTS

INTRODUCTION

"Those who do not look upon themselves as a link connecting the past with the future do not perform their duty to the world."

– Daniel Webster (*1820*)

"A great civilization is not conquered from without, until it has destroyed itself from within."   – Will Durant

Throughout history, powerful forces have changed the direction of civilizations and impacted the quality of life for those generations to come. Some of the forces behind these changes, such as wars, famines, plagues, and major technological, scientific, or engineering breakthroughs, were quite apparent to those who lived through them.

At other times, however, humanity failed to see the changes a force was making on society, even as those changes were occurring. The automobile, for example, made possible the suburban shopping center. But as it did so, it eroded core city shopping districts and contributed to the urban blight of empty and decrepit buildings. It enabled us to live further from work, but it took years for us to realize that our payment for that would be clogged freeways and poisonous brown sky.

Even subtler, less apparent forces had significant, though often unrecognized, impacts. Their effects were recognized only by later generations, even when those effects were often greater – either more beneficial or more devastating – than those occasioned by traumatic events. The Dark Ages, the Renaissance, and the early history of Christianity had undeniable impacts on the future of the world and everyone in it, but in the early stages, those who would be most effected by these movements were completely unaware of the dramatically altered futures with which they and their children would be presented.

Today there are also subtle forces at work that will have major impacts on the future. For example, most of us like

1

stability in our lives, especially when it comes to such phenomena as the daily appearance of the sun. So it can be unsettling to learn about the global forces that make our planet inherently unstable and unpredictable.

Such is the case with the earth's magnetic field. Every so often, our planet's magnetic poles reverse position. Compass needles have always pointed north; if the magnetic poles reversed, it would cause a reversal, and they would point south. We can take comfort in knowing that these reversals happen only infrequently – on the average, once every 250,000 years. However, the last reversal was over 700,000 years ago, and the next may be on the way. The reversal of the magnetic compass is subtle and imperceptibly slow. Therefore, it is not likely to impact our generation or the next few that follow.

But this example is illustrative of how subtle forces might dramatically impact the physical world; in this case they would do so by reversing our magnetic compass. This book is about the major impacts on Western values and thought brought on by subtle changes in belief systems and ideas. **Over the past five decades there has been a complete reversal of the world's moral compass. This reversal of values and beliefs is a trend that is having a negative impact on today's world, and will prove to be an even stronger negative force in future generations.**

Being a professional futurist for over 30 years, I'm usually way ahead of society in identifying and tracking trends. Not many things surprise me. But I am shocked almost daily by my dissonance with the conclusions and perceptions I hear in the media about issues, people, events, and other subject matter. Often these opposite viewpoints are poles apart from my view of reality. At times I feel as if I have woken up on another planet, where black is white and white is black.

Indeed, there is profound confusion about such basic dichotomies as what is right and what is wrong. What is true and what is false? Who is doing good, and who is doing evil? Daily media couches the confusion in such questions as: Did Bush or Joe Wilson lie about Iraq's attempts to buy uranium for WMD? Is Jessie Jackson an admired leader or a greedy opportunist? Are groups like the ACLU, Amenity International, and the UN positive and impartial organizations? Is the Civil Rights Movement a positive or negative force? And so on.

As someone who has been paid for over 30 years to be an objective observer of our world, it became a mission for me to understand why my usually accurate view of reality was differing so much from today's younger generation and 'mainstream' media. My conclusions about why the moral compass has been swinging wildly for so long, and my ideas for a corrective calibration, are presented in this very clear book.

I've concluded that today, we live in a period where many of our most important beliefs are simply wrong! Yet, we have a cabal of headline-grabbing pseudo intellectuals, politicians, professors, special interest groups, professions, organizations, and clergy who continually inculcate our society with false creeds. These beliefs are today's idols, worshipped with the same dangerous, unquestioning, irrational fervor as ancient man-made images of golden calves. They have indeed become our 'idol threats.'

The hated Nazi propaganda minister, racist Joseph Goebbles, helped develop and promote the beliefs that the Aryan race was superior to other races, that Hitler was Germany's savior, and that the Jews caused all of Germany's economic problems. Millions of people lost their lives before Goebbles and Hitler were toppled and the threat to world stability ended. Goebbles said, "A lie told often enough becomes the truth."

On the other hand, my late uncle Tony, a decorated WWII veteran, would cock his head and look up with an unforgettable twinkle in his eye when confronted with lies and beliefs that did not compute with his real world view. The next words out of his mouth would always be, **"You don't believe that shit, do you?"**

If Uncle Tony were living today, he would be flabbergasted, as I am, at the lies that so much of humanity believes as truth. There are ten significant beliefs that many of us accept as true that are actually today's big lies. These big lies have been told so often by today's self-serving high priests and the media that the lies have become the gospel for the new millennium. This book will present the scores of small lies that, when taken together, combine to become the Ten Great Lies.

Their devastating implications are spotlighted in the chapters of this book:

Lie 1 – Diversity Benefits the US: Unmasks the lie that diversity is our country's greatest strength.
Lie 2 – The Left Is Right: The Left wing is a danger to society, not society's social conscience.
Lie 3 – The Right Is Right: Conservatives are compassionate.
Lie 4 – The UN Is Not Unfair, and Other Arabian Fables: Discloses the UN as a biased and corrupt organization that does little to promote world peace or justice, and questions basic concepts relating to the Palestinian people.
Lie 5 – Economists and Other Pundits: Why the Experts are Missing It: Highlights the lie that economists understand the economy.
Lie 6 – Government Is for the People: Identifies the people really served by politicians.
Lie 7 – Mass, Not Mess, Immigration: Questions the lie that illegal immigrants are good for our country.
Lie 8 – Justice Is Just: Disputes the fairness of our legal system.
Lie 9 – Media Smear and Malice: Provides examples of how the media's own agenda reinforces global conflict.
Lie 10 – Man Is Listening to Mother Nature: Discusses the refusal of scientists, politicians, and others to tackle the global environmental problems that are already impacting our planet.

Who I Am, and Why I Have Written This Controversial Book

For more than 30 years, including ten with Stanford Research Institute (SRI), I have been paid by scores of organizations all over the world to identify opportunities and threats to their companies and governments. I have been paid to be an objective observer and to always "tell it like it is." This has given me a real world prospective on where we are today, how we got here, and where we are heading.

My previous book, *Future in Sight*, published in the 1990's (Simon& Schuster Macmillan), accurately predicted more then 100 of the most important trends, their implications, and

4

opportunities for the new millennium. I appeared on "Larry King Live" to debate the economy with then-editor Robert Bartley, of the *Wall Street Journal*. One publication, *Critical Factors*, called me "a candidate for guru of the decade."

I predict that if left standing, the ten lies presented in this book will appear in future history books as main reasons for the decline of Western civilization. Already, nearly four in ten babies born last year were to unwed mothers – an all-time high. This year is predicted to be the warmest year in history. Muslim clerics are suing airline passengers who reported what they thought was suspicious behavior, and some schools refuse to talk about the Holocaust, for fear that they will offend Muslim student sensitivities. These are a just few signs of the many problems ahead.

Although I understand that people do not get involved unless personally impacted, and that it is probably too late to reverse the negative impact of the "great lies," I feel an obligation to my beloved country and future generations to help right our societal decline. In the Epilogue of this book, I make some very specific suggestions for doing just that.

I expect and encourage the controversy that this book will engender. Some of the belief systems and high-profile people I pursue have become icons to millions of people. I am quite aware that many of the personal opinions I will express run counter to mainstream thought and the views of many respected experts. Therefore, I strongly recommend that the issues I raise present opportunities for discussion and fact finding.

It is also very important to state up front that I view most Blacks, immigrants, Muslims, students, and other groups as victims, not targets, of scorn. Indeed, my goal is to help these groups by spotlighting and attacking those forces that, in pursuing their own agendas, use these people as pawns on a geo-political chessboard.

I'm also very aware that some of the organizations and people highlighted in this book throw punches in the media and then duck behind frivolous lawsuits and other forms of intimidation to avoid getting counterpunched with the truth. Indeed, I salute heroes like David Horowitz and other truth seekers, who stand up to a conspiracy of legal attacks brought by a new cabal of Islamic, Left-wing groups and academics. These people, through a ruthless campaign of legal intimidation, are trying to silence anyone who criticizes their malevolent agendas. A dangerous trend that is helping to undermine the foundation upon which America is built is when judges forget the First Amendment of speech protection, and allow lawyers to misuse libel and slander statutes. There are a brave few who seek to serve our country by exposing the organizations and individuals that undermine our security and societal values by their words and actions. Lawyers who are no longer forced to follow the First Amendment are being allowed to intimidate and harass the very people who are trying to protect our nation.

How I Work

As I speak or consult with groups around the world about future trends, I find it helpful to explain the trends and insights that have led to my predictions. It helps to demystify how professional futurists work, and separates us from the charlatans and crystal ball set. Let me try to help you, the reader, understand something about how I think.

My strength as a global management consultant and futurist stems from my broadly diverse 35 years of real-world experience. My instinctual (right brain) ability allows me to quickly analyze numerous complex multidimensional situations, though they are shrouded in the fog of confusing times. I then use my rational (left brain) ability to separate out significant factors as foundations for the clear objective conclusions, predictions, and action steps that I present to my clients.

I have an internal computer that has proven over the years to be a valid, reliable, sensitive, and trusted instrument. When something I hear or see feels very right or very wrong, I get a gut (right brain) reaction. Most of the time I do not understand why I had such a strong visceral reaction. Later on, however, my left brain kicks in and I'm finally able to present the logical rationale for my initial agitation.

For example, while watching CNN International one morning, visceral alarm bells went off as I listened to the CNN anchor interrupt a young Iranian correspondent, who had limited English skills. The anchor shoved her confrontational agenda into speaking gaps to get agreement on Iran's right to have nuclear weapons like other countries in the area. She looked over her notes, and nodded her head up and down to indicate 'yes' as the right answer. I grabbed a pencil and paper to record the journalistic offense.

As examples of media and other bias came up, I started to record them, as well as the accounts of others who also observed examples of misinformation and bias. My right brain alarm was going off so often that I felt compelled to organize these abuses and lies in a personal journal, which became the outline for the ten chapters of this book. I apologize to readers who may be offended by my emotional use of the graphic, instinctive, and colorful language that at times surfaces in the text.

As the chapters came together, it became clear to me in an "ah ha!" moment that a larger message was emerging, greater then the insights in each of the chapters. **Simply put, a random series of events and actions beginning in the 1960's unleashed a cascade of negative, unintended consequences that few, if any, people understand or can explain.** *The impact of those subtle events is great enough to have reversed the moral compass of the entire world.*

The generation gap is a consideration raised by my son Brett, who wrote much of Chapter 3, "The Right Is Not Right." I've realized that those of us who are old enough to have experienced the 1960's personally have a prospective of those times that has been lost to later generations, who too often rely on academic and media revisionist presentations. Sadly, his generation never experienced the 'happy days' of the 1950's and 1960's that my generation envisions as America's homeostatic norm. America's thermostat needs to be reset to the values of those days for all people.

But America's values continue to suffer because media bias determines what stories are covered on the news; what is not being said, who is being asked for commentary, what topic, organization, profession, or person is politically correct, and what harmful actions are swept under the rug? Today's generation is TV trained and brainwashed.

Added to the mix is the fact that later generations were too young to experience the Civil Rights Movement or understand its current reversal and manipulation for personal gain and glory. My son's lost generation did, however, experience the rare event of America losing the unpopular Vietnam War. Like radioactive material, Vietnam continues to have low-level, long-range negative impacts. For example, Brett, who is 40 years old, is very aware that his generation, unlike mine, is suspicious of people who are perceived as too patriotic. They also believe that my generation is made up of 'old farts' that cannot be trusted.

Where did his generation acquire such beliefs? He certainly didn't get them at home. I suggest that the suspicion of patriotic flag waving can be traced in part to Left-wing 60's radicals who infiltrated and then used our universities and media as power bases. I am now very aware of how that trend continues to negatively impact our world. But like so many of us, I was unaware at the time of the perverting influence that the large influx of Left-wing professors and reporters hired in the 1970's would have on the belief systems of our kids.

I've concluded that we live in a world where a large percentage of the population has been brainwashed as thoroughly as the Chinese "Red Guard" generation that was lost to Maoist propaganda. The brainwashing has been very effective because many of the people and institutions we have been taught to trust have slowly instilled their views over decades. For example, instead of objectively highlighting the glory of our democracy, the media treats America as a totalitarian pariah whose few faults and problems are continually exaggerated and highlighted by biased, overpaid, egotistical TV anchors. On the other hand, those people and groups that hate American values and try to destroy them are presented as victims who deserve a media platform to spew hateful propaganda

I have identified those individuals and organizations on both the Right and Left that are manipulating,

controlling, and brainwashing a generation around the globe to pursue their own agenda – some for profit and some not. They are destroying Western values and dimming all hope for a bright future.

Try to clear your mind and open it to theories that will challenge your closely held belief system. Please read this book with the assumption that through years of subtle manipulation, your views of the world do not jive with reality. **You have indeed been brainwashed! You can, however, reverse the process, if you read this book with an open mind.** Do you have the courage to check your automatic emotional responses at the door and recalibrate your assumptions and beliefs?

I wrote this book to help move the world toward a better future, and to help right our moral compass, by providing a voice to the suppressed silent majority of fair-minded independent thinkers. Moreover, I have provided a manifesto that will hopefully fortify students with facts before they are subjected to university brainwashing. I wrote this book against the advice of many of my family members and friends, who do not share my views. I alone take full responsibility for what is written. Unfortunately, I have an inner voice that has kept me in front of this damn computer for ages, and will not let this messenger rest until the message is delivered. I have learned to trust that voice, and to do as it suggests.

Be very clear that this book is designed as a platform to express my opinion. This journal of my personal beliefs and life experiences is supplemented by supporting evidence, as collected by my best attempt to compile accurate and authoritative information in regard to the wide variety of subject matter covered. However, this book is presented with the clear understanding that most of the research material presented is based on thousands of secondary sources of unknown and varied reliability. Therefore, as the author, I must insist that all readers use particular caution before they accept or reject my personal opinions or secondary source comments and conclusions. This is particularly true of the specific people and organizations mentioned in this book. Both my publisher and I specifically disclaim any liability, loss, or risk, personal or otherwise, which is incurred as a consequence, directly or indirectly, of the use of any of the contents of this work.

I have collaborated with some colleagues and experts to develop certain chapters of this book. I want to thank Frank Jewitt for his input into Chapter 1, on diversity. Geraldo Joffe's insights contributed heavily to the chapter on the UN and the Arabs. Dale McGlothlin, and the Federation for Immigration Reform, offered input on immigration that proved invaluable to that chapter as well. I also want to thank Don Wolfe for his help on the legal chapter, and offer thanks to my son, Brett Jordan Minkin, and Arthur T. Heist for their thoughts on the Right wing chapter. Moreover, as I scoured thousands of articles, I have added the thoughts and words of many others when they illuminate a point.

Chapter 1
DIVERSITY BENEFITS THE US

We must topple one of our new idols: the misguided belief that diversity is strength. In order to protect our country and society, we must see diversity as the threat and danger that it has become. By using diversity as the weapon of choice, the high priests of diversity have successfully infiltrated our legal, media, governmental, political, business, financial, cultural, and most importantly, our educational sectors. Their success continues to come at great cost to our country's well being.

Many of America's Blacks have strayed too far off Martin Luther King's trail to the mountaintop. They have instead been rolled down the less strenuous hill toward victim-hood. Indeed, recent generations have grown up believing that they live in a hostile, alien nation. Encouraged by their leaders to act like dysfunctional children, many Blacks have learned that they can get what they want by stomping their feet and throwing temper tantrums at all forms of authority. And government has allowed them to do just that, time and again. For example, instead of responding firmly to illegal minority actions like the looting in New Orleans after hurricane Katrina, or the race riots in Watts, government at all levels continues to look for excuses to rationalize the causes of minority crime, poor school scores, and job performance.

Moreover, politicians have allowed the might of powerful government departments such as the Department of Justice to be usurped by minority leaders, for use as weapons to bully businesses and schools into giving them opportunities they could never earn on their own.

In this chapter, I will explain how extremists, demagogues, and extortionists hijacked the Civil Rights Movement and the basic good will of all the American people in order to benefit themselves and to promote their radical ideology. In the name of diversity, we have damaged existing institutions, brainwashed a whole generation of our youth, and silenced public outrage.

PART 1 – WHO IS TO BLAME?

In January 1961, I watched the inauguration of John F. Kennedy, our youngest president ever. He brought a vital energy and enthusiasm that was contagious. His rallying cry, "Ask not what your country can do for you, but what you can do for your country" inspired young people to participate in the world's greatest democracy and mold a new vision of the future. JFK brought the Peace Corp into being, and was immensely popular at home and abroad. He even promised us the moon! But before JFK could lead us to a world of peace and prosperity for all, he was assassinated. For many of us, the killing was a rude awakening from a collective American dream.

My World in the 1960's

I heard the news about the Kennedy assassination while I was working as Employment Supervisor for Coca-Cola Bottling Company of New York. I was devastated because I knew what a rare person JFK was, and that the world had lost a great leader.

As a newly degreed Industrial Psychologist at the time, I prided myself on my objectivity and my professional use of testing and interviewing tools to hire the best people for this NYSE-listed company. After a period of interviewing and testing, I found a good applicant for an accounting supervisor job. He was Black, but I didn't give it a second thought. Perhaps I should have.

I brought the candidate to the accounting manager's office. The manager's secretary said that the manager would be right back. I left the test results, my extensive interview form, and the applicant with the secretary. On my way back to my office, I stopped walking because I heard someone yelling behind me. As I turned around, I saw the red-faced accounting manager throw the candidate's paperwork at me and scream, "When you hire one of them, then I will!" I was quickly learning that by presenting a Black candidate, I had crossed an unacceptable boundary.

The elderly chairman of Coca-Cola rarely strayed from his office, which occupied the whole fourth floor of the building. So you can imagine my shock the next day when this red-faced old geezer threw open my door and stomped into my office. "You're Jewish. You know how to talk to them. Make them go away!" he shouted. The "them" that he referred to was a group from the NAACP, who were picketing the Coca-Cola headquarters because of the incident the day before.

I quickly walked downstairs and talked with the demonstrators, explaining that I was the person who had recommended the applicant, and was ashamed and disgusted at what had transpired. After they understood that I was a recent hire and was attempting to change this ingrained culture, they began to see me as an ally. I accepted their invitation to become a member of the New York Urban League Job and Economic Development Committee, and they agreed to abandon their protest against Coca-Cola.

Later on, at one of the Urban League committee meetings, a problem surfaced. A number of Black applicants had failed a test required to get jobs in the then-racially closed airline industry. Being a testing maven, I asked what test was given. It was the Bennett Mechanical Comprehension Test that I also used as part of my standard test battery. I then asked which scoring scale was used, and received some blank stares. I explained that there were scales for those with two years of high school, high school graduates, and those with a college education. Upon checking, we learned that the HR person at TWA was using a college scoring scale for Blacks and a high school scoring scale for Whites, when both groups had only high school educations. Faced with that information, it was amazing how willingly and how quickly the airlines began to hire Blacks.

The point of this history is to show by example that in the early 1960's, there was real discrimination. Blacks were indeed being discriminated against. Most Black people were poor and often faced discrimination in employment, including the despicable practice of putting racial notations on application forms. (Our government now uses similar notations to promote Affirmative Action.)

Black leadership, at that time, included great people like Roy Wilkins, who welcomed the continuing gains the Civil Rights Movement was making, and welcomed the White liberal power base that was at the forefront of the movement. The Jews, who made up a large percentage of the Civil Rights Movement, felt particular kinship with the movement; their children had also been discriminated against when they applied to universities, businesses, and country clubs throughout the US.

By 1973, I was working as Assistant to the President, for a brilliant, liberal businessman and political aspirant involved in many worthwhile causes, including civil rights. As his assistant, I participated in numerous benefits and committee meetings, and did so enthusiastically. However, at one of these meetings a subtle change occurred that would alter history. Few understood that the hot air being vented by the speaker would mushroom into such a damaging storm.

I cannot remember the date, but the speaker was Stokley Carmichael, Chairman of Student Non-violent Coordinating Committee (SNCC). As he spoke, the crowd, which was split between Blacks and Whites, cheered his fiery rhetoric. I had also been cheering, but at some point became aware of a dramatically different tone and theme.

The focus of the talk shifted to the need for a Black power movement to create awareness among Blacks of their ability to change their own circumstances, without reliance on the White power structure. Though there was some logic to his argument, his tone and words made me feel defensive, unwelcome, and confused at a gut level.

Carmichael's SNCC position paper confirmed his "Whites not welcome here" attitude.

No matter how much money you make in the Black community, when you go into the White world you are still a nigger. Any white person who comes into the movement has concepts in his mind about Black people, if only subconsciously. He cannot escape them

14

because the whole society has geared his subconscious in that direction... One White person can come into a meeting of Black people and change the complexion of that meeting. If Blacks feel intimated by Whites, then they are not liable to vent the rage they feel about Whites in the presence of Whites. This is not to say that Whites have not had an important role in the movement. In the case of Mississippi, their role was very important in that they helped give Blacks the right to organize, but that role is over, and it should be. The charge might be made that we are racists but Whites that are sensitive to our problems will realize that we must determine our own destiny.

Carmichael used the term "Black Power" to label the movement that he was advocating.

While most of the White liberals just continued cheering, my gut and my objective mind were once again telling me that something was changing very dramatically. The bottom line was that many people, Black and White, felt that the Civil Rights Movement was achieving significant economic, social, and political liberation. But some Black radicals, disgusted with the slow pace of reform, decided to speed things up through in-your-face confrontation. Indeed, once again in world history, a subtle new belief system was about to spin out of control with enormous consequences to society.

The Black Revolution
Black Muslims

Among the most outspoken Black people who changed the "civil" rights agenda was Malcolm X, formerly Malcolm Little. He was a guy in trouble with the law. This Black Muslim extremist demanded not only equality, but also a Black revolution, as a response to the oppression and inequality Black people experienced. Malcolm X looked at the history of the Black people in America and pointed out how the country was still suffering from a slave mentality on the part of both the White establishment and Blacks' thinking. Malcolm somehow identified with the Muslim faith, although the Qur'an condones slavery, and Arabs had long been the major slave traders in Africa.

Black Panthers

Eldridge Cleaver made the issue literally black and white. "All of us must take a stand for or against the freedom of your people. You must be with your people or against them. You are either part of the solution or part of the problem." In his book, **Soul on Ice**, Cleaver aired Black grievances against White society, and like Malcolm X, pointed out that Black anger was rooted in hundreds of years of psychological oppression by Whites. Cleaver went on to become the Minister of the Black Panther Party.

Huey Newton, along with Bobby Seale, embraced the teachings of Malcolm X and founded the Black Panther Party, which is when the counter-culture enemies of America began their ongoing guerrilla war. "We have two evils to fight, capitalism and racism. We must destroy both racism and capitalism," said Newton. Their agenda was nothing less than revolution!

To protect Blacks from alleged police brutality, the Black Panthers advocated arming Black people with weapons with which to defend themselves. Cleaver made that clear when he said, "No force can stop us from achieving our goal. If it is necessary to destroy the US of America, then let us destroy it with a smile on our faces."

Furthermore, Cleaver's attempt to destroy the morale of Black troops in Vietnam was a blatant act of treason that was never pursued by authorities.

I am the Minister of Information of the Black Panther Party, and I am speaking to you for the Party, but I want to put a personal note into this because I know you niggers have your minds all messed up about Black organizations, or you wouldn't be flunkies for the white organization – the USA – for whom you have picked up the gun… Either quit the army, now, or start destroying it from the inside… You need to start killing the racist

16

pigs who are over there giving you orders. Kill General Abrahams and his staff, all his officers. Sabotage supplies and equipment, or turn them over to Vietnamese people... You should start now weeding out traitors amongst you. It is better to do it now than to allow them to return home to help the pigs wipe us out.

The Panthers' preaching of revolution and armed struggle was a very credible threat to American society. They were well organized, highly motivated, well armed, and trained. And unfortunately, the new tough talk appealed more to the gut of the Black masses than the slow, steady gains and the reasoned and inclusive work of the Civil Rights Movement. Indeed, a *Wall Street Journal* poll of four metropolitan areas in the late 1960's indicated that a clear majority of Blacks strongly supported both the goals and methods of the Black Panthers.

Their supporters were happy to parrot some of the irrational nonsense of the revolutionary group. Many are now highly paid professors in public universities. Their party line included:

- Exemption of all Black men from military service
- Freedom for all Black men in all jails
- A UN plebiscite for a Black colony, with the purpose of determining the will of the Black people as to their national destiny
- Forty acres and two mules as restitution for slave labor and mass murder of Blacks

The angry Black rhetoric, which can still be heard in today's rap, became the chorus of other groups looking to overthrow the status quo. The Young Lords Party Platform sounded a similar note to that of the Panthers for a Puerto Rican / Latin audience.

In every way we are slaves of the gringo... Our Latin brothers and sisters, inside and outside the U.S., are oppressed by amerikkkan (sic) business. All the colored and oppressed people of the world are one nation under oppression.... No Puerto Rican should

17

serve in the U.S. Army against his Brothers and Sisters, for the only true army of oppressed people is the people's army to fight all rulers... The time has come ... for revolutionary war against the businessman, politician and police.

The unrealistic Black Panther Platform of 1966 helped set the stage for the acceptance of closed and hyphenated groups such as African-Americans, Asian-Americans, and Arab-Americans, who identify themselves first by race, national origin, religion, and gender, and rarely as proud Americans. Our country could now be symbolized as a tattered patchwork quilt, rather then the melting pot that turned immigrants and natives into the steel that built America's businesses and fought fascism. Moreover, as rational thought was silenced by political correctness, the minority squeaky wheel whined on and on, demanding more oil to quiet its shrill sound.

Though the Black Panther leaders were eventually either killed or incarcerated, they managed to inspire many Blacks, other ethnic and protected groups, and their Left-wing supporters, to continue to angrily fight, disrespect, and undermine the greatest democracy the world has ever known. The class warfare and victim mentality that still permeates the Black community spread to the new Left wing, Hispanics, disabled, and Women's Rights movement.

Moreover, our brainwashed children are now being taught to respect and legitimize radicals such as Malcolm X. Malcolm X didn't mince words. "I'm not an American!" he sputtered. "America is a nightmare! America practices slavery! The white man is the common enemy!" Naturally, *Time* magazine heralded him during Black History Month. And let's not forget other radical troublemakers, such as Eldridge Cleaver and Bobby Seale, who are now presented as role models to our brainwashed students.

I have watched with horror as our schools celebrated the schism they call diversity, not seeing that it rips apart the moral fabric that binds us together as Americans. While minority groups are using diversity as a weapon to slice the

American whole into separate, angry, unmanageable pieces, many of us long for the togetherness of the cohesive and proud country that was propelled by the vibrant energy of President Kennedy. He spoke of a new generation of Americans, participating in the world's greatest democracy to create a new vision of the future.

The Tattered Patchwork Quilt

Though Kennedy's legacy and dreams have faded, the seeds of irrationality, reverse discrimination, blackmail, negativity, diversity, threat, and extortion sowed by the Black extremists around the same time continue to sprout weeds. As radical and revolutionary dialogue and action were being introduced and accepted by a large percentage of the population, the whole USA, rather than just a few individuals, Southern states, or specific businesses, was seen as the enemy. I watched sadly as Black reverse racism permeated the North, at a time when we should have been celebrating how racism against Blacks was declining dramatically in the South and the rest of the country.

Part of the Kennedy legacy was his call for Congress to bring forth civil rights legislation. Lyndon Johnson, a master politician fearful of Black tension and aware of the need to eliminate discrimination, passed the Civil Rights Act of 1964. The Civil Rights Act was groundbreaking legislation, aimed at ending all forms of discrimination based on race, color, gender, religion, and national origin.

Title I of the Act guarantees equal voting rights. Title II bans discrimination in public accommodations involved in interstate commerce. Title IV calls for the desegregation of schools. Title V of the Act establishes a government agency, the Equal Opportunity Commission (EEOC), to enforce the provisions that prohibit discrimination by employers dealing with the Federal Government or interstate commerce. Title VII deals with discrimination in employment. Title IX requires equal school spending in athletics for women. Congress also debated the issues of racial preferences and proportional representation. The result of the debate was the adoption of

Section 703(j) of the Act, which states that nothing in the Act "shall be interpreted to require any employer ... to grant preferential treatment to any individual or group because of race ... of such individual or group" in order to maintain a racial balance.

Senators Clark and Case, who steered that section of Title VII through the legislative process, left no doubt about Congress's intent in their statement at the time.

> Any deliberate attempt to maintain a racial balance, whatever such balance might be, would involve a violation of Title VII because maintaining such a balance would require an employer to hire or refuse to hire on the basis of race. It must be emphasized that discrimination is prohibited to any individual.

Like so of the many best intentions, few of us who celebrated the passage of the Civil Rights Act realized how it would be bastardized into a weapon of mass destruction. No one guess that it would someday be used to legitimize reverse discrimination against Whites, or to have quotas based on skin color and race used as a substitute for picking the most qualified person for the job or for admission to school. Moreover, no one could have predicted that Black politicians and leaders of the EEOC, and other government agencies, would misuse the legislation to help them extort business, media, and associations with deep pockets.

It is no wonder that Latinos, Asians, Arabs, women, gays, and the handicapped have expropriated the Black approach to dealing with society and the government for themselves. The US is at war with itself, as cooperation has given way to confrontation, and irrational thinking has replaced logic in race relations.

Solidifying Mediocrity, and Reverse Discrimination

For a brief, shining moment, the principle of colorblind justice was recognized as the law of the land. But all too soon, that principle was thrust aside by the Nixon administration, to make way for a system of race-based entitlement. The critical events took place during the Nixon Administration when the so-called Philadelphia Plan was adopted. It became the prototypical program of racial preferences for federal contractors.

In February 1970, the US Department of Labor issued an order that the Affirmative Action programs adopted by all government contractors must include "goals and timetables to which the contactor's good faith efforts must be directed to correct … deficiencies in the utilization of minority groups."

This construct of goals and timetables clearly envisioned a system of proportional representation in which group identity would be a factor – often the decisive factor – in hiring decisions. Embodied in this misguided bureaucratic verbiage was a policy requiring that distinctions in treatment be made on the basis of race.

This language has allowed a newly protected class to become reverse racists and use fear of our own government's equal opportunity laws to bully fearful executives and administrators. They are seeding their diversity apostles into the power positions in our schools, government, and businesses. They, in turn, follow the party line and hire, promote, and contract with their less-qualified insider buddies. Later in this chapter, I will highlight the Boeing case, where race rather then performance or experience determines hiring and pay grade.

The Bad Guys Are Now the Good Guys

Minority criminals and illegal aliens are now seen as victims that should be given healthcare, schooling, childcare, support, and other benefits not available to law-abiding citizens. Gangster illogic has become chic to the Left. This logic states that we (minorities) are victims of society, so if we commit crimes on society, we should not go to prison. We (minorities) should not be profiled, though statistically we are much more likely to commit crimes. I'm looking at a description of a suspect who stabbed a 14-year-old girl after stalking her.

Nowhere is the race of this suspect mentioned, because the local police and newspaper find that it is more important to be politically correct then to take dangerous criminals off the street.

Because minorities are more heavily represented in prison than in the general population, they contend that there must be something unfair about the system. They do not consider the obvious fact: that minorities commit more crimes. And how sad to watch the destruction of our legal system as the oversupply of lawyers, many paid by our government, try to prove the one creed that all prisoners share – that they are innocent.

Teen Idle

Other blessings to society from the diversity idol include minority pop culture idols that are foul mouthed and inarticulate, with large gold chains, diamonds, and other "bling," and who wear baggy pants that are great for concealing weapons. These losers, who extol drugs, nice asses, and violence while playing with themselves on TV, have been allowed to become role models for our children. Over 60% of our youth say that their role model is either from Hollywood or the sports arena. Indeed, our youth are like Pinocchio who, after a time of out-of-control indulgence on Pleasure Island, was slowly turned into an ass by unscrupulous profiteers.

Signs of our youth being becoming jackasses abound. For example, the most searched person on Google in 2006 was Paris Hilton, the diva of overindulgence and material values. The reversal of our moral compass is assisted by the so-called reality TV shows that, with their crude and distorted presentation of reality, continue to brainwash and pander to teens, who are becoming sexually mature at younger ages. And how about the popular movie Jackass 2, which makes many of the previous crude movies seem PG-13 rated. What has happened to all those consumer companies? They take pride in their social responsibility programs, yet promote these losers, and help them to reach target demographic audiences.

Our Brainwashed Generation

Like the generation of children who grew up brainwashed under Mao, or children who are currently studying terrorism in the Madras' of Pakistan or the Jew-hating classrooms in Gaza, Saudi Arabia, and Iran, we in the US have lost a generation of our children to the prophets and profits of egotistical Black males and their blackmail. Our children have even accepted the growing trend of schools to have separate proms for Blacks, Hispanic, and White students.

We Have Silenced the Good Hearts and Minds of America

Furthermore, the majority of Americans have bottled up their anger and become silent, for fear of saying something that would go against our government-protected classes. Someone who said "say monkey" to a Black family to get them to smile for a picture – a word he has always used for his own family pictures – was fired from his job at Southwest Airlines for "racial insensitivity." A Black professor / rapper, Cornel West, is criticized by the President of Harvard for missing classes, grade inflation, and neglecting serious scholarship political activism; in this case, spoken word poetry is of course played up as a victim, while the university president is subjected to unrelenting faculty and media criticism. Finally, the media called for the firing of a football coach for saying that Black people run faster than Whites because his comment was considered "insensitive and racist."

Wake up, people, and see the growing danger of Affirmative Action, the (Un) Civil Rights Commission, inept, trouble-making and immoral Black leadership, and ass-kissing White leaders. The silent majority must get a voice and speak up clearly, before this un-equal favoritism rips apart the most basic tenants of America.

Frank Jewett is a popular local TV host, community activist, Navel officer, friend, and a contributor to this book. In the words of the late Secretary of Commerce, Ron Brown, he calls himself, "an American who happens to be of African decent." Frank, like most fair-minded people, believes that giving advantage solely because of race or national origin is simply wrong, and the very definition of un-American, even if our own Supreme Court has forgotten the basic tenant upon which this country was built.

The following section exemplifies how and why a damaged belief system is being exploited to our country's detriment.

PART 2 – THE GOVERNMENT GETS INTO THE ACT

The bloated Federal government has unleashed a rat's nest of lawyers, causing a plague that is destroying our businesses and economy. Using its legitimacy as an arm of the Federal government, the Equal Opportunity Commission (EEOC), which grew out of the landmark Civil Rights Act of 1964 and was intended to help prevent discrimination against Blacks, has instead become the home base for reverse discrimination against Whites.

Government lawyers have helped Jesse Jackson and other opportunists successfully use threats and intimidation to achieve large cash settlements and forced employment of Blacks from deep-pocket organizations throughout the country. These organizations are willing to pay off Black leaders and their cadre of lawyers and consultants in order to prevent spurious boycotts, lawsuits, demonstrations, and other problems.

EEOC

The EEOC is one of most dangerous organizations in America. It has done irreparable damage to our businesses, schools, and government institutions. I first became aware of the EEOC when, as the head of Labor Relations for a New York company, I was asked to appear before the Commission regarding a complaint by an employee who had recently been fired. The employee, a Hispanic union member, was let go after several months of the normal grievance process, and with the agreement of the union. His

24

argument was that he was discriminated against because he was Hispanic. I explained to the Commission members that this claim was nonsense, because about three-quarters of our union employees were Black or Hispanic.

The logic of my argument should have produced a win for my company; it was instead a no-brainer that highlighted that the all-minority panel consisted of no-brainers. The EEOC insisted that we had discriminated, and that we must rehire the troublemaker with back pay. These irrational, one-sided, unjust rulings, I was to later learn, were the rule rather then the exception with the EEOC. The legacy of this worthless department continues today.

Protect Illegal Aliens

When Ida Castro, a Latino female, became EEOC chair, it was the Hispanics' turn to swing with the EEOC paddle and try to break apart an American piñata, filled with jobs and cash payoffs just waiting to fall into what the Federation for Immigration Reform (FAIR) called "unclean hands." She quickly sought protection for the undocumented workers who illegally entered the country while thousands who followed the law waited for a chance to immigrate legally. Her policy called for the undocumented workers to be entitled to wrongful termination, back pay, damages, and legal costs. According to FAIR, this policy "appears to be sanctioning people who have unclean hands, people who break our laws willingly and knowingly, and people who are bidding down the wages of all Americans."

Payoff for Not Speaking Our Language

If you're still not convinced that the EEOC should be shattered and swept into the dustbin of history, the following case will change your mind.

A private Catholic university in San Antonio, Texas did a tremendous favor for its Hispanic housekeepers when it told them to speak English on the job – not because the workers learned to speak the language of the US, but because the EEOC then helped the housekeepers win a $2.4 million legal settlement. Note that 71% of the students at the University of the Incarnate Word are minorities. Their tuition dollars now line the pockets of people who couldn't bear the thought of speaking English.

In this case, it didn't matter that it is legal for employers to have English work rules; in this wacko world, the EEOC insisted that there was a violation of the 1964 Civil Rights Act on the grounds that they discriminated against people on the basis of their national origin. Similar language case boondoggles have shot up 500% over the last few years. It is another one of the typical EEOC cases, where everyone loses except the people who should have.

If you are *still* not convinced that the EEOC and the quota business should be shut down and padlocked, the following case might shock you.

Boeing

Boeing, the huge aerospace and government contractor with over $18 billion in contracts, was brutalized by the growing quota industry to aggressively exclude non-minorities. **The aerospace giant spent $1.3 billion on race-based and gender-based programs, to ensure that Boeing's employment policies specifically favor minorities in hiring and promotions.** Moreover, Boeing suppliers and subcontractors must be in the correct race, gender, and ethnicity classes in order to do business with the aerospace giant.

Our bloated, duplicative, wasteful Federal government sends no fewer than three huge federal agencies to monitor Boeing's employment practices regarding selected minorities: the US Department of Justice, the US EEOC, and the US Department of Labor. This virtual army of tax-supported lawyers and analysts combs through Boeing's personnel files to verify the total number and pay scales of each of the following categories of Boeing preferred employees and suppliers: Black, Asian Pacific-American, Sub-continental Asian-American, Hispanic-American, Native-American, and females of any ethnicity.

26

In their analysis of Boeing's "enforced diversity," the US Department of Labor does not take into account seniority or years of service. As a Federal contractor, Boeing must prove to the Federal bureaucracy that it has hired the correct proportions for all of these preferred race, ethnic, and gender classes, and that they have been paid the same as their White counterparts, regardless of performance or seniority. The government also requires Federal contractors such as Boeing to aggressively ensure that people of the "correct" race and gender are their suppliers and subcontractors ("correct" is a code word for Blacks and other protected minorities).

Race and Gender-Motivated Lawsuits against Boeing

Since 1997 alone, at least five discrimination lawsuits have been filed against Boeing on behalf of Black, Asian, and female employees. Boeing chose not to contest the two largest suits, and instead agreed to pay a total of almost $20 million to settle disputes.

In response to a lawsuit filed by Black Boeing employees (Staton v. Boeing), Boeing settled for $15 million in January of 1999. Jesse Jackson figured prominently in brokering the $15 million deal. It has been reported that his various tax-exempt organizations "profited handsomely from his interference." In fact, Boeing Chairman and CEO, Phil Condit, made a point to announce the settlement in a joint news conference with Jesse Jackson. However, on November 26, 2002, the US Circuit Court of Appeals ruled that the method of distributing the $15 million among the individual plaintiffs, as well as the compensation to be paid to the lawyers, was suspect, and sent the case back to the District Court for review.

Women and minorities won a second settlement for $4.5 million in November 1999, in a case concerning alleged pay disparities among female and minority workers. The settlement was agreed to after the US Department of Labor launched no fewer then ten burdensome and contentious audits of Boeing's pay practices around the country.

Also, as part of the deal with former President Bill Clinton's Department of Labor, Boeing must collect and report race and gender data on anyone who merely expresses an interest in working at Boeing, not just the people Boeing actually interviews.

The US Department of Labor's Office of Federal Contract Compliance Programs (OFCCP) analyzed Boeing's compensation data, and determined that some women and minorities were earning less than the median pay scale, as compared to White males in their particular jobs. The OFCCP analysis never took into account length of time on the job or how well individuals did their jobs.

These class actions by minority employees are significant for two reasons. First, the cases illustrate that the racial quota industry is able to exploit huge concessions and preferences from large employers. In virtually all cases of this type, the employer *never* goes to the expense of proving itself innocent in a court of law. In fact, no major civil rights lawsuit of this type in the past decade has ever gone to trial! Second, the dollar amount, both on the books ($15 million) and off the books (over $1.3 billion) is far larger than in other cases.

Boeing's concessions to the quota industry, as reported in the press, are: Employees must have worked at Boeing for at least one year to be eligible for awards, and since Boeing had previously bought McDonnell Douglas and Rockwell, the settlement also included former McDonnell Douglas and Rockwell employees. The Black workers got a total of $6.65 million, while various attorneys involved were to receive $7.7 million. This contested amount is puny compared to the huge off-the-books payments.

Public records reveal that Boeing has made race-based payments of $1.3 billion to the quota industry. One wouldn't be surprised if this was done specifically to keep "Jessie James Jackson," as he has been called, and his gang (Department of Labor, EEOC, et al), off their backs.

A partial list of Boeing's off the books racial payments is:

- $800 million – In the first nine months of 2001 alone, Boeing boasted that it had issued $800 million in contracts and supply orders to minority and woman-owned businesses as part of their "Supplier Diversity Program."

- $500 million was reported for contracts to three minority-owned investment banks that have financial ties to Jesse Jackson's Chicago-based Rainbow / PUSH coalition, for contracts to manage the Company's pension funds and defined benefit trusts.
- $3.7 million was spent for equal opportunity and diversity training initiatives.
- $1 million was paid to the National Minority Supplier Development Council Business Consortium fund, which provided contract financing to certified minority businesses across America through a network of local participating certified lending banks and regional councils.
- $250,000 – For his Boeing intervention, Jackson reportedly received at least $250,000 for his CEF fund.
- $225,000 was reportedly paid to Boeing-appointed Rosalind Crenshaw, a supplier diversity specialist, who acted as Boeing's liaison to Jesse Jackson's Rainbow / Push organization, with 25% of Ms. Crenshaw's salaried Boeing job being devoted to Rainbow /PUSH activities.
- $150,000 – Four scholarships are provided annually by Boeing St. Louis for owners of minority businesses to attend the Kellogg School of Business and Northwestern University, and two scholarships are provided to attend the Minority Business Executive Program at the expensive Dartmouth University.
- $100,000 – Reportedly, Boeing "donates" hundreds of thousands of "off-the-books funds" to Jesse Jackson for sponsorship of Jesse Jackson fundraisers, conventions, and dinner galas.

One such dinner gala, a Black-tie event for which Boeing had paid over $100,000 in sponsorship fees, raised an additional $2.1 million in a race-based shakedown of corporate America to support Jesse Jackson's Citizen Education Fund

(CEF). The CEF is the fund from which Jesse Jackson cut a $40,000 check to his mistress, Karen Stanford, who bore his out-of-wedlock child.

The IRS subsequently ruled that Jackson's use of these tax-exempt funds to avoid a lawsuit was a permissible use of taxpayer funds! This is an example of how the virus carried by the diversity business moves back into the protection of a government agency once it has infected the host company, in this case Boeing.

These companies are paying to assure that they will continue to be ripped off. According to the *Seattle Times*, during Washington State's Initiative 200, a campaign to overturn racial preferences, Boeing contributed $50,000 to opponents of the initiative, who wanted to retain racial preferences in the state. In spite of Boeing's efforts, the voters, by an overwhelming majority, approved Initiative 200. Boeing's unnecessary involvement and support of the University of Michigan's use of racial quotas in admissions is another example of how the parasitic racial preference groups made Boeing their personal bitch, and used their cash machine to push their agenda.

As the Judicial, Legislative, and Executive branches, along with infected businesses and liberal media, try to legitimize these horrible wrongs, other groups also identifying themselves as victims literally begin to follow suit – lawsuit that is. Moreover, the Left-wing / minority-dominated extremists at the EEOC expanded their sphere of influence, making areas such as sexual harassment a profitable growth business for their friends. Their success brought forth headlines such as "Ford settles harassment case for $7.5 million," making it the fourth-largest sexual harassment case in EEOC history.

Business Learns To Roll Over

The diversity business has spread like a cancer throughout many industries. Having a "diversity officer" to assure that minorities get a leg up when applying for a job or competing as suppliers is now the latest form of featherbedding and influence peddling offered by the "un-civil rights" mob offers to their "good fellows." Businesses who unquestionably give the most are called socially responsible for allowing part of their shareholder profits to be siphoned off to these unproductive leaches. The Jackson group's latest target is big oil, including BP, which is a sponsor of the Jackson "circus," but still became a target to shoot at. An exception and another hero is T.J. Rodgers. When Jessie Jackson tried to shake down T.J.'s company, his board originally said, "Don't make waves – go along to get along." Originally, he was going to adopt the "under-the-desk" reaction like the board wanted him to. But after listening to Jackson saying outrageous things on the radio, T.J. got ticked off. He challenged Jackson to a debate about the facts in Jackson's racial discrimination claims. Rodgers offered to hire any well-qualified Black candidates Jackson sent him. But of course, it is not the needs of the Black community in which "Me-first Jackson," as some call him in Chicago, is primarily interested. His close circle, however, does get its payoffs – beer distributorships for his sons and millions of dollars for about two dozen of his closest friends.

Author Ken Timmerman had a number of CEO's come up to him and actually tell him that paying Jessie Jackson $400,000 to $500,000 was the price of doing business. I guess it's cheaper than being involved in a lawsuit, but it is we, the shareholders and the consumers, that are being ripped off. Shame on the CEO's who don't have the balls to stand up against what talk show host Geoff Metcalf calls extortion.

The Mexican American Legal Defense Fund (MALDEF) has immigration reform at the top of their legal agenda, and has also learned that it is good to have friends with deep pockets. Some of the largest corporate / foundation contributors to this Latino organization in the year 2004 were:

- $100,000 – Anheuser-Busch Companies, Ford Foundation, The State Bar of California, University of Notre Dame
- $50,000 to $99,000 – Wells Fargo, AT&T Foundation, Bank of America, Disney Corporation

31

- Other contributors listed on their website are General Motors, AARP, BP, SBC, Ford Motor, and Fannie Mae

With such strong support for immigrant rights, the ridiculous growing trend of having to "press one" to speak English in America may soon be a way of life for our children.

Forcing Diversity on the Media

Having planted people in power positions in business, educational institutions, and government, it is time for minorities to try to get more control of the media. The quota industry egotists would then have more airtime to spread their propaganda and to balance the rare negative media attention. Black leaders get on fair and balanced news programs to launch their transparent tactic of playing the race card as an excuse for unacceptable Black behavior.

We watched as Jesse Jackson called for widespread consolidation in the communications industry, saying that the "re-segregation of ownership" was a threat to democracy, when it really was a natural byproduct of competition, and industry consolidation as correctly characterized by Ken Johnson, the press secretary to Rep Tauzin.

Another Black strategy, when possible, is to bring the lambs to the lion's den. Why in the world did Boeing move its headquarters to Jackson's stomping grounds in Chicago? Moreover, FCC Chairman William Kennard appeared, bearing gifts, at a two-day conference in Chicago that was organized by Jesse Jackson. To rousing applause, Kennard told the conference that he would "complete a proceeding to explore new incentives for minority owners." But as Ken Johnson correctly warned afterward, "We do not believe it is within the scope of the FCC to dictate quotas for broadcasting licenses."

Jackson's Rainbow / PUSH coalition previously announced that it would form a rating system to evaluate performance opportunities at media companies. Of course, one must always question Jackson's motives when he is backed by armies of tax payer-funded lawyer hit men in the

Department of Justice and the Department of Labor, all drooling over alleged grievances about minority employment and job training.

NAACP President Mfume also used a challenging, confrontational style, calling TV programs an "outrage ... a virtual whitewash," because of the lack of minority representation. The need to write in more roles for minorities under court threat is pure chutzpah. How about counting the number of minority players on baseball, football, and basketball teams, and insisting that some Black players be dropped because there seems to be a virtual blackball of White players? How about redirecting the disproportionate amount of NFL philanthropy from Black colleges to White-only universities?

Who is going to stand up to this absurd illogic, and throw this extortion, protection, and numbers racket onto the rubbish heap of history? It should be our government, but they have become so politically correct (PC) that even the Republicans are now adding to the problem. Since President Bush took office, Republican reverse discrimination has only intensified. Bush has appointed an African-American Secretary of Education who had never held office above the county level. When Bush's first choice for Secretary of Labor bowed out, he selected another non-White woman. In the wake of Trent Lott's mugging and downfall, which was hastened by a big push from the Black establishment, Republican National Chairman Marc Racicot will very likely hire Blacks over more qualified Whites from now on. Can anyone say quota?

Where is it written that we must have a quota of minorities, often less qualified, in every segment of business, education, media, and government? What has happened to the concept of equality and competition? The US becomes a very scary place when our basic values are under threat.

Affirmative Action

All discussions of affirmative action should begin with the reading of the definition of discrimination. According to the *Random House College Dictionary*, discrimination is "treatment or distinction based on individual merit in favor or against a person, group, etc."

By promoting a system of race-based entitlement, Affirmative Action is keeping America from evolving into a colorblind society where people are judged by their abilities rather than the color of their skin. Affirmative Action is a system of racial preferences and quotas that denies opportunity to individuals solely because they are not members of a preferred race or ethic group. By locking deserving Whites out of schools to make room for minorities with much weaker records, Affirmative Action exacerbates racial divisions.

Affirmative Action is in fact a smoke screen for discrimination. In Europe, it is called "positive discrimination," but even the judges on our Supreme Court continue to rationalize its use of. "A racially diverse and ethnically diverse student body produces significant educational benefits such that diversity constitutes a compelling government interest," wrote Judge Patrick Duggan in his justification of the University of Michigan's use of racial preferences in its admissions policy.

In actuality, Affirmative Action is primarily a powerful force for perpetuating preferential treatment and discrimination based on race, sex, ethnic origin, or some other approved badge of victimization. It does not assure equality of opportunity, but rather judicially enforced equality of outcome. As Ken Smith wrote in the *Washington Times*, "Skin color quotas are just quotas by another name. Henceforth, judges will be looking over the shoulders of school administrators to determine when the skin color bonus is too high or perhaps not high enough."

Since the University of Michigan's own expert studies confirm that the value of ethnic diversity is slight, the University is just trying to get a racial mix for its own sake. This is illegal. Why should an individual be required to give up a chance to attend a state-run school solely because their skin color is not right for the current racial mix? Recently, an Appeals Court stuck down an admissions plan that resulted in a 15-year-old White girl being denied admission in favor of lower-scoring Black and Hispanic students. It should be made clear that school officials lack the authority to assign students by race to achieve a desired racial mix. Michigan voted for Proposal 2, which would add this language to the state constitution.

> The state shall not discriminate against, or grant preferential treatment to, any group on the basis of race, sex, color, ethnicity or national origin in the operation of public employment, public education, or public contacting.

These words, which were once the foundation of the Civil Rights Movement and our country's laws, are unacceptable to the "civil wrongs" puppet masters, who spent $3 million in their unsuccessful attempt to defeat the measure by using sick ads like this one on Detroit radio.

> If you could have prevented 9/11 from ever happening … would you have? If you could have prevented Katrina from ever happening … what would you have done? On November 7, a national disaster headed for Michigan … the elimination of affirmative action. And on November 7, there's only one way to stop this disaster … by voting no on Proposal 2.

When will young people stop being puppets of the Left wing and the civil rights con men, and realize that their naïve support of Affirmative Action will negatively impact their lives and generations to follow? Why bother continuing an illegal, immoral, and divisive program when the Educational Testing Service expects college enrollment to swell over the next 15 years with Black, Hispanic, and Asian students accounting for 80% of the growth? Will Whites, then the minority on campuses in California, the District of Columbia, Hawaii, New Mexico, and soon thereafter in Texas, become a protected class, and be given all the racial preferences currently offered to other minorities?

Dummying Down our Universities

Education officials worry that the number of minority newcomers will not be sufficiently prepared for the rigors of higher education. How do the NAACP and other minority organizations like the University of California Latino Eligibility Task Force respond to the fact that Blacks and Latinos don't perform well on College Board Tests? They employ what I call a "color the facts" strategy, which highlights the differences between Whites and protected groups.

First, they hire an expert booster, who they know will support their position. The expert then prepares a slick statistical presentation of the obvious. Scores for Blacks, Latinos, and American Indians were drastically lower then those of Whites and Asian-Americans. They then play the victim card and present a series of lame, illogical excuses for the poor performance of minorities that would be laughable if the problem wasn't so serious.

For example, the Director of the *Princeton Review* attributed lower test scores by minorities to stereotypes that result in a self-fulfilling prophesy: minority fear of tests resulted in their avoiding them, waiting until the last moment to prepare, and not preparing adequately. Thus, the NAACP wants the importance of the College Board tests reduced, rather then having minorities compete fairly with other students who cared more, studied longer, and got better grades.

Another reason the minority establishment wants to abolish testing is that exit exams rightly expose grade inflation as a cruel hoax. Just ask Bridget, a Black student, who was graduating as the class valedictorian from Fortier High School in New Orleans, Louisiana. Despite her superior grades, she could not pass a math proficiency test required for graduation. In states without such tests, she would have received a scholarship to some prestigious university. Bridget is not alone; four out of ten freshmen from Louisiana's public high schools must take remedial, noncredit courses in college, according to the Council for a Better Louisiana.

The arrogance and incompetence of today's crop of Black leaders have blinded them and their fellow underachievers in the educational bureaucracy. Always acting the victim to milk the system makes some leaders rich, but will never boost Black student performance. If the NAACP and groups representing Hispanics win the battle and lower the bar, the quiet contempt and stigma towards minority students will be reinforced, as will ideas of inferiority harbored by Blacks and Hispanics themselves.

As Thomas Sowell has pointed out in his article "Patterns of Black Excellence," there is a tradition of Black achievement that dates to well before the civil rights era. From the post-Civil War era to the 1950's, pupils at some leading all-Black schools in Atlanta, New Orleans, Brooklyn, and Washington DC more then held their own against White high school students. This was despite run-down facilities and fewer teachers in some of the schools. Sowell credits teachers' high expectations of Black students for these scores, rather than bowing to the excuses for poor performance, as is often the case today.

As in the past, it is better not to lower standards. Studies show that Black students from low-income families benefit dramatically from schools where standards are set high, more personal instruction is involved, and teachers are held accountable. This was the conclusion of a report issued by the organization Education Trust. The group took a close look at 366 elementary and secondary schools where students performed above average on math and reading tests in spite of poverty levels that qualified them as Title I schools, eligible for Federal assistance. The success factors included teachers and staff who were held accountable and increased time allotted for reading and math.

Texas did a better job than most states in closing the achievement gap between students of different races. Analysts believe they know why: schools have no choice. To earn a recognized rating, each school has to make sure that 80% of each racial group passes state tests. This differs from rating schools using average test scores, which allows schools to focus on higher-performing students. The

Texas system forces principals to make sure that every group of students is learning.

In the end, no amount of Affirmative Action can make up for 12 years of a poor education. Washington, DC is the epicenter of what was once called the soft bigotry of low expectations. Almost two-thirds of DC's ten year olds cannot read with any degree of understanding, and the district sits near the bottom of the national educational rankings. Poor Black residents are searching for change. Several congressmen think school vouchers are the best way to force failing schools to perform better, and give minorities more control over their education choice lives.

Quotas versus Quality in the Workplace

The reason for the decline in the US worker correlates directly to the decline in our educational system. We are turning out high school students who can't pass a basic competency exam. Then we give them a free pass to college, where they double major in Hate America Revisionist History and Hyphenated Studies Programs. Minority recruiters then recruit these incompetents for employment. This is hardly a formula for success in the work place, or for the US to compete on the global stage.

Black Studies

Around the time of Malcolm X's rule, Black students on college campuses were demanding classes that focused on Black history and minority studies rather then the traditional White version of history. This has made it difficult, if not impossible, to reverse the brainwashing going on in our schools or to fire the professors that are using these worthless programs as bully pulpits to pump their delusions of grandeur and one-sided anti-American extremist views at the expense of basic education.

In high demand by our public supported colleges are former Black Panther criminals and Left-wing radicals who, as professors, inculcate our impressionable students with their distorted views of history, making themselves heroes against

38

"the man." This educational system, which makes heroes out of criminals, encourages some of our best college athletes to make gang signs on national TV after winning championship football games. We were recently treated on TV to an overpaid Ivy League professor dressing like a pimp to support of his "brother" Harry Bellefonte's right to call the President of the United States the world's greatest terrorist.

Sadly, the current Black leaders do not have the character or moral strength or earned respect of someone like the late Roy Wilkins Jr. of the NAACP. In an encounter with James Farmer, the founder of the Congress of Racial Equality (CORE), Wilkins summed up the traditional view of the Civil Rights Movement, and how it differs from what is believed today.

> I have a problem with the whole concept [Affirmative Action]. What you are asking for is not equal treatment, but special treatment to make up for unequal treatment of the past. I think that's outside the American tradition and the country won't buy it. I don't feel at all comfortable asking for special treatment; I just want to be treated like everyone else.

The Sorry State of Black Leadership
Jessie Jackson

Jessie Jackson, in my personal opinion, is the worst of the Black leaders. His ego, need for control, greed, and stamina keep him looking for the next mark or opportunity to exploit. He uses his high profile to promote racial division, and to support the American haters at home and abroad for his own enrichment and promotion.

We have reviewed his greed earlier in this chapter, but his chutzpah, inflated ego, and self-serving opportunism continue to both amaze and scare me. He is so obvious as he tries to costume his addiction to headlines, respectability, and money with his colorful poetic preacher rhetoric. This hypocrite, known to have a mistress, counseled President Clinton after the Lewinsky affair. Jackson and Clinton did have

39

something in common, according to Ken Timmerman, author of *Shakedown* – they are both compulsive liars.

Timmerman outlines lies about Jackson's athletic and academic achievements, as well as the spin regarding his actions during the assassination of Martin Luther King. For example, Timmerman reports that Jessie Jackson was not on the balcony when King was killed, when Jackson and his camp have tried to show a picture of Jackson up on the balcony with King. The picture in question was actually taken the day before. It was in fact a publicity shot.

Though never elected, this troublemaker often goes over the President's head to get his unwelcome oar into foreign policy areas. It appears that if he can embarrass the US and get a few bucks while visiting a foreign dictator, like Omar Khadafi in Libya, it is all the better. His meetings at the United Nations with Kofi Anon to discuss Iraq undermined our State Department. His visit to Castro's buddy, Hugo Chavez, provided support for this anti-US radical. Jackson also tried to influence how Venezuelan oil is distributed and priced in the US. He showed up to direct the flow of billions of Federal funds to storm-ravaged New Orleans. Like the Black Caucus, Jackson was quick to assign racially motivated blame for the way the disaster was mishandled. Lately, he even suggested that attacks on Barry Bonds' records are also racially motivated, rather then caused by alleged steroid use.

Jessie Jackson Accused of "Racketeering" by Top Black Businessman

One of America's wealthiest African-Americans, asked by Jessie Jackson to assist with Jackson's "Wall Street Project," said that the tactics used by the civil rights leader amounted to "racketeering." Harold Doley, Jr, a broadcasting executive, rated as one of the country's 100 wealthiest African-Americans by a newsletter covering Blacks on Wall Street, said that he was the victim of intimidation at the hands of Jackson. Doley is fighting the Federal Communications Commission's efforts to block the sale of his television stations.

After initial exuberance about Jackson's stated goal of "making corporate America look more like America from the entry level to the board room," Doley became disillusioned. Jackson, who seems to believe he has an inalienable right to get a piece of someone else's pie, went after the multi-trillion dollar pension fund industry. He sought legislation that would require that 10% to 15% of the nation's pension funds be brokered or managed by minority firms. Doley, like most standup people, disapproved of the methods Jackson employed in persuading the pension industry to aid minorities. "What worried me was the way he operated, dealing with those veiled threats," Doley stated.

He soon realized that Jackson was actually "directing an enormous income from pension [funds]," by channeling them to "roughly ten firms that qualify." Doley doubted that most Americans knew "that they [were] paying and putting money in Jessie Jackson's coffers to the tune of $170 million in commissions a year, 10% of which is going to Jackson." These antics might seem all too familiar to those who have followed Jackson's career.

Al Sharpton

Democrats should always be nervous when Reverend Al Sharpton, infamous New York agitator, takes his racist political circus onto the national stage. Sharpton, who made his name by fueling racial discord, stepped into the spotlight after his one-time mentor, Jessie Jackson, fell from grace through financial and personal scandals. Many fear that if he is not shown the proper obsequiousness by the party, Sharpton will use his oratorical gifts and trademark grievance policies to convince minority voters to stay home. In spite of his history, Sharpton is often used as a commentator on racial and political issues by the media.

Indeed, I listened intently as naïve CNN Barbie Doll Paula Zahn, in her best drama queen voice, seriously announced to straight man sheep-in-Wolf's-clothing Blitzer that there would be a special on the serious topic of racism in America. But then I fell off my chair laughing, when unbelievably, she stated that the two experts selected to discuss the problem were the we-deserve-no respect duo of Jessie Jackson and Al Sharpton. Having people who some have labeled as being compulsive liars, hypocrites, and racist profiteers discuss racism is as useless as plastic vegetables in a soup kitchen. Some people seem to enjoy this dynamic duo, with their "what a racist country we live in" comedy routine, and "I cry all the way to the bank for racial justice" is one of my favorite song and dance numbers.

But seriously, these men are considered by others to be near the top of a list of the most dangerous racists in the country. Instead of having the balls to confront race-baiting hypocrites and profiteers of the reverse discrimination game, CNN bends over backwards to provide perpetrators with a platform to attack the true victims of racism in White America. By legitimizing rather than strongly condemning these two racists, CNN continues to be a major contributor to the moral decline of this country. CNN programs continually brainwash a naïve public into making heroes of the bad guys. By doing this, CNN bears a major responsibility for completely reversing our moral compass and negatively impacting the future of our society.

Representative Maxine Waters

Maxine Waters understood the power of reverse discrimination and cronyism early on, as a legislator in California. I once sent a proposal in response to a request for a small business consulting opportunity. On follow up, I was told I that would have to hire a Black person to lead the project. I explained that a woman in my office would lead it, and it was at best only a two-person job. I was told that my bid would not be considered. Outraged, I asked who came up with this stupid policy. I then heard the name of Maxine Waters for the first time. I asked that she call me regarding this matter, and she did get back quickly. When I explained how unfair and wasteful the policy was, she commented, "That's tough," and then she hung up. I have watched her on cable TV with the Congressional Black Caucus, and was reminded of the French saying what roughly translates to "those who assemble resemble." Waters was in her element with this poor excuse for Black leadership.

The Black Caucus

How sad it was for me to watch as the opportunistic cabal of Black leaders wielded the ax of discrimination with the same frenzy as the White racists of antebellum times. Some of the greedy members, like their White counterparts, nose their way into the free-flowing pig trough of public money to find opportunities for families and friends. No wonder the Bush administration did not want to meet with them. They will, however, get all the pork they want from Nancy Pelosi. Why isn't the Black Caucus speaking out against the tobacco, junk food, and alcohol companies that prey on the nation's young and old alike?

Could it be because Anheuser Busch, Heineken USA, Miller Brewing Company, PepsiCo, Philip Morris, R.J. Reynolds, and Coca-Cola give big dollars to the Foundation, and Ms. Tina Walls of the Miller Brewing Company sits on the board of the Black Caucus Foundation? This "Foundation " provides the Caucus with a way to get its cut of the corporate and Fannie Mae hush money pie for its pet projects.

Talk about allowing the wolf to guard the chicken coup: the Black Caucus will be hosting the Presidential candidates debate. Rather than allowing a true debate that might criticize diversity, which is the very opposite of the togetherness and victimization, these self-segregated, self-serving pork hunters will likely use this platform to pressure candidates to commit to their dangerous PC world, where black skin color counts over competitive performance in business and education.

Representative Cynthia McKinney

Need an excellent example of the Black Caucus attitude? How about the chutzpah of this former Black congresswoman, who played the worn-out racist card after hitting a Capitol policeman? She had been confronted for refusing to stop and identify herself at a security checkpoint. McKinney, like other minority losers, demands respect even while she loses the public esteem by participating in egotistical self-serving actions. Perhaps she should have been identified as someone who had lost her grip on reality, when she began hosting numerous panels on September 11 conspiracy

43

theories, and suggesting that President Bush had prior knowledge of the terrorist attacks but kept quiet about it to allow friends to profit from the aftermath. Unbelievably, she also introduced legislation to establish a permanent collection of rapper Tupac Shakur's recordings at the National Archives, and called for a Federal investigation into his killing.

Representative John Conyers

Aide Deanna Maher recapped allegations that Dewayne Boyd, a former top aide to John Conyers, used Conyers' congressional office to obtain a fake passport after being convicted of fraud, making false statements, and government theft in 2004. Sentenced in 2005 to 30 to 46 months in prison, Boyd fled to Ghana before being recaptured and extradited to the United States. Moreover, Conyers' Congressional aides sent letters to the House Ethics Committee and to the FBI alleging that they were forced to baby-sit and chauffeur his children. Conyers must agree with Mel Brooks, who said, "It is good to be the king."

Lately, Conyers is trying to do more damage to our country by introducing legislation against racial profiling. This plays right into the hands of Islamic terrorist supporters in the US, who play the racist card to try to loosen up security at our airports for their terrorist buddies.

Representative William Jefferson

Court papers documented a videotape of this Louisiana Democrat accepting $100,000 from an FBI informant. Instead, of condemning this betrayal of his office, the Black Caucus and Congressional leaders Nancy Pelosi and Dennis Hastert initially came out in support of the alleged crook, even after the "frozen assets" were found in the representative's freezer.

Senator Barack Obama

Finally, there is the "Great Black Hope," Barack Obama. I like this young man's thinking and spirit. But why in the world would this inexperienced freshman Senator be considered a Presidential candidate? If his name was Joe Smith and he was

White, with exactly the same education and experience, no objective observer would ever even consider him for this role.

Arab-Americans Learning the Game

The Arab-Americans are now learning from the civil rights gang, and realizing that playing the victim pays big money. I recently watched a conference where an Arab-American organization had a Black civil rights lawyer, who bragged about the billions of dollars she had secured for clients. No wonder the Islamists have jumped into the diversity business in a big way.

Another lesson that the second generation Islamists have learned from the Left and the Civil Rights Movement is to maintain their status as a "hyphenated group" rather then to merge into the American culture. Except for a respected and truthful scholar like Fouad Ajami from Johns Hopkins, and Arab-American psychologist Wafa Sultan, US-based Islamic leaders rarely speak up against the killings of Americans and Westerners by Islamic terrorists, or the need to destroy the medieval thinking that many immigrants had been infected with in their former homelands. Our own government reinforces their backward culture by allowing local cable programs to broadcast news in Farsi (often anti-US propaganda) from countries like Iran, a sworn enemy of our nation.

Moreover, Arabs and Persians have quickly learned to use the universities, their associations, and the media as pulpits and meeting places to blame and target others for the evil their brethren inflict all over the world in the name of their religion. Arab-Americans continue to hurt their public image and their adopted country by not having the courage to stand up and condemn Islamic terrorism. Instead, they rationalize or deny its existence.

They have made places like Dearborn, Michigan into press boxes for bigotry. Too often, they abuse our free speech rights by spewing hatred in sermons at Dearborn's mosques. Radical clergy should have been deported years ago because of their views. Instead, they use free press rights for Holocaust denial and to express support for America's enemies, like the lunatics who currently run Iran, and their homicidal proxies, Hezbollah and Hamas.

These groups are just one more example of the subtle reversal of our moral compass, and its dangerous consequences for the future. Inexplicably, however, our "PC" Justice Department encourages the spewing of this garbage as part of the ongoing FBI program to "build bridges to these communities." Where do they think the next terrorist attack will come from? But of course the FBI should not do profiling. Instead, FBI agents will soon be social workers that speak Arabic and carry ACLU cards.

To "build bridges," the FBI has engaged in sensitivity training with the Council on American-Islamic Relations (CAIR). It is unimaginable that while we are fighting a war on terrorism, our FBI is being trained by a group that US Senator Richard Durbin said is "unusual in its extreme rhetoric and its associations with groups that are suspect." It would serve the American-Muslim community and the US government well to review the motives and backgrounds of those so-called moderates who claim to be messengers promoting "interest and understanding among the general public with regards to Islam." CAIR claims, "We are similar to a Muslim NAACP." Many in the public disagree with this statement, and others suggest that the American-Muslim community consider another messenger.

Ex-navy man, Andrew Whitehead, is an American hero who runs an anti-CAIR website. Whitehead called CAIR a "terrorist front organization that was founded by Hamas supporters, and was working to make radical Islam the dominant religion in the United States." CAIR filed a libel suit against Mr. Whitehead. The suit was dismissed.

Media coverage of CAIR's background has been frighteningly scarce, perhaps because of the new Left-wing trend to make flagrant lawsuit abuse a weapon to silence opponents. Perhaps the FBI and the administration were therefore unaware of TV commentator and best-selling author Daniel Pipes' observations. Pipes wrote on October 1998 that CAIR demanded the removal of a Los Angeles billboard describing Osama bin Laden as "the sworn enemy," finding this depiction "offensive to Muslims."

Also in 1998, CAIR denied bin Laden's responsibility for the twin, Eastern African embassy bombings. As CAIR spokesman Ibrahim Hooper saw it, those explosions resulted from some vague "misunderstandings of both sides." (A New York court, however, blamed bin Laden's side alone for the Embassy blasts.)

In 2001, this group, trying to "promote understanding with regards to Islam," did just that by denying bin Laden's culpability for the September 11th massacre, saying only that, "if [note the "if"] Osama bin Laden was behind it, we condemn him by name." (Later on, in December, was CAIR finally embarrassed into acknowledging his role.)

CAIR also consistently defends other militant Islamic terrorists. The conviction of the 1993 World Trade Center bombing perpetrators was deemed "a travesty of justice." The conviction of Omar Abdel Rahman, the blind sheikh who planned to blow up New York City landmarks, was called a "hate crime." The extradition order for suspected Hamas terrorist, Mousa Abu Marook, was labeled "anti-Islamic and anti-American."

True to form, and continuing to "promote" Islam, CAIR backed those who financed terrorism. When President Bush closed the Holy Land Foundation for collecting money used to support the Hamas terror organization, CAIR decried his action as "unjust and disturbing." CAIR has included at least one person associated with terrorism in its own ranks. In 1995, US Attorney Mary Jo White named Siraj Wahhaj as one of the "un-indicted persons who may be alleged as co-conspirators" in an attempt to blow up New York City monuments. Yet CAIR deems him "one of the most respected Muslim leaders in America," and included him on its advisory board.

Some former FBI officials do get it! The FBI's former chief of counter terrorism, Steven Pomerantz, concludes, "CAIR, its leaders, and its activities effectively give aid to international terrorist groups."

Terrorism is not the only disturbing aspect of CAIR's record. Other problems include:

- *Intimidating moderate Muslims* – In at least two cases (Hisham Kabbani and Khalid Duran), according to Pipes, "CAIR had defamed moderate Muslims who reject their extremist agenda, leading to death threats against them."
- *Embracing murderers* – CAIR responded to the arrest and conviction of Jamil Al-Amin (the former H. Rap Brown) by praising him, raising funds for him, and then denying his guilt after his conviction for the murder of an Atlanta policeman. Likewise with Ahmad Adnan Chaudhry of San Bernardino California; CAIR disregarded his conviction for attempted murder, declaring him "innocent" and setting up a defense fund for him.
- *Promoting Anti-Semitism* – The head of CAIR's Los Angeles office, Hussam Ayloush, routinely uses the term "zionazi" when referring to Israelis. CAIR co-hosted an event at which an Egyptian militant and Islamic leader, Wade Ghunaym, called Jews the "descendants of apes."
- *Aggressive ambitions* – As reported by the *San Ramon Valley Herald*, CAIR Chairman Omar M. Ahmad told a crowd of California Muslims, "Islam isn't in America to be equal to any other faith, but to become dominant. The Koran … should be the highest authority in America, and Islam, the only accepted religion on earth."

Daniel Pipes concludes (as should our government, universities, Muslims, and all Americans), "CAIR must be shunned as a fringe group by responsible institutions and individuals throughout North America." As incredible as it sounds, your tax money is being paid to this group, whose abuses are highlighted above, to train law enforcement personnel. The following list includes some of the government agencies that are using your tax dollars to support CAIR's activities:

48

(This information comes directly from the CAIR website.)

- CAIR-Arizona: Conducts quarterly diversity training for the City of Phoenix. Training sessions often include enforcement officials. FBI and local police attended a CAIR-Arizona banquet.
- CAIR-Michigan: Member of Building Respect in Diverse Groups to Enhance Sensitivity (BRIDGES), which brings state and Federal law enforcement officials and leaders in the Muslim and Arab-American communities together for monthly meetings to discuss mutual concerns.
- CAIR-California: CAIR officials graduated from the FBI Citizens Academy, and participated in a dozen diversity training programs for the Orange County Sheriffs Department, including several diversity training sessions for more then 180 law enforcement officers at the Anaheim Police Department, as well as for the Hawthorne, Brea, and Laguna Police Departments.
- CAIR-Florida: Conducted sensitivity trainings for the FBI in Orlando and Jacksonville.
- CAIR-New York: Conducted cultural sensitivity training at the Nassau and Suffolk County Police Departments.

What a great opportunity to spread the CAIR message to law enforcement and get paid to do it with taxpayer money. Remember, this is the same organization that, according to US Senator Charles Schumer, "has ties to terrorists." Americans can smell hypocrisy from sea to shining sea. Do "moderate Muslims" really want to have CAIR represent them to the American public, even as TV ads try to disassociate American-Muslims from the perception that many are terrorist supporters?

Exporting the Affirmative Action Virus

Our Canadian neighbors are reaping the deadly harvest of years of lax immigration and assimilation programs. Recently they uncovered a serious Islamic terrorist threat when they caught 17 Islamic terrorists planning attacks in Canada. All of these homegrown killers, I suspect, were overfed on overly liberal policies, and then allowed to vomit out their hateful speech in out-of-control universities and mosques. Indeed, in 2002, former Israeli Prime Minister Benjamin Netanyahu was scheduled to lecture to a group at Concordia University in Montreal. A large mob of students shouting anti-Semitic slogans appeared and violently prevented Netanyahu from approaching the university, smashing a plate-glass window in the process.

The frenzied mob, the hate-filled slogans, the flagrant attempt to stifle free speech, and the glass smashing reminded onlookers too starkly of old familiar anti-Semitism. But the similarities went much farther. At this university, an overtly anti-Semitic political party had taken control of the Student Council and had outlawed Hillel, the Jewish students' organization, for the first time since the 1930's in Austria.

Is homegrown terrorism a major at Concordia University? Assdem Hammoud, who confessed to plotting an attack on New York train tunnels, has allegiance to bin Laden, and studied for seven years at Concordia in Montreal before getting his Bachelor's Degree in 2002, the year of the anti-Semitic riot.

But when it comes to Muslims, Canadian law enforcement seems terminally political correct. A clueless spokesman for Canadian law enforcement said with a straight face that the terrorist raid does not reflect negatively on any particular ethnic group. You hear that shit, Uncle Tony? Though we hear about Islamic terrorist acts everyday, it is not okay to reflect about the religion, ethnicity, culture, or education systems that continue to populate the civilized world with these losers.

Moreover, ever since 9/11, Europeans have been encouraged to believe that the big new problem for their continent is discrimination, particularly Islam phobia, and a prejudice against the European Union's estimated 15 million Muslims. Unfortunately, the biggest profile critic of ethnic preferences in Europe would appear to be Jean-Marie Le Pen in France. With fascist and anti-Semitic views, he is not a

50

credible opponent of the "positive discrimination trend," as Affirmative Action is called in Europe.

The Netherlands has what appears to be the most ambitious Affirmative Action regime in the European Union. On center stage is the country's wordy "Act on the Stimulation of Participation of Minorities in the Labor Market." It requires that companies and public agencies build their labor forces so that they reflect the ethnic composition of the areas. The Netherlands also has an Equal Treatment Commission that enforces a 1994 law barring employment discrimination based on race, sex, martial status, or workers' political ideas. The European Union is in the process of adding ten more countries, mostly from Eastern Europe, and these entrants will have to meet the European Union discrimination standards before they are allowed in.

However, Europe is already beginning to suffer the consequences of their naïve Left-wing policies, as witnessed by the killings and riots in the Netherlands, where rioters questioned the Dutch country's most liberal immigration policies. Riots in France by Muslims who have remained as a separate culture led to damage in this Left-leaning country. As in the US, Affirmative Action in Europe is an innately unfair policy that will eventually tear apart the cultural and moral fabric of any country that participates in this failed form of social engineering.

Hope for the Future

As I write this book, I'm aware that many Blacks get it. Black leadership would do some good for their people and this country if they embraced the insights of Black author John McWhorter. McWhorter has clearly detailed in his writings that the problems in the Black community are cultural rather than structural. He presents examples ranging from jobs and education to the justice system. He knocks the legs out from the arguments that it is the "system" that is holding Blacks down, rather than their own efforts, or more accurately, their lack of effort.

Shelby Steele is another Black hero who, like McWhorter, will be called an "Uncle Tom" for telling the truth. He believes that America is no longer a racist country. Steele knows that Blacks are indeed free to pursue all opportunities available to other Americans, and that exploiting "White Guilt," as his latest book is called, has been used and abused to get Blacks unbelievable concessions.

Bill Cosby cares enough to act the father figure, telling the truth to Blacks. Is racism the cause of the close to 90% Black illegitimacy birth rate in some cities, and the divorce rates double that for Whites? It will take more than diversity programs to put the Black family back together, and to then educate them on how to succeed in the real world without having to play the tattered and overused race / victim card.

Another hero, Angela Parker, a black reporter from Chicago, did research and discovered that Jessie Jackson was fiddling with the money from the Southern Christian Leadership Conference Breadbasket. This was after Martin Luther King was shot. When Parker covered a Jackson Operation PUSH event after her discoveries, he pointed a finger at her, saying, "This woman has been destroying Black leadership." She was hooted and howled out of the meeting. When she went home, she had to have bodyguards because people were picketing her house. She moved from her house because Jackson unleashed a movement of hate against her, when all she had done was to be a good reporter.

It will take leaders like McWhorter, Steele, Bill Cosby, Condoleezza Rice, Roger Craig, Colin Powell, Starr Parker, and Ward Connerly to continue to tell the truth. I'm waiting for a great celebration of racism's move from the center of White America to the lunatic fringe of society.

Good for us! America is the greatest force for good in the world today. But why tell the truth when it is easier to play the victim, demanding ever bigger payoffs? Resurrecting, perpetuating, and embellishing the racist victim myth is another example of a subtle, amazing, but unrecognized powerful force that is shaping our future.

The Choice for the Future of Blacks is Clear

Listen to people of truth, or continue to embrace the "victim con" perfected through continual practice by a damaged crop of Black leaders. In the next chapter, I will show how liberals play the co-dependent role to the victim / diversity addiction by hip-hopping to the Left wing's "the US is an imperialist and racist country" song and dance.

Chapter 2
THE LEFT IS RIGHT

Mix the confrontational, militant, anti-American Black struggles of the early 1960's with the anti-war movement, the pot-smoking hippie lifestyle, modern-day anarchists, comedians turned pundits, authority-hating liberals, impressionable students, day dreamers, unions, peace-at-any-cost politicians, do-gooders, Hollow-wood losers, remnants of the socialist and communists, militant subversives, ACLU lawyers, America-can-do-no-right professors, graying clergy misfits, and of course, advocates for women's liberation, illegal immigrants, and welfare rights, and you will envision the myriad of faces carved on the totem pole of the new Left that will be toppled in this chapter.

PART 1 – HISTORICAL TIDBITS

The toxic mix that ignited and melted into the new Left in "Berzerkely," California in 1964 quickly mushroomed into a critical culture-changing clash. Cops, just returning from their battles with local Black militants, drove onto the Berkeley campus to arrest a student at an illegal Civil Rights table. Hundreds of students trapped the cop car for two days, until hundreds of cops freed the car. A peacenik writer at the time, Michael Rossman, gave the irrational but poetic rationale for using violence: "We're being roasted in the oven of our culture's violence."

The on-campus radicals quickly drew on the off-campus Left-wing community, as well as the Black Panthers, and laid claim to a section of Telegraph Avenue near the university. The joining of this unholy trinity was another of those subtle events that changed history. There was a palpable and growing desire among the students and their community supporters to claim this piece of turf as the birthplace of an amorphous new culture that they wanted to grow and control.

On April 9, 1967, about 3,000 pot-smoking people, unmolested by police, closed the street and listened to music.

Their laying claim to this piece of turf was accompanied by the shouts of the Black Panthers' revolutionary language, goals, and tactics. The Left quickly adopted this chic gang mentality, dress, and confrontational speech. Looking into my retroscope, this moment in time was still another example of a subtle cultural change that would impact history, though at the time most Americans thought it was little more than a Berkeley freak show.

These idealistic, pot-smoking, middle-class peaceniks wanted to experience new paradigms and to create a more diverse, humane, creative, and joyous community, but they lacked the models for getting there. Across the country, many people experimented with utopian types of communities such as farm collectives, raising the level of free love, but growing little in the way of produce. Buddhist and Hindu-style teaching centers led by self-appointed gurus were also popular. But after the successful closure of Telegraph Avenue, the Left adopted the confrontational Black Panther approach to political action. At that moment and place, the mushroom culture that changed history and our society became deeply and permanently rooted in nonsensical manure. It was painful to watch the cultural vacuum suck up good middle-class kids and morph them into violent, hate-filled radicals.

The old Left wing in the academic community tried to portray the conflict in Vietnam and the establishment at home as two fronts of an imperial war. Beginning with this warped premise, the New University Conference (NUC), an organization of radical faculty members and graduate students, labeled the Secretary of Health, Education, and Welfare (HEW) "a military officer in the domestic front of the war against people." Those heroic academics who disagreed with this nonsense were considered to be elitists who had "sold out" or been compromised.

Partisan political pronouncements by groups invoking the authority of their profession are treacherous exercises. They cast a chill on academic discourse by suggesting that there is a party line. This kind of politicization of academic professional groups is a fairly recent event in the United States, and can be blamed on the Left wing. Various Left-wing academics disrupted professional meetings and developed organizations of radical faculty members like the NUC in order to "join the struggle for a democratized university and to radically transformed society." In 1969, at the American Sociological Association convention in San Francisco, around 100 students and faculty members took over the microphone, interrupting the keynote address by the association president, to conduct a memorial service for Ho Chi Minh, who had died a day before.

The same year, at the annual meeting of the American Historical Association (AHA), a "radical caucus" led by Staughton Lynd and Arthur Waskow attempted to have the organization pass an official resolution calling for American withdrawal from Vietnam and the end of "repression" of the Black Panther Party. Radical historian Eugene Genovese, who had become a national figure when he publicly declared support for the communist Viet Cong, led opposition to the resolution. He opposed the radical call for such a resolution as a "totalitarian" threat to the profession, and to the intellectual standards on which it was based. Genovese defeated the resolution with the help of H. Stuart Hughes, a Congressional peace candidate, who asserted that any anti-war resolution would "politicize" the AHA.

How and When the Left Took Control and the Brainwashing Began

The insights of Martin Kramer in his recent book provide an excellent example of a subtle event that has had, and will continue to have, mind-boggling implications to global society, but slipped completely under the radar of those who lived through the changes.

Kramer's example deals with the subversion of Middle Eastern studies. The way was cleared for academic revisionism in the Middle East studies establishment when the late Edward Said's *Orientalism* (1978) promoted his biased views. Said, a member of the ruling council of terrorist Yasser Arafat's PLO, quickly became one of the most powerful academics in America. Eventually he headed the Modern

Language Association, the largest professional organization of academics, which had 40,000 members.

Months after the World Trade Center bombing, Said wrote an article for the *New York Times* with the revealing title "The Phony Islamic Threat." Said's title summarized the intellectual shift in Middle East studies during the previous decade. The new perspective infiltrating the field defined terrorist threats from Islamic radicals as expressions of "Eurocentric" or racist attitudes by their Western oppressors. As I look up to the sky, I can't help thinking out loud again, "Yes Uncle Tony, these academics really do believe that shit."

Said bestowed academic license on Left-wing professors in the full range of phony, harmful, hyphenated culture departments (Latin-American, African-American, Asian-American, Islamic, and Women's Studies). They then argued that all previous scholarship, including that on the Middle East, was hopelessly biased because it had been written by White Europeans and was thus "racist." **I would advise taking a course in propaganda from Said, because the only area where the PLO excels is in propaganda. (See Chapter 4 about the UN and the Arabs.)**

How about this piece of Said's generalized bullshit for turning truth and our moral compass backwards? "All Western knowledge of the East was intrinsically tainted with imperialism." In one sentence, Said discredits all previous scholarship in the field, paving the way for its replacement by radicals like him. With the help of his Left-wing academic allies, Said's extremist viewpoint created the climate and context for a revolution in Middle Eastern studies.

His views were reinforced by the pro "multi-cultural" attitudes of the university, as well as the racial preference policies in faculty hiring, and the widespread recruitment of political Leftists and biased foreigners placed in history, human resources, administration, and all hyphenated culture departments. They would better serve the university by teaching fiction, since fiction is the basis for most of what is presented by these arrogant soapbox jockeys.

We take back the control from the Left wing cabal of administrators charged with faculty hiring and student admission. Before the Said fiasco, "3.2% of America's Middle East area specialists had been born in the region. By 1992, nearly half came from the Middle East." This demographic transformation consolidated the conversion of Middle Eastern studies into Islamist / Leftist anti-Americanism. Eventually, objective professors with no axe to grind were replaced by anti-American Leftists. Left-wing radicals now constitute a teaching majority in hyphenated programs, and are the major reason that our students come out of universities sounding like Marxist wind-up toys, while those who still comprehend truth and morality are becoming an endangered species.

The Middle East Studies Association, the professional group representing the field, even refused to describe the perpetrators of the World Trade Center attacks as "terrorists," and pre-emptively opposed any US military response. Georgetown professor John Esposito, a former president of the now infamous Middle East Studies Association, made his name by following Said's example. After disparaging concerns about Islamic terrorism as thinly veiled anti-Muslim prejudice, he was made a foreign affairs analyst for the Clinton State Department.

Georgetown University continues to provide a forum for Palestinian and other Arab propaganda. The Center for Muslim-Christian Understanding at Georgetown has been renamed for Saudi Prince Alwaleed bin Talal after he donated $20 million for the center. And while that may be just the tail, the dog appears to be moving away from its historic Catholic and Jesuit teaching philosophy too. Leaders say that the center now will be used to put on Islam workshops fostering exchanges with the Muslim world, addressing US policy towards the Muslim world, working on the relationship of Islam and Arab culture, addressing Muslim citizenship and civil liberties, and developing exchange programs for students from the Muslim world. Although the University has a 200-year history of higher education based on its Christian founding, the Center's projects are now conspicuous because of the absence of Christian focus in the ten-year plan that has been posted on the Internet.

An objective measure of the magnitude of the damage caused by the academic earthquake that hit our universities is found in the fate of the celebrated Sproul academic freedom clause. This clause, written by the University of California president Robert Sproul for the Academic Personnel Manual, governs faculty behavior.

> Essentially the freedom of a university is the freedom of competent persons in the classroom. In order to protect this freedom, the University assumes the right to prevent exploitation of its prestige by unqualified persons or by those that would use it as a platform for propaganda... The function of the university is to seek and to transmit knowledge and to train students in the processes whereby truth is to be made known. **To convert, or to make converts, is alien and hostile to this dispassionate duty**. Where it becomes necessary in performing this function of a university, to consider political, social or sectarian movements, they are dissected and examined, not taught, and the conclusion left with no tipping of the scales, to the logic of the facts...

In July 2003, the Faculty Senate of the University of California, by a 43-3 vote, removed this clause from the university's academic freedom provisions. **The Sproul clause was removed because it was in conflict with a course called "The Politics and Poetics of Palestinian Resistance," taught by a political activist who had been arrested for conducting illegal demonstrations on the Berkeley campus.** This candidate for my America's Academic the Hall of Shame, Shingavi, issued a warning advising conservative students not to take the course – not a history or political science – but rather an English writing program required of all freshmen.

A secondary infection caused by yanking academic freedom out of the university is the corruption within the hyphenated studies programs. As always, the bloated University of California system is among the worst of the offenders. In the insulated playground called the University of Santa Cruz, a group of femmes fatal changed the Women's Studies Department to the Department of Feminist Studies. They use taxpayer money for the recruitment of students to radical causes. I can't help chuckling to myself when I read this nonsense, imagining the brew this covey of witches were drinking to come up with this shit.

> **Employment Opportunities for Feminist Studies Majors: With a background in women and minorities' histories and an understanding of racism, sexism, homophobia, classism, and other forms of oppression, graduates have a good background for work with policy-making and lobbying organizations, research centers, trade and international associations, and unions. Graduates' knowledge about power relationships and injustice often leads them to choose careers in government and politics, because they are determined to use their skills to change the world...**

The politicians and UC Regents who continue to piss our away our money on such crap should be tarred and feathered, and made into a May pole for these "Earth Mothers" to dance around.

The Left Agenda: Brainwash Students by Historical Revisionism

Another subtle act that swung our moral compass around and will continue to have a major impact on future generations was the migration of 1960's radicals into our universities, where they politicized and polarized much of the academic curriculum and administration.

Thousands of members of the radical Left wing are now overpaid, taxpayer-funded professors. Indeed, 72% of college faculty describe themselves as liberal – a figure that is up from 39% in 1984. About 93% of faculty donations from the top 25 colleges went to John Kerry in the 2004 Presidential campaign.

Moreover, only 12% of universities require students to take even one course in American history.

These losers, who I would never hire for a job in the real world, are the role models indoctrinating our children on high school and college campuses. We must organize the forces of rational thought to break into these academic fortresses, which are closely guarded by Left-wing radicals and those who owe their existence to their Affirmative Action godfathers.

"In the first place God made idiots," observed Mark Twain. "This was for practice. Then he made school boards." The decision by the San Francisco Board of Education to abolish the Junior Reserve Officers' Training Corps program (JROTC), which has been active in the city's high schools for 90 years, certainly supports Twain's view. Moreover, in an ongoing effort that will result in San Francisco continuing to turn out another generation of dumb, brainwashed anti-American marching robots, the city has decided to continue undermining our security, culture, and democracy from within. A local anti-war activist has donated 4,000 copies of *Can't Kick Militarism*, in comic book format, to the district.

According to Pete Hammer (who exemplifies Mark Twain's scorn for school boards), who approved it for use in the San Francisco Unified School District, this unabashedly biased Left-wing look at the United States and its involvement in foreign wars throughout its history is a topic that a lot of teachers would have an interest in bringing into the classroom. To truly open the minds of our children, we need courageous teachers, willing to stand up to these Left-wing vampires and shine the light of commonsense. To save Western values and our country's truth and fairness, we must free future generations from the current anti-American, pro-radical syllabus. Parents must question why they shell out a small fortune to schools that have substituted Left-wing propaganda for education.

There was a lot of competition to become the poster boy for Left-wing academics, but we do have a whiner / winner. In many people's opinions, our winner could be University of Colorado professor Ward Churchill, who wrote, among other things, that the people in the World Trade Centers deserved to die on September 11, 2001. They were, Churchill said, "little Eichmanns," comparing them to Adolph Hitler's right-hand butcher.

Others have told me that a close competitor for my off-the-wall Professors' Hall of Shame is Kevin Barrett of the University of Wisconsin. He believes 9/11 was an inside job, and is able to teach his ridiculous views in an Islamic studies course. One might ask how a respected University would allow a dangerous view like that to be taught, when it reinforces and gives credence to the conspiracy paranoia beliefs of too many Muslims and brainwashed Left-wing students.

T. Kenneth Cribb, Jr of collegiatenetwork.org produced some other examples to show independent thinkers how off-the-wall radicals are using our own universities to try to brainwash America's greatness and moral values out of our kids. Cribb mentions Professor Nicholas De Genova of Columbia University, who wished for a million Mogadishus to visit our soldiers and Marines in Iraq. And the eyes of Texas should be on University of Texas Professor Robert Jensen, who says, "The United States has lost the war in Iraq, and that's a good thing," and "I welcome the US defeat … it's essential the American empire be defeated and dismantled." How about North Carolina State University's Professor Kamau Kambon? He has this to say: "We are going to exterminate white people because that in my estimation is only conclusion I have come to. We have to exterminate white people off the face of the planet." Finally, Yale University tarnished its reputation by actively recruiting the ex-Deputy Foreign Secretary / Ambassador for the Taliban for their freshman class. "I could have ended up in Guantanamo Bay. Instead, I ended up at Yale," he says.

Unfortunately, this obnoxious, ridiculous thinking is de-rigueur on our campuses today. The silent majority of Americans are unaware of how radicalized and controlled our schools have become. Hiding in their ivy towers, overpaid, under-worked, Left-wing faculty cabals are totally invested in academic control in order to inculcate students with their distorted view of the world. Our universities allow the hogwash sampled above to exist under the banner of academic freedom,

but these same university fascists refuse David Horowitz'
Freedom Center ads, which publicize important and well-
researched publications like **Big Lies** by David Meir Levi and
What Americans Need to Know About Jihad by Robert
Spencer.

If you still think I'm exaggerating, you will see I'm not
after you read the following example of a failed attempt at
brainwashing. An article written on January 6, 2005 for
FrontPage Magazine.com highlighted just how extreme the
swing has been in our moral compass, and the kind of Left-
wing propaganda to which our kids are being subjected in our
taxpayer-funded colleges and universities. In this case, the
Board and administration of a well-funded, local community
college received a timely wake-up call about taking back
control of a faulty faculty. A courageous student, Ahmad Al
Qioushi, knows right from wrong, even under pressure from
what some might call the "I hate America losers."

Dissident Arab Gets The Treatment
(By Ahmad al-Qloushi)

I am a 17-year-old Kuwaiti Arab Muslim and a
college freshman studying in the USA... I arrived in the
United States for the first time 5 months ago with
tremendous enthusiasm to study the political institutions
and the history of this extraordinary country.

I enrolled in Foothill College in Los Altos Hills,
California and immediately registered for "Introduction to
American Government and Politics." I was shocked by
my Professor's singularly one-sided presentation. Week
after week, I encountered a lack of intellectual and
political diversity that I would have more commonly
expected to hear on the streets of pre-liberation Iraq. **In
this particular class I heard one consistent refrain:
America is bad.**

A week before Thanksgiving Professor Woolcock
assigned us a take home final exam. The final exam
consisted solely of one required essay: "Dye and Zeigler
contend that the Constitution of the United States was
not 'ordained and established' by 'the people' as we

64

have so often been led to believe. They contend instead that it was written by a small, educated, and wealthy elite in America who was representative of powerful economic and political interests. Analyze the US constitution (original document), and show how its formulation excluded the majority of the people living in America at that time, and how it was dominated by America's elite interest."

When I read the assignment I remembered back to my high school in Kuwait. Many of my best teachers were Palestinian: they hated America, they hated my worldview, and they did their best to brainwash me. I did not leave my country and my family to come to the United States to receive further brainwashing. I disagreed completely with Dye and Zeigler's thesis. I wrote an essay defending America's Founding Fathers and upholding the US constitution as a pioneering document, which has contributed to extraordinary freedoms in America and other corners of the world – including my corner, the Middle East. Professor Woolcock didn't grade my essay. Instead he told me to come to see him in his office the following morning. I was surprised the next morning when instead of giving me a grade, Professor Woolcock verbally attacked my essay and me. He told me, "Your views are irrational." **He called me naïve for believing in the greatness of this country, and told me "America is *not* God's gift to the world."** Then he upped the stakes and said, **"You need regular psychotherapy."** Apparently, if you are an Arab Muslim who loves America you must be deranged. Professor Woolcock went as far as to threaten me by stating that he would visit the Dean of International Admissions (who has the power to take away student visas) to make sure I received regular psychological treatment.

This scared me, I didn't want to be deported for having written a pro-American essay, so as soon as I left his office I made an appointment with the school psychologist. She let me go with a comment that I don't need regular therapy. As I left her office, I couldn't help thinking that even my Palestinian high school teachers had never tried to silence me or put me in therapy.

I have since learned that mine is not an isolated case. Many students in American uni-versities are being indoctrinated and silenced by biased professors who hate America. America saved my life and the lives of my family. How can I not speak out?

The local media picked up the story of what happened to me. Professor Woolcock then filed a school grievance accusing me, under Section 5 of Foothill's grievance code, of an "act or threat of intimidation or general harassment." If you are con-fused by this, so was I. Foothill's Dean of Student Affairs, Don Dorsey, would not let me see the grievance as filed but he summarized it for me by saying, "Professor Woolcock feels harassed by your having mentioned his name to the media." As a result of growing media attention I am told that Foothill's Board of Trustees has received hundreds of e-mails. I came to this country to study American political institutions and I have certainly been getting a crash course. I've discovered that, as a taxpayer funded college, Foothill has a 5-member publicly elected Board of Trustees who care passionately about education.

Ironically, as I was going through all of this I learned that California State Senator Bill Morrow was introducing the Academic Bill of Rights to the State Legislature to defend academic freedom and intellectual diversity on California's campuses. As a result of my own experience and the many stories I have heard from other Foothill students, I am helping to form a chapter of Students for Academic Freedom to get my college and my state to adopt this bill. You can encourage Foothill's Board of Trustees to pass the Academic Bill of Rights as official school policy by emailing them.

Ahmad al-Qloushi

Ahmad Al-Qloushi was born and raised in Al-Shaab, Kuwait, where he attended English language school. He became President of Foothill's College Republicans, and is a Political Science major at that college.

As any government and politics professor should know, sending dissidents to an asylum to silence them or brainwash them to accept dogma was a popular punishment used by Russian Communists sadists for decades. In this case, it is the professor that should have been sent for therapy and fired for his actions. Ahmad and others who stand up against this tyranny of minorities and the Left inspire fair-minded independents to learn more about the dangerous consequences of the Ten Great Lies. Independent thinkers must unite and prevail if there is to be any chance of reversing the decline of our great country. Professor Woolcock sent a rebuttal to *FrontPageMagazine*, which I've put after the following David Horowitz statement. The rebuttal is followed by Ahmad's response and my final thoughts on the matter.

Statement by David Horowitz
I have met Ahmad al-Qloushi, a 17-year-old Kuwaiti student who was in this country less than five months when these events occurred and exactly five months when he came to see me. Ahmad spoke English so flawlessly that I thought he was a California native, which is but one indication of his precocious intelligence. I asked him to write an article about what happened at Foothill, which he did and which can be read here. Ahmad's article required no editing and appears as it was written.

FrontPage Magazine publishes articles by writers twice Ahmad's age who are native born that require editing and are not nearly as articulate. The fact that this student was failed (and in an environment of such rampant grade inflation that students hardly get C's anymore) is an indication of how disingenuous Ahmad's professor is in the attached letter. Professor Woolcock is in fact the leader of a very ugly campaign, abetted by left wing websites to destroy a student's reputation. Just imagine if Ahmad was an Arab professor under this kind of attack – the ASAP, CAIR, and the entire blogosphere of the left would be up in arms about his persecution.

One other point, Professor Woolcott's claim that he was solicitous about Ahmad's "high anxiety" is equally spurious. Ahmad told me that Professor Woolcock told him he would send him to the Dean in charge of student visas if he refused to take the counseling, a clear threat to have him deported. This whole episode is a disgrace and an indication of why colleges need to defend students' academic freedom.

David Horowitz

Professor's Woodcock's Denial

I have been asked by a number of news and web based organizations about my interaction in late November 2004 with a Foothill College student Ahmad al-Qloushi. This is my response.

In mid-November 2004, Ahmad al-Qloushi came to see me at my request to discuss the outline of his Final Research Paper assignment in the course: "Introduction to American Government & Politics." He had failed to write the mid-term assignment and had chosen to write his final paper on a topic we both agreed would be a challenge for him. Recognizing that he would have difficulty completing the assignment, I offered him the opportunity to write his paper on a less challenging topic from the mid-term assignment list of topics. We agreed that should he take up the offer, I would not only discount the points he failed to earn at mid-term, but I would also work with him on the outline, and on the review of a draft copy of the paper before he submitted it for grading. Mr. al-Qloushi agreed to do that. However, he turned in his final written assignment without returning for the assistance, which we had agreed on earlier. When I read the paper, it became clear to me that it did not respond to the question.

In late November, after grading all final papers, I asked Mr. al-Qloushi to come and discuss with me the grade. During this meeting, I sought from him his reasons for reneging on our earlier agreement. In response, he expressed in great detail, concerns and feelings of high anxiety he was having about certain developments, which had occurred over ten years ago in his country. Some aspects of his concerns were similar to certain concerns expressed in his paper.

Based on the nature of the concerns and the feelings of high anxiety, which he expressed, I encouraged him to visit one of the college counselors. I neither forced nor ordered Mr. al-Qloushi to see a counselor; I have no authority to do so. My suggestion to him was a recommendation he freely chose to accept and which he acknowledged in an e-mail message to me on December 1, 2004.

Foothill College counselors are competent and highly respected professionals capable of providing professional services to students, and faculty members are always encouraged by the college administration to make such referrals to college counselors as the need may arise.

In my conversation with Mr. al-Qloushi, I did not make any reference, explicitly or I implicitly, to the Dean of International Students or to any other Dean.

In my conversation with Mr. al-Qloushi, I did not make any reference, explicit or implicit, to Mr. al-Qloushi's status as an international student. At the time of our conversation, Mr. al-Qloushi was still enrolled in my class, but after he met with the counselor, he never returned to the class.

I deny unequivocally all the allegations Mr. al-Qloushi has attributed to me regarding my suggestion to him that it might be helpful for him to discuss his long-standing concerns with a college counselor, as I have described here. All the other allegations made are false and have no basis whatsoever in fact.

Professor Joseph A. Woolcock

Ahmad al-Qloushi's Response

My complaint is not about how technically good or bad I am as a student. If I failed that class based on my performance, then so be it. I wrote my midterm but was not permitted to turn it in because it was two hours late. That's fair enough. My complaint instead is that I was attacked for my political beliefs that I expressed in my final exam. I was sent to counseling because I love America, and that makes me "naïve" in the words of Professor Woolcock. That, precisely, is my complaint; it has nothing to do with the technical merits of my essay at all.

Professor Woolcock asked each student to choose what he or she wanted to write. Professor Woolcock suggested that I write on a topic that he himself chose. There absolutely was no agreement that I would do so. Why am I suddenly the only person in the class that is not permitted to choose my topic? If choosing the topic in fact is the problem, why was I the only person in my class that was sent to counseling for doing so? If we were not supposed to choose our topic, shouldn't every one of my classmates be sent to counseling as well for choosing their topics?

Finally, even if choosing my own topic was not permitted, wouldn't the solution be to give me a bad grade? I suspect if you ask the professor, he'll tell you that he doesn't send every student who writes a bad essay or doesn't meet course requirements to psychological treatment. So you see, the facts just don't support the professor's claims.

My essay is passionate about America, but it is not "emotional." Finally, the claim that I was sent to counseling for a war that occurred 15 years ago is just, well, convenient.   **Ahmad al-Qloushi**

70

Final Thought

What helped me (the author) decide that al-Qloushi's version of events was probably more accurate was a quote in the *Washington Times* by Keith Pratt, an English professor at the college. Pratt said he was pretty appalled upon hearing about the incident, and told Ahmad to go through channels. Pratt added, "There was never one hint that he [Ahmad] had any axe to grind. I know the guy and have had many conversations with him about the atmosphere in the classroom, but he never engaged in any character assassination."

The Left Wing Diversity Business Continuum (LDBC)

I believe the therapy theme, though abhorrent in the way Woodcock may have used it, does serve as a tongue-in-cheek metaphor for how delusional some of the Left-wingers and the diversity gang are from the real world. To free students from Left-wing mind control and help them see the light, we need a diagnostic reality check tool. We could call it the Left Wing Diversity Business Continuum (LDBC).

Using a point scale and this tool, the more hateful your views are about America, the more points you would receive. For example, a Professor would get points for hating America, and more points for being in a power position where he is able to brainwash students. Someone else might be in the diversity business, where they could con big-budget agencies like the FBI to spend taxpayer bucks on "sensitivity to Arabs" training. If these trainers know enough not to believe their own "we are victims" propaganda, they would move up on the diversity business scale. If they really believe they are the victims of the US and Israel, they would also receive the "I hate America" points.

Possible LDBC questions could include:
(Please answer yes or no)
- O.J. was innocent.

- Bush is worse than Hitler.
- America is a terrorist nation.
- 9/11 was justified.
- America exploits the Third World.
- Illegal aliens should be given full coverage for healthcare and education.
- Israel intentionally kills innocent Palestinians.
- The UN should impose sanctions on the US for invading Iraq.
- Bush lied about "weapons of mass destruction" to go to war.
- The Patriot Act should be scrapped.
- There should be a Black, Hispanic, Asian, and woman on all admissions committees.
- The Black Panthers and Malcolm X were American heroes.
- Most Blacks are in jail because they are victims of the system.
- America indiscriminately bombs innocent civilians.
- Iraq was better off without American interference.
- Zionism is racism.
- Jews control the media.
- It is OK for organizations that have links to terrorists to train US law enforcement.
- Racism in the US is getting worse.
- An Arab who thinks the US is a great country must be mentally ill.
- American history and literature should be scrapped and replaced by Black, Native American, and Hispanic history.
- America is a racist and imperialist country.
- The freedom of speech of Left-wing professors is under attack.
- The press is being muzzled.
- Big Brother is listening to the phone calls of average Americans.

- Fox News is biased, but BBC, CBS, MSNBC, CNN are fair.
- Israel should negotiate with Hamas even though they have sworn to destroy Israel.
- Iran having an atomic bomb is all right with me.
- Nancy Pelosi is a winner and Donald Rumsfeld and UN Ambassador Bolton are losers.
- We should talk to the leaders in Iran to help us in Iraq.

IF YOU ANSWERED YES TO 20 OR MORE OF THE ABOVE STATEMENTS, YOUR BRAINWASHING IS COMPLETE AND THERE IS LITTLE CHANCE OF RECOVERY

Possible Diversity Business Power Scale questions could include:

(Please answer yes or no)

- I provide diversity training to the government and big businesses with annual gross sales of over $1 million.
- I am a civil rights lawyer and I have brought in over $1 billion in diversity business, including lawsuits and diversity-training dollars.
- I help bring millions of dollars to minority-owned business.
- I'm a former radical who is now a college professor.
- I make sure all professors I hire have progressive views.
- I help get minorities hired as professors and administrators.
- I believe that students must take Black, Hispanic, and Middle East studies only from Blacks, Hispanics, and native-born Middle Easterners.
- I work to get illegal immigrants and minorities with lower scores into public colleges.
- I believe John McWhorter and Shelby Steele are a threat to my diversity business.
- I work for rights and benefits for illegal aliens.
- I am a member of the New Black Panthers.
- Jessie Jackson and Al Sharpton's views about race are good for America.

- We should insist that professional sport coaches have the same racial mix as their players.
- It is not a concern of mine that better-qualified White students are not admitted to universities.

IF YOU ANSWERED YES TO 10 OR MORE STATEMENTS IN THIS SECTION, YOU ARE A STRONG NEGATIVE IMPACT ON OUR COUNTRY'S FUTURE.

America Is Always Wrong

George Orwell commented that the Left-wing intelligentsia of his time was "markedly hostile to their own country," and that what distinguished Left-wing newspapers was "their generally negative, querulous attitude." Nothing has changed!

Today's Left is a self-hating, spiteful group undergoing a mental breakdown. Symptoms are manifest in many areas. For example, there is the spasm of barely concealed glee that "America had it coming" after September 11th, the dismissive attitude as progress in Iraq is reported and chemical WMD are discovered, and the willingness to disclose details of our security programs while insisting on rights for our enemies that give them more protection against surveillance then a common drug dealer. The acceptance, gloating, and permission the Left gives Palestinian violence and the Iranian bomb is one more example of this mental illness.

In other countries, the government, people, and press inflate virtues of their nation but downplay the vices. In the United States, it's just the opposite. The Left would like the world to believe that America stands for killing Iraqi civilians, lying to its own people about the reasons we went to war, being racist in hiring and education, putting minorities in jail with undue process, torturing prisoners, exploiting developing countries, and committing atrocities in war.

Thankfully, the American silent majority can see through the Left-wing media fog of national self-hate. We value being American, and are proud of our country's courage against murderous and deranged evil dictators now and in the past. When it comes to aid, immigration, and equal opportunity, we know that we are the most generous nation that ever existed. We marvel at our country's continuing record of achievements in medicine, science, technology, and commerce.

Provide Public Relations for Terrorists

We regret that too many people in the Arab world live deep in the Dark Ages, where the spark of freedom and humanity ignited by US sacrifices may take years to kindle. While we are offering the precious gift of freedom, self-serving Muslim leaders and cleric perverts profane their religion by sending a naïve generation of dumbshit religious students to blow themselves up using Iranian-made bombs. Rather than providing sanctuary, support, and excuses (like that everything is Israel's fault) for these Islamic cowards, religious / political leaders and media must as I do – strongly revile and mock them as the sick mass murders of women and children they are. But instead, these scumbags (not "shahid," as these criminally insane losers prefer to call themselves) are sheltered and trained in Mosques, where real heroes are not allowed to follow. While the professional forces of the United States and Israel suffer more casualties simply because they both have values that prevent killing civilians who act as human shields, neighboring countries such as Iran, Syria, Pakistan, and Saudi Arabia continue to send an endless supply of bombs and more disposable human containers.

These brainwashed idiots have been taught to believe that increasing the death count of innocent people and killing any hope for all children to live in freedom is worth dying for. I guess any promise of a better life in the next world is preferable to living in their wacko world of veils and veiled threats. I only wish that they were all sent quickly to pig paradise in the next world, and away from civilized people. Moreover, as these low-life criminals commit cold-blooded acts in the name of Allah, they continue to demean their Prophet in the eyes of the civilized world, by presenting him as an accessory to murder.

Meanwhile, a subjective world press graphically presents the number of victims as little more then scores in a bizarre game controlled by Islamic killers to get publicity. More media coverage of terrorist kill rates, coalition troubles, and discontent in the US provides these butchers with unrealistic expectations of victory, directly aiding the recruitment of new Koran-fed, mentally defective bomb wrappers throughout the world.

I grimace as the Left-wing media gives succor and hope to evil people by accentuating negative US images, while eliminating the positive ones. I cringe at the impact and damage caused by the negative reporting of American activities. CNN and BBC chose to highlight for months the fraternity hazing of murderous terrorists at Abu Ghraib prison. Left-wing agitators and fiction writers like the UN and the "Amnesty" crowd ignore the special meals and treatment given these captured killers at "Hotel Gitmo" in Cuba. These child killers never had it so good. I, for one, would have preferred an eye for an eye or, more accurately, a head for a head approach to these terrorists.

The media's subjective coverage that allows their dumb-assed, naive reporters to equate our military activities with the daily killing, maiming, and beheading of innocents by the Islamic fanatics plays right into the terrorists' game plan. By blaming the forces of good and providing cover for terrorists, we can be assured that the world will never have the balls to stand up to the next global menace. Will Russia be pressured to stop supplying weapons to the Iranian eunuch puppet masters and their sadistic Iraqi and Lebanese puppet militias? Will the rich and duplicitous Saudis be forced to discontinue using religious events, like the hajj pilgrimage to Mecca, as coverage for illicit money transfers to the resistance in Iraq?

Provide Cover for Tainted Minority Leaders

Similarly, how can someone like Jessie Jackson be the darling of the Left? This hypocrite's infamous racist "Hymietown" remarks give insight into this "great pretender." The high Black priest recently invited Michael Richards, aka Kramer from the Seinfeld show, to confess his sins and ask for forgiveness on his radio show. It seems Richards used the "N" word as a retort to a group of black hecklers intent on interrupting his act at a comedy club. It was also reported the Blacks called him a "cracker," but of course using racial epithets against Whites is a regular part of the acts of certain Black and Hispanic "comedians." These hecklers, as predicted, were so upset that they hired a lawyer and are looking for a payday and more from Richards.

When there is well-publicized racial tension and an opportunity to exploit it, we can expect Jesse Jackson and Al Sharpton to be there to "search for justice." There has not been much of a search for justice in the media when it comes to Reverend Jackson's past. This paragon of virtue to some has been called a "compulsive liar" by author Ken Timmerman (another truth-telling hero I recognize in this book), and as previously noted, Jackson has been involved in a scandalous extramarital affair, numerous questionable financial transactions, and dangerous foreign affairs meddling. More about Jessie, role model of the Left, follows.

Hail, Hail the Gang's all Here
Gangsta Rap in Chicago, and the Reverend's Songs of Praise for World Dictators

Jackson was closely tied to Jeff Fort, the head of the Blackstone Rangers, one of the biggest gangs in its time. The Rangers were the most violent street gang in Chicago, involved in the killings of more then 200 people. Jeff Fort was eventually sentenced to life in jail for his involvement in a plot that took $2.5 million from Libya. He was planning to blow up US government installations on behalf of a Jackson contact, Colonel Omar Khadafi. Other highly praised Jackson dictator buddies include Fidel Castro and Hugo Chavez.

Did you miss this episode of "All in His Family?" Well it seems that Jackson's half brother, Noah Robinson, with Jackson's help, became a businessman in Chicago, getting lots of contracts from the ill-conceived minority set-aside piggy bank. Robinson, who was reportedly introduced by Jackson to Jeff Fort, was arrested and convicted of murder for hire, drug trafficking, and racketeering, all while role model of the Left, brother Jackson, was running for President.

Affirmative Action

Affirmative Action was discussed in the first chapter. I mention it again here because it is embraced by the politicians of the Left, and particularly by those who support and are supported by the diversity gang.

I received a letter from a "Black man," Ward Connerly, a Regent of the University of California, asking me for assistance. I would like to quote from the letter to again highlight what hustlers, lawyers, and Left-wing politicians use as a basis for reverse discrimination, and how they have hijacked good-intentioned law.

> Dear Mr. Minkin,
>
> The Civil Rights Act of 1964 is often referred to as the most important US law on Civil Rights since reconstruction. We established as law the "civil right" of every person in this dear country of ours to be treated as equal without regard to race, color, or national origin.
>
> Every government agency in every village and hamlet of America thereby acquired the duty and the obligation to make no distinction between its citizens on the basis of the color of their skin or the origin of their ancestors when those citizens interact with their government.
>
> One June 23, 2003, the highest court of the land, with the stroke of a pen, essentially said that the Equal Protection Clause of the Fourteenth Amendment … is meaningless…
>
> I cannot describe to you the anger and humiliation that fills me as a Black man to be viewed with such misplaced pity and misguided patronization. I believe the Supreme Court decision was unjust…
>
> And I witnessed the tears when a young lady with a 4.2 grade point average and a 1480 SAT score was denied admission… And her parents' resentment when

78

they reached the conclusion that the "diversity" objective mentioned in their daughter's letter of denial was a code word for affirmative action…

Perhaps this woman was denied admission because of the insane policy of the California State University system that has recruiters visit Black churches on Sundays to look for Black students to recruit. Yes, Uncle Tony, there is certainly a lot of material for a video called the "Left Gone Wild."

World Government

The left preaches the concept of world governance in their perverted "Commissions on Global Governance." Let me sum up the agenda of world government by quoting from their documents. This commission "has been established to contribute to the emergence of global order…", "…the United Nations will play a central role…", "…regimes empowered to force compliance…", "…an era that responds to the collective will…", "…old notions of … citizenship, sovereignty, and self-determination are being challenged…", "Sovereignty must be exercised collectively … particularly … the global commons …", "The task of governance is … to help those less privileged and needing comfort", "…major changes in economic practices must occur."

Also wanted by the Left:
- Expansion of the Security Council to shift power to developing nations
- Elimination of the Security Council veto
- Elimination of permanent council seats for the US and others, Compulsory jurisdiction of, and binding decisions by the world court in matters of UN concern

Why is the Left so naïve as to believe that responsible people will make their laws and government actions subservient to world governance through the UN or some other international body? Indeed, why change the status quo? We have all the corrupt, ineffective, inept, bloated, biased bureaucracy we need in Washington today without super-sizing our problems by giving power to an organization of losers like the troubled United Nations.

Kill the Death Penalty

According to the Left, murders and criminals are victims of a White racist society and should be protected from being put to death. Indeed, almost every prisoner in the world says that they are innocent, and the idiot Left is out to prove them correct. There are many more O.J. Simpsons out there, who beat the system using lawyer games and DNA experts with a Left-wing, prisoners' rights agenda. Moreover, this nonsense about a lethal injection pin prick being a "cruel and unusual punishment" for these cold-blooded murders is another example of the stupidity of Left-wing judges, who are overly concerned that death row trash not suffer any discomfort for their crimes.

Who is against the death penalty? No surprises, just look for the usual suspects out to promote this Left-wing cause:

- ACLU Capital Punishment Project
- Amnesty International, USA Program to Abolish the Death Penalty
- American Friends Service Committee
- Campaign to End the Death Penalty
- Church of the Brethren
- Citizens United for Alternatives to the Death Penalty
- Equal Justice USA / Quixote Center
- Feminists for Life of America
- Friends Committee on National Legislation
- Human Rights Watch
- National Association for the Advancement of Colored People
- National Association of Criminal Defense Lawyers
- National Black Police Association
- National Conference of Black Lawyers
- National Lawyers Guild

- National Legal Aid & Defender Association
- National Urban League
- People of Faith Against the Death Penalty
- Project Hope to Abolish the Death Penalty
- Seamless Garment Network
- Southern Center for Human Rights
- Southern Poverty Law Center
- Conference of Catholic Bishops
- United Church of Christ

Undermine National Security

The Left were hypocrites when they tried to blame the Republicans for the 9/11 attacks. As David Horowitz, a keen observer of the Left, noted,

> **The root cause of the nation's security problem is that, beginning in the 1960's, the political Left aimed a dagger at the heart of America's security system, and from a vantage of great power in the universities, the media and the Democratic Party were able to press the blade home for three decades prior to the World Trade Center disaster.**

The only places the CIA can recruit the linguists and computer scientists it lacks are America's universities. But the universities have long since become the political home base of a Left that has not given up its fantasies of social revolution and deep hatred of America and its purposes.

Using frivolous lawsuits with hopes to get some bloated fees is standard ACLU practice. These cases (including their latest attempt to make a mountain out of a mole hill – NSA phone surveillance) clog up our courts, cost taxpayers millions, and seriously undermine national security. The ACLU bulldog has even initiated a series of lawsuits against former Secretary of Defense Rumsfeld (by far the best Secretary of Defense this country has ever had) and his top Generals.

It was the Left that for years slashed the military. While Defense Department budget cuts forced military families to go

81

on food stamps, the DOD was spending enormous amounts of money to re-equip ships and barracks for co-ed living. In addition, "consciousness raising" classes regarding gender, diversity reform, and rigging physical standards for women helped undermine moral and the merit-based benchmarks that are crucial for fielding the best fighting force available.

The Left dissected the CIA and then blamed it for 9/11 intelligence failures. African-American, and Leftist, Ron Delliums, the top Democrat on the Armed Services Committee from 1993 to 1997, cast all eight funding cut amendments for less intelligence funding. He pushed to get Barbara Lee, his "protégé" and Left-wing, Black Caucus loser, elected for his Berzerkly, California seat. Nancy Pelosi, the current speaker of Democrat-controlled Congress, voted to cut intelligence funding three times, even though she herself was a member of the Intelligence Committee. They also opposed the projection of military power into terrorist regions like Afghanistan and Iraq.

The hypocrites and proponents of the political Left are still putting our security at risk by opposing essential defense measures like wiretaps of terrorist suspects, detaining them, or imposing immigration controls. They keep us in danger by rejecting airport security that is based on racial profiling. Based on statistical information as to who commits terrorist crimes, it is foolish to stop and search an 80-year-old, White grandma while an Arab in his 20's walks on past unquestioned. But I can see why Black and Hispanic politicians do not want racial profiling, when Blacks and Latinos commit such a high percentage of crime in the US.

In his worst nightmare, Uncle Tony could never have imagined people in the US during WWII driving around with bumper stickers reading "hands off Germany and Japan." But the Left's latest bumper stickers, "Hands off Syria and Iran," unfortunately suggest that the Left in our own country will continue to protect the world's worst terrorist states and the sworn enemies of our country while they attack America. The Left should not be seen as Hollywood or Berkeley chic, but a dangerous, negative force, subverting our country's security and reputation without a constructive "real world" idea of their own. No wonder Democrats show up high on groups suffering from depression.

Worship the Principle of Sovereignty

The Left teaches us not to trust government, and that government exists primarily to serve the rich and powerful. In spite of their distrust, the Left also worships the principle of sovereignty, which means that every government respects the right of other governments to do, with impunity, whatever they want to do to the people inside their borders. The Left believes that even though the leader of a country can be a complete lunatic (killing hundreds of thousands of their own people, as was the case in Iraq, and is the case in North Korea), we must respect that person and his government's right to exist.

Graying Out Evil

The Left sees evil in terms of shades of gray when it comes to issues like terrorism, which they believe is the result of victimization and occupation. Terrorists are often called freedom fighters. People like bin Laden and Arafat, and organizations like Hamas, are seen as complex. They may sometimes do evil things, but they are always excused by the Left as justifiable. These killers of innocent people are never seen by the Left as purely evil people. It is embarrassing to listen to the Left-wing intelligentsia like Jimmy Carter, the latest Southern Baptist propaganda minister for the terrorist enclave called Palestine, coolly and calmly give logical, well-thought-out, but misleading and factually wrong, reasons for every terrorist thought and action. It is infuriating that Left-wing media allows Carter to perform his one-sided Sunday school sermons that try to obscure the simple truth that these terrorists, like his late buddy Yassir Arafat, represent the very essence of evil.

Indeed for the Left, the only truly bad, evil people are people on the Right, who they see in black and white terms. Not even the President of the US or the former Secretary of Defense have any redeeming qualities, and, when compared to bin Laden, are seen as the real terrorists. Some Leftists have gone so far as to say the people killed indiscriminately in the World Trade Center were not innocent victims, however those Iraqis killed accidentally while the US fights terrorists are.

Support Labor Unions

There are rare occasions when a traditionally Left misperception is made right by one of their own. Here's an example shared by contributor Don Wolfe.

Perhaps one of the reasons why America prospers and her hard-working people enjoy the liberties and bounty of our gifted land is due to the keen patriotism of some of those chosen to lead the American labor movement.

One of these men for whom I have high respect is George Meany (1894 -1980), who was elected as national president of the AFL / CIO in 1955. Meany was a major factor in merging the American Federation of Labor (AF of L) and the Congress of Industrial Organizations (CIO).

My father, William F. Wolfe, Sr., told my brothers and me about an incident that is not well known but that he witnessed first hand. My father met Meany when they were both local labor leaders in New York City in the 40' and 50's. Meany, a native of the Bronx, had been president of the Plumbers Union and my father was a leader of local #891 of the Operating Engineers Union – a part of the New York City Board of Education Bureau of Plant Operations and Maintenance.

What impressed my father about Meany was the insight that he held and expressed about the special nature of America.

In a meeting of a small group of local labor leaders that my father attended with Mr. Meany came this story. Meany, then president of the national AFL / CIO, was regarded – and accurately so – as the top leader of the labor movement in the United States. As such, he was invited all over the world to meet with and

84

have discussions with national labor leaders from various countries. He enjoyed that role and was pleased to do so.

While on these visits, he observed that the leader of workers in Italy, for example, was the chairman of a major political group known as the Labor Party, and was an avowed Communist. In France it was the same thing. In England, it was the Labor Party that represented those who toiled by the sweat of their brow and its leader was a Socialist. Each of these men urged Meany to join in humming "The International," the anthem of the communists and socialists, and become a Marxist brother.

But Meany told my father and his fellow New York union leaders that he answered by refusing and asked, "Why should I?" His reasoning was that American workers are the best-paid workers in the world; they are the best-fed and freest workers on earth. They have more opportunity then others around the world. And why? It is because of the free enterprise system. "Why should I," he asked, "endeavor to overthrow it? Why not strengthen it – get our fair share of it and its benefits, of course. But why destroy free enterprise? We're Americans! Let's keep it and thrive."

So this was the patriotism of a plumber from the Bronx that kept the American labor movement from drifting too far to the Left. I wish the current crop of labor leaders had similar convictions and intelligence.

As time went on, Meany became even more dedicated as an anti-Leftist. He defied the union tradition of supporting Democrats when he refused to support George McGovern's 1972 presidential candidacy, precisely because of McGovern's Left leanings.

Labor unions simply should not be allowed in public sectors such as education, police, and fire fighting. These unions pose a long-term economic danger to the communities that do not have enough politicians to stand up to those overpaid, overstaffed union members.

Moreover, in San Jose, where a back-door garbage deal got the mayor in trouble, the teamsters employed by the current waste contractor told companies who wanted to bid for the next contract that they must include the same benefits in their bids with the city "to assure labor peace." This smells of extortion, and reminds me of the threats made by mob-related unions in the past. This kind of nonsense must be stopped. Hopefully, the mayor and the contractor in this case will be persecuted to the full extent of the law.

Develop Anti-American Coalitions

The strange new anti-American coalition of godless Leftists and Islamic radicals, who believe God is a procurer of virgins and bombs, is a clear and present threat to Western civilization. As a futurist, I cringe as a cabal of European, Spanish, African Union, US Islamic, and Leftist leaders voice support for Hamas, Hezbollah, Chavez, and Ahmadinejad. Indeed, pictures of Chavez are hanging alongside Hezbollah leader Nasrallah in the Middle East. It is insanity to support people who are like growing tumors that slowly destroy the very values of western civilization.

PART 2 – LEFT-WING MYTHS

"The trouble with our liberal friends is not that they're ignorant; it's just that they know so much that isn't so."
– Ronald Reagan

Myth – The Industrial Military Complex Is the Reason We Went to War in Vietnam

The Left masses know little of the workings of the military or big business. They naively believed that US business interests got us into the Vietnam War, rather than the communist North Vietnam attempting to take over capitalistic South Vietnam. These drama queens love to hear their own colorful crude rhetoric, the rap of that time. One self-described American terrorist, named "Revolutionary Force 9," called companies like IBM, GTE, and Mobil Oil "enemies of life" that made profits from the suffering and death of human beings. He goes on to say,

They profit from the racist oppression of Black, Puerto-Rican, and other minority colonies outside Amerika (sic), from the suffering and death of men in the America army, from sexism, from exploitation and degradation of employees forced into lives of anti-human work.

Today this dialogue, which belongs in a Saturday Night Live skit, can still be heard regularly at rallies in San Francisco, Beirut, Berkeley, and throughout Europe. Indeed, community activists, teachers, politicians, union organizers, and others who pander to the Left wing keep this nonsense alive.

Like so many things in life, people who are on the outside of a group often have mistaken perceptions about the people and activities within the group. This is especially dangerous and misleading to those who depend on activists, politicians, teachers, and talking heads that haven't spent any time working with either the military or industry for enlightenment.

For over three decades, I have consulted for scores of companies, as well as the Department of Defense and other government agencies. I was always paid to be an objective observer and speak the truth, no matter how detrimental it was to the organization. In one case, I told the members of a Board of Directors who already spent $4 billion on a project that the project was completely unnecessary. The point is that I have no axe to grind when I say that for the most part, the people I have met within the military industrial complex have been people of the highest moral integrity, intelligence, and foresight, and certainly would never promote war for profit. Nor would they go to war just to control Iraq's oil fields.

The strategic vision of Donald Rumsfeld and Paul Wolfovitz to re-create the military has been brilliant, in spite of the Left wing, the media, generals without vision, and the dead-enders in our own military. If you were privy to the strategic vision, as I was when I was invited to participate in an Office of the Secretary of Defense (OSD) seminar titled the "Future of War," you would understand that there was an urgent need to modernize our armed forces and move thinking away from the Cold War battle of giants toward creating the lean, mean, custom fighting machine that rolled across Iraq.

Politicians, media, and military personnel concerned with their own special interests have been fighting the changes. They use the fact that there have been more casualties in the occupation phase than in the active phase of the Iraqi war as an argument for the failure of the war, rather than focusing on the fact that there was a historically low number of casualties in the active phase. The Left and the old guard military are, of course, not accountable for their predictions of tens of thousands of casualties expected during the initial phase of the war. Our country is weaker because naïve Leftist forces just "do not get it." Because of this, they ended up pressuring the best Secretary of Defense in our nation's history to resign.

Myth – Bush Lied About WMD to Take Us to War

Every intelligence organization in the whole world, and most of "Sodamn Insane's" own top military officers thought that Sodamn (who is now thankfully always at ambient temperature) was telling the truth when he repeatedly threatened to use his weapons of mass destruction. After all, he did use WMD against the Kurds, and over 500 containers of WMD were found as recently unclassified documents were disclosed. Bush didn't lie; Sodamn lied, and ended up caught in a rat hole because of it. In fact, Bush is a very moral man, who is not a liar, while the Left's heroes, Jessie Jackson and Bill "I never had sex with that woman" Clinton, are compulsive lairs. But facts never disturb the Left, as they continue to lie and slander our President with help from the media hyenas. Here is another clear example.

Joe Wilson's cover Is Blown – He, Not Bush, Is the Liar

This Left-wing speaking circuit junkie claimed to be a truth teller, a whistle blower, and a victim of a Right-wing conspiracy. The Left-wing media of course bought and promoted this crap. In this case, **a bipartisan Senate Intelligence Committee report concluded that former Ambassador Joseph C. Wilson had been telling lies.**

For openers, Wilson insisted that his wife, CIA employee Valerie Plame, was not the one who came up with the brilliant idea that the agency send him to Niger to investigate whether "Sodamn Insane" had been attempting to acquire uranium. "Valerie had nothing to do with the matter," Wilson says in his book. "She definitely had not proposed that I make the trip." In fact, the Senate panel found, she was the one who got him the assignment. The panel even found a memo from her.

This dandy enjoyed his wife's free junket present and some government spending money. After all, this is a guy who couldn't get further in our foreign service then the jungles of Gabon, considered a diplomatic backwater for those going backwards in their careers. Joe was indeed qualified to sit on his ass for eight days "drinking sweet mint tea and meeting with dozens of people." On the basis of this "in-depth investigation," he confidently concluded that there was no way Sodamn sought uranium from Africa. Wilson didn't bother to write a report, but gave an oral briefing instead. Moreover, he was not required to keep his mission or conclusions confidential, and was happy to write an op-ed for the *New York Times*, charging the Bush administration with "twisting," "manipulating," and "exaggerating" intelligence about Iraq's weapons program to "justify invasion." In particular, he said that President Bush was lying when, in his 2003 State of the Union address, he pronounced these words: "The British government has learned that Saddam Hussein recently sought significant quantities of uranium from Africa."

We now know for certain that Wilson was wrong and that Bush's statement was entirely accurate.

Though not covered by the media, the British consistently stood by that conclusion. In September 2003, an independent British parliamentary committee looked into the matter and determined that the claim made by British intelligence was "reasonable." British spies stand by their claim to this day. Moreover, French Intelligence also reported an Iraqi attempt to procure uranium from Niger.

Even the *Financial Times* (*FT*) has reported that illicit sales of uranium from Niger were indeed being negotiated with Iraq, as well as four other states. *FT* reported that

> European intelligence officers have now revealed that
> three years before the fake documents became public

[there were forgeries planted probably as a ruse to discredit the story of a Niger-Iraq link], human and electronic intelligence sources from a number of countries picked up repeated discussion of an illicit trade in uranium from Niger. One of the customers discussed by the traders was Iraq.

Lying Joe, the poor little rich boy victim, whose nose keeps growing, was again caught in a lie. As reported in the *Washington Post*, **"Contrary to Wilson's assertions and even the government's previous statements, the CIA did not tell the White House it had qualms about the reliability of the Africa intelligence."** The Senate report put it bluntly:

Wilson lied to the media. **The Senate panel found that "Wilson provided misleading information to the** *Washington Post* last June. He said then he concluded the Niger intelligence was based on a document that had been clearly forged because the dates were wrong and the names were wrong.

The problem is that Wilson had "never seen the CIA reports and had no knowledge of what names and dates were in the reports." The article continues, "The documents – purported sales agreements between Niger and Iraq – were not in US hands until eight months after Wilson's made his trip to Niger."

Well, facts do matter to most, but not to Wilson and his Left-wing followers, who lie about the "lies" to discredit the way we went to war. Once more, with feeling – **the facts say that Bush did not lie, but truthfully presented the facts**. A bipartisan **Senate investigative committee has now established that Wilson had very few facts in his possession**. Yet, this is another example of the lies that are still being sung by the gospel choir of the Left, tearing our country apart.

Myth – Iraq is Another Vietnam

Many Americans watched with pride as our newly streamlined professional military rolled into Baghdad in world record time, and without anywhere near the 10,000-plus casualties predicted by pundits on the Left. Years later, we cry for every precious loss, though our casualty figures are less than 3,000. Let's give this sad number some perspective. The Left always wants to compare Iraq to Vietnam. OK, let's compare: US losses in Iraq are less then 5% of the US solders killed in the Vietnam War, and less then half the number of brave Marines killed in the three weeks it took to capture Iwo Jima in WWII.

Most Americans, unlike the Left, are not deaf to the clear bold plan our leaders continually outline to promote democracy in Iraq, and we know the necessary milestones that must be met before our troops come home. We are proud that the best of America's youth, kids we identify with, are serving in Iraq.

Myth – America Doesn't Care About the Rest of the World

The little traitor and so-called American Taliban, John Walker Lindh, sent a letter to his mother questioning her loyalty to America. Lindh wrote asking what America had ever done for anybody. The Left, like Lindh, believes that the answer to this is "not much."

The truth that the brainwashed Left doesn't want to discuss is that America has given more then $500 billion in aid to foreign countries since World War II. No other country comes close. But, in many places, struggling nations express their gratitude by chanting "Down with America" and burning our flag, actions often associated with our own darlings in the American Left.

Myth – Christians are Intolerant

The secular Left hates Christianity's influence on American society because it is an "intolerant" religion. Yes, the US is a predominately Christian country, but I can't think of many other places outside America where you are able to practice your faith with almost no restrictions. Moreover, when it comes to supporting charity in America, the conservative Right continually outperforms the liberals.

Myth – America is a Racist and Xenophobic Country

The real problem we have here in America is reverse racism, where we discriminate against Whites. This "racist" country spends more money than any other to aid the undeveloped world, including places like Africa. It is a financial black hole that does not serve either our defense or economic interests.

The Left would like the US to stand up to the Arab killers in Sudan Africa and send military help, but the same people are against the US pursuing killers of Arabs in Iraq. These wackos really believe we are the bad guys and the homicidal maniacs, and that the Arab world is the victim. How much more proof does one need that we have been brainwashed to accept lies for logic? Wow! How far the moral compass has swung! Yes, Uncle Tony, they believe this shit! Welcome to the new Dark Ages.

Myth – The Rest of the World Knows What They are Talking About, and We Should Care What They Think

From my world travels, I've learned that the knowledge most foreigners have about America is consistently wrong. Often, the political fringe and controlled media color their views about us. Moreover, the quality of leaders in most countries (England, Denmark, Australia, and Israel excluded) is dismal and self-serving at best.

But for some reason, the Left thinks that what the rest of the world thinks about us is very important and relevant. The US did the right thing by getting rid of Saddam, even though in most of the globe besides the UK, Israel, and India, less then 10% of the people support the US invasion. The Bush administration, to their credit, didn't change values just because the global majorities of brainwashed, uninformed, prejudiced people had different values and morals, or in John Kerry's case, because public opinion polls shifted. Poll dancer Kerry wanted us to get yet another round of UN approvals, despite years of ignored UN-sponsored resolutions against Iraq. Also, Kerry would have tried to get France and Russia to support our decision to go into Iraq. Now, after the liberation, we continue to learn about bribes received by the French, Russians, and the UN from the Oil for Food program, that may have influenced their UN votes.

The US morals and values have been the global gold standard for decades. But perhaps the Left could offer some foreign example of a more moral country or a better economic model then capitalism. Would they like us to be like the France, whose united Left students and unions have just doomed the country to the economic toilet? Perhaps a communist country should be our model? Maybe the largest left-wing country, Communist China, could be a model? That could work if you are one of the corrupt elite, who doesn't mind watching as China's economic growth tips the global environment into a global disaster. How about the Left's hero, Fidel? Perhaps he will share his Swiss bank accounts, valued at more than the Queen of England's, with his struggling people. Venezuela's Hugo Chavez is another leftist pinup boy that is re-making the democratic country of Venezuela into his own Banana Republic dictatorship.

Has there ever been a foreign Left-wing leader whose verbose verbiage translated into any thing positive? I objectively cannot think of a better country in the world then the US of A. If the Left disagrees, let them move to that new country ASAP. If they can't come up with a better country, they must stop playing their no-win game of trying to destroy this country with asinine words and actions. The simple truth is that the masses are now brainwashed asses that believe and spit up whatever the media prepares for them, and nothing they serve up is good for the health of the world.

Myth – Vast Right-Wing Conspiracy

Another hallmark of the lunatic Left is to see Right-wing conspiracies and fascists throughout the government. The Left wing believes that our media reports only what the government allows it to publish, and that vocal opponents such as Martin Luther King, Bobby Kennedy, and Paul Wellstone died under mysterious circumstances.

An important reason for writing this book is to highlight the far Left's collective paranoia, which is very dangerous, and a growing byproduct of years of brainwashing. Going beyond their flying saucer and crop circle comrades, some in the Left unbelievably deny al-Qaeda's own admission of responsibility for the World Trade Center attacks. They are so far out in the loony-sphere that they are actually suggesting that the 9/11 terrorist attacks are some type of conspiracy, involving top government officials and others who would gain somehow from the insurance claims, gold, and creating a reason to go to war in Iraq.

I'm continually amazed at the depth of the brainwashing the Left must have endured to envision good people, their own elected government, maliciously tapping into our phones and bank accounts, sending forces in black helicopters to eliminate Left-wing leaders, and torturing enemy combatants in secret locations around the world.

It is time to take the videogame chips out of their heads. People with similar beliefs have been put in insane asylums in the past, not on the pages of the *New York Times*. But as Henry Kissinger said, "The presence of paranoia does not prove the absence of plots and plans."

Myth – Terrorists are Freedom Fighters

The bombing of the Red Cross headquarters in Baghdad on October 27, 2003, and the daily homicide bombings of innocent Iraqis, exposes yet again the absurdity of the Left's attempt to portray the violence in Iraq as anything other then a vicious and calculated campaign of terror controlled by outsiders. Hopefully, the freedom-fighting label for the Muslim fanatics around the world is finally wearing as thin as Jimmy Carter's grasp of Mid-East reality.

Myth – 9/11 and All Bad Things Happen Because Of US Actions

The naive Left believes that terrorism, and indeed all evil, has its root cause in social conditions, and that the US is usually the cause of the problems. Therefore, they think that 9/11 was not an evil cowardly act on humanity, but instead "an attack on the world's self-proclaimed superpower, undertaken as a consequence of specific alliances and actions…"

In fact, when al-Qaeda terrorists first engaged US troops, it was in Somalia in 1993. At that time, the Americans were there to feed the starving people in this Muslim country. It was the Left and the Black Caucus that spearheaded the pressure for Bill Clinton to send forces to this country, which had no national or strategic importance to the US. Our goodwill ambassadors were ambushed, 18 were killed, and 80 wounded. We all remember a dead US solider being dragged through the streets as a spectacle. The terrible American offense that they were protesting was having brought food for the hungry.

The idea that the US is somehow responsible for global distress has been a common theme among the Left wing. After Monica Lewinsky, and sermonizing by womanizer opportunist Jessie Jackson, Clinton embarked on a hand-wringing trip to Uganda with a large delegation of freeloading African-American leaders. There the President apologized for the crime of American slavery. This was offered despite the fact that no slaves had ever been imported to America from Uganda or any East African State. In fact, slave trading in Africa, conducted by Arabs, precedes any American involvement by 1000 years. America and Britain were the two powers responsible for ending the slave trade. America had abolished slavery 100 years before Clinton's visit – at great human cost – while slavery persists in Africa without protest by African governments to the present day.

But if you tell the truth, there is no longer any reason to shower the continent with our tax dollars, or to continue the nonsensical arguments about reparations for US slavery to those who want an uncivil right to the nation's wallet. As for the positive impact of the boondoggle trip and crocodile tears apology, four months after Clinton left Africa, al-Qaeda terrorists blew up our embassies in Tanzania and Kenya.

Organizations, Foundations, and Friends of the Left
Amnesty International
It has been said that Amnesty International panders to the Left, and acts as a hit man to attack those targets identified by the Left. Their conclusions and motives, which should be carefully scrutinized, are always promoted as gospel by Left-wing professors and media like the BBC, who are always looking for ammunition to unjustly attack the US, Israel, and other undeserving targets. Amnesty International has been exposed as having had an obvious and definite Left-wing bias since the 1980's, when they were the subjects of French journalist Hughes Keraly's book.

Keraly exposed the organization's infiltration by communists and discovered that Amnesty director Derek Roebuck was an active communist himself. Keraly investigated Amnesty claims and found that though at times they did good work exposing human rights abuses around the world, their work was severely tainted. He noted that problems arose from their agenda that magnified and, in some cases, manufactured the abuses of freedom-loving regimes, while minimizing and ignoring the abuses of regimes of the totalitarian Left.

This is instructive regarding the danger of placing monitoring responsibilities into the hands of so-called "Non-Governmental Organizations" (NGO) like Amnesty International and Human Rights Watch. Amnesty affiliates with the United Nations. This affiliation, in effect, grants this un-elected and un-accountable bureaucracy an appearance of authority and legality.

In his study of thousands of files, Keraly discovered Amnesty practices such as listing terrorists working with Ugandan dictator Idi Amin as "victims of political oppression," a title similarly used by Amnesty for Palestinian terrorists. At that time, Amnesty had done nothing to investigate the torture and concentration camps of the Soviet Union, Cambodia, or Cuba. In fact the group had little to say at the time regarding Leftist abuses.

Amnesty International still pursues a radical Leftist agenda today. They support such things as the communist-inspired "UN Declaration of Human Rights," which calls for the transfer of capital from productive Western societies to Third World dictators and a guaranteed right of employment: a typical Bolshevik idea.

Now they are championing the cause of Muslims who have experienced "discrimination" in the US since September 11th, and the al-Qaeda prisoners at Guantanamo Bay, Cuba. As if the most humane country in the world needs a lesson about human rights from a group that has little to say about Leftist Palestinians and their terrorist offshoots.

Once again, those willing to concede that they may be victims of years of Left-wing brainwashing might begin questioning their sacred Amnesty International as to why America, the fairest and freest country in the world, should be subjected to the dirty lens of the Amnesty International microscope, while the politically oppressive Islamic world is often ignored.

Human Rights Watch (HRW)

This leading international human rights NGO has earned its stripes with its Left-wing buddies (such as Amnesty International) by demonizing Israel, and stays in business by avoiding any criticism of Israel's enemies. HRW's lack of objective reporting on governments in the region is demonstrated by its inability in the past, despite an annual budget of $22 million, to produce a specific report on human rights abuses in a country like Libya, or the relative paucity of attention given to states with appalling human rights records like Syria and Saudi Arabia as compared to Israel.

So there should be no surprise when HRW wrongly describes Israel as violating international legal norms by labeling the killing of terrorist leaders like Ismail Abu Shanab

and Sheikh Ahmed Yassin "liquidation" or "assassination."
International law does not protect all enemy combatants from
being targeted before judicial process, or grant them immunity
from military operations when they use civilians as human
shields.

Human Rights Watch's lack of objectivity and its
complicity with Left-wing buddies was highlighted during the
UN's infamous racist circus called the "anti-racism" conference
held in Durban, South Africa. Some noted that HRW Executive
Director Ken Roth telegraphed his real convictions rather than
his public face in an interview on US National Public Radio
(August 14, 2001), when he said, "Clearly Israeli racist
practices are an appropriate topic."

So in the lead up to Durban, HRW fanned the flames of
racial intolerance, notwithstanding the fact that one-quarter of
Israel's citizens are actually Arab and enjoy democratic rights
unlike anywhere else in the Arab world. That world has
systematically forced hundreds of thousands of Jews from their
countries, or killed them outright, as in the case of the Iranian
Revolution.

At Durban, one role of HRW seemed to be to exclude
representatives of Jewish lawyers and jurists from over 40
countries (IAJLJ), who, as members of the NGO caucus, had a
right to vote on the final NGO document. The draft included
egregious statements equating Zionism with racism, and
alleging that Israel was an "apartheid" state guilty of "genocide
and ethnic cleansing designed to ensure a Jewish state."
Having the courage to speak out against the tide of hate
directed at Israel and the Jewish people by the Left and by the
Arabs is not one of the strengths of Human Rights Watch,
while avoiding criticizing Israel's enemies is something at which
they seem to excel.

The American Civil Liberties Union (ACLU)

The joke goes, "How do you get the ACLU to stop
defending enemy terrorists who vow to kill Americans? Tell the
ACLU that the terrorists are really Boy Scouts." Unlike Amenity
International, the ACLU was at one time an important protector
of human rights. But like NATO after the Cold War, it appears

to have lost its focus and direction. There is an important need for the organization to seriously re-examine and change the activities that do more harm than good, such as defending extreme people and values that undermine society. The media recently reported attempts to stop members from publicly airing their disagreements about the direction and targets of the organization. Aren't attempts to control internal and external criticism the hallmark of a totalitarian regime? But then the ACLU is big business.

They have certainly lost the forest for the trees when they fight against American institutions like the Boy Scouts and memorials to our veterans. Like the Civil Rights gang, the ACLU could become a serious impediment to American values and justice.

Do they go after our values because they make big money pursuing the Civil Rights con? Like the "people of color" extortionists discussed in Chapter 1, the ACLU profits from the disgusting abuses of the Civil Rights business. Indeed, they make millions of dollars in taxpayer "attorney fee awards" by turning authorization under the Civil Rights Act into a piñata of lawyer goodies. I discussed in Chapter 1 how Civil Rights con men and women have exploited a well-intentioned law. These diversity groups welcome the ACLU to join them in feeding at the money trough, while the taxpayers keep picking up the tab.

Elected and appointed officials at the local, state, and Federal levels have been literally terrorized about standing up to the ACLU, for fear of enormous attorney fees being imposed by un-elected judges not answerable to the tax payers. I don't know of a single American judge who has had the guts to exercise discretion by denying attorney fees to the ACLU.

And attorney fees do seem to motivate the ACLU. The American Legion called on Congress to end judges' authority to award attorney fees in cases brought to remove or destroy religious symbols. In 1934, a private citizen strapped two pipes together to form a cross and mounted it to a rock outcrop on private land in the Mojave Desert. The purpose of the cross was to honor WWI veterans. In the year 2000, President Clinton incorporated the area into a Mojave National Preserve.

The ACLU vultures swarmed in and filed a lawsuit to remove the cross, picking up some $40,000 in attorney fees. Legislation was passed to exchange the one-acre site for five acres from a private owner, placing the monument on private land. But the ACLU appealed against this legislation and picked up an additional $63,000. They ruled that the plaintiff, who later moved to Oregon, suffered a Civil Rights injury because he saw the cross when driving back on visits.

International ANSWER (Act Now to Stop War and End Racism)

ANSWER, one of the leading organizers of anti-war protests in the United States, has begun to openly and vociferously support Palestinian terrorists. They have played a key role in inserting anti-Israel sentiment into the anti-war movement, which has led to extreme invective against Israel during protests. ANSWER was created by the New York-based International Action Center (IAC), often attracting protestors by the tens of thousands.

Its largest and most disturbing event was the "National March for Palestine Against War and Racism," in Washington, DC. The rally attracted nearly 200,000 demonstrators, and served as a vehicle for supporters of violence and anti-Semitic terror. The flag of the Iranian puppet Hezbollah flew from the speaker's podium. This same Hezbollah is currently tearing Lebanon apart, bombed the US Marine barracks in Lebanon in 1983, killing 241 US Marines, hijacked a TWA flight in Europe in 1985, executed a US Navy diver, bombed the Jewish community center in Buenos Aires in 1994, killing 85, and blew up the Khobar Towers housing complex in Dhahran, Saudi Arabia, killing 19 American servicemen in 1996. A retired, covert US intelligence officer with years of experience in the Middle East noted that Hezbollah teams have regularly done surveillance on US Embassies in Europe in case they're activated to strike.

Our counter terrorism efforts against this Iran-linked group should actively pursue and prosecute the leadership of those Left-wing groups and churches who support Hezbollah and other terrorist organizations. Hiding behind a curtain of free speech and the peace movement are traitors to our country, who are giving support to our enemies in the war on terrorism.

Left-Wing Money and Mouths
Moveon.org

Move On is a web-based grassroots political network of more then 2 million online activists whose general goal is to push the Democratic Party to the Left. More than a website, Move On is a catalyst for a new kind of grassroots involvement tailored to attract young net-savvy Democrats. They succeeded in harnessing popular entertainers to their cause in the form of rock concert fundraisers. This group does damage to the Democrats as it moves the party further to the Left, and toward losers like Denis Kucinich, and away from winners like Joe Lieberman. Moreover, Move On efficiently spreads and reinforces the lies and hateful propaganda of the Left to our already brainwashed youth.

Noam Chomsky

Noam Chomsky is the left's "intellectual," and a perfect example of how one can become blind to common sense when one practices too much mental masturbation. To many he seems like a fool with a high IQ when he tries to rationalize the al-Qaeda terrorist attacks on the United States. The death toll, he argues, was minor compared to the list of Third World victims of the far more extreme terrorism caused by United States foreign policy. The more hate-America rhetoric he dribbles out, the more popular Chomsky becomes among the academic and intellectual Left. His willingness to present the rationale for the past and future terrorist actions of our enemies makes him a campus superstar. Even our next generation of warriors at West Point has allowed him to shoot holes in our foreign policy.

Ramsey Clark

A former US Attorney General, Ramsey Clark, also gives a false sense of moral legitimacy and cover to terrorists.

Along with ANSWER and the IAC executives, he helped organize a conference in Cairo, where hundreds of international and Arab activists gathered to support "acts of resistance in Iraq and Palestine." The ANSWER delegation met with Osama Hamdan, head of Hamas' operation in Lebanon, and an open supporter of suicide bombing. The event sponsors, the International Campaign Against US and Zionist Occupations, a movement co-founded and partly led by the IAC, invited Hamdan. ANSWER is the anti-war arm of the IAC.

Clark also found it very important to represent and try to delay justice to the hundreds of thousand victims of mass murderer Sodamn Insane. Hopefully there will be many replays of his hanging with other Islamic terrorist trash, since that is the only justice respected in that part of the world. Clark's support for terrorists and enemies of the United States has helped damage the country that he swore to defend as Attorney General.

Hollow-wood Looney Prunes

Hollywood has also played a major role in the brainwashing of a whole generation around the globe. There is nothing new in their thinking, as shown by the slide in ticket sales.

How about a positive movie about our great country, rather than one turning homicidal maniac terrorists into innocent victims or freedom fighters? I would buy a ticket to a movie that deals with reverse discrimination and how Civil Rights leaders extort money from our biggest companies, or how a drunk, Black stripper with a criminal past schemed with the help of the Left-wing media, Black Panther Party gangsters, and an immoral DA with political ambitions to ruin the reputation of 40 innocent White lacrosse players.

Another suggestion would be a political science fiction thriller, perhaps directed by a born-again Michael Moore. In it, an evil cabal of Left-wing professors, Left-wing media, and Hollywood have systematically brainwashed a whole generation into thinking the good motives, actions, and dreams of the best country in the world are some kind of evil conspiracy, and the hero who uncovers the plot is an conservative family man.

In other words, how about telling the truth – something the Left has not done since the days when Ed R. Morrow dealt with the real problem of McCarthyism, and when Black Civil Rights needed protection, decades ago. Today, as White civil rights are being trampled by the Civil Rights business and government, Hollywood is stuck watching old movies and playing old roles.

I express my disdain of Left-wing slander regarding America's greatness with the power of my ticket sales and by avoiding sponsors and studios supporting Leftist propaganda. I cannot make the emotional swing from being upset by the hate-America speech of Left-wing stars to feeling comfortable about watching them perform. The self-inflated egos of stars and their need to be in the spotlight only serve to highlight their worn-out Leftist scripts. Though they really have nothing new or of value to say, they stay on the stage as long as the Left-wing media gives them a microphone. A brief composite of unsubstantiated online web reports and my commentary about the "not politically" correct comments and attitudes of the Hollywood left follow.

Harry Belafonte – joins the Hollywood loonies by embracing Hugo Chavez, the latest Castro puppet attempting to undermine the Western Hemisphere. Perhaps Harry's expertise counting bananas will help this dictator turn Venezuela back into a Banana Republic. Source: Media Research Center.

Susan Sarandon – On President Bush and the death penalty: "We stand a chance of getting [in the 2000 election] a President who has probably killed more people before he gets into office than any President in the history of the United States." Source: Counterpunch.org

Janine Garofalo – thinks "Our country is founded on a sham: our forefathers were slave-owning rich white guys who wanted it their way. So when I see the American flag, I go, 'Oh my God, you're insulting me.' That you can have a gay parade on Christopher Street in New York, with naked men and women on a float cheering, 'We're here, we're queer!' – that's what makes my heart swell. Not the flag, but a gay naked man or woman burning the flag. I get choked up with pride." Source: HollywoodInvestigator.com

That kind of naïve thinking would be funny if the kids listening to her didn't take her seriously. Again, the problem is that these people have little or no interaction with the highly moral, honest leaders we have in business, government, and the military, so they blindly throw mud from afar.

Margaret Cho – has enough of her own problems to be making Hitler / Bush comparison jokes. Her Left-wing Moveon.org audience laughs wildly as our President is compared to a man who killed six million people. Hey, try telling the joke by comparing the current president of China with Mao and Stalin, since they are both great communist dictators. Another good laugh was the Japanese raping the Chinese at Nanking during the same war – lots of great material for Cho there. Source: the 2003 MoveOn.org Awards

Woody Harrelson – "This is a racist and imperialist war. The warmongers who stole the White House (you call them 'hawks' but I would never disparage such a fine bird) have hijacked a nation's grief and turned it into a perpetual war on any non-white country they choose to describe as terrorist." Source: Brainyquote.com

Does he really believe we are in a racist, imperialist war and that we go to war with any non-White country the White House chooses to describe as terrorist? Who says a White man can't jump? Woody would have to jump over all logic and play the dumb bartender again. How many hundreds of thousands of your non-Whites must be killed by Sodamn Insane and other terrorists before you call the US liberators and patriots rather then warmongers?

Ed Asner– "They're sheep. They like Bush enough to credit him with saving the nation after 9/11. Three thousand people get killed, and everybody thinks they're next on the list. The President comes along, and he's got his six-guns strapped on, and people think he's going to save them." Source: Brainy Quotes

Does Asner think that we are sheep for hoping our President will save us after 9/11? What I am afraid of is that the Left is continually getting in the way of securing our borders, hurting our military by giving hope to the terrorists that we will soon abandon the mission.

Ben Affleck – "The Bush administration has continued to push a dangerous Right-wing agenda, which has included increasing encroachments on civil liberties, particularly with the questionable and aggressive use of the Patriot Act." Source: NY Daily News

What he and the Left don't seem to understand is that if the US does not stand up to the truly evil people that exist in the real world, these Islamic terrorists will kill more innocent people in our country and around the world in order to meet the elusive Muslim virgins these losers can't seem to find in reality.

Tim Robbins – seems an angry jump up and down Lefty who doesn't seem to have the smarts to come up with a quotable line without an old script such as left canard that we go to war to earn profits at the cost of human lives. "Our resistance to this war should be our resistance to profit at the cost of human life. Because that is what these drums beating over Iraq are really about. This is about business." Source: Brainy Quotes

Danny Glover – is someone I met at a dinner party. He sees our great country as the enemy and Marxism as the answer. One month after 9/11, Glover told an audience at Princeton University, "One of the main purveyors of violence in this world has been this country, whether it's been against Nicaragua, Vietnam or wherever…" Source: Speech at Princeton University

George Clooney – has recently joined other producers who put a paranoid Left spin on movies and guest appearances. They give voice and vision to terrorist propaganda about victim hood and present a negative role of the US in world affairs. On the movie *Syriana*: "They (the terrorists) are, in a way, the most sympathetic (characters in the movie), but I think that's important. Because if you are going to fight a war on terror, which is not a state that you can go and bomb, then you need to understand what it is that creates the people that would do such horrible things, rather then just saying-labeling them as evildoers." Source: Media Research Center

Sean Penn – visited Iran and then played the role of biased reporter as he condemned the US for using "inflammatory rhetoric, like the 'Axis of Evil'…" and tries to protect Iran from "increased sanctions and potentially unjustified military action from the US and Israel."

Is Penn so naïve as to believe Iran is not building WMD but nuclear energy for internal use? Why haven't we heard from the "mouth that roars" about the Iranian president's inflammatory remarks about the Holocaust, destruction of Israel, and unleashing Iranian controlled terrorists against Western interests if provoked? When asked if he considered himself to be a patriot: "I am more patriotic than this President we have (Bush), who I consider a traitor of human and American principles." Source: MSNBC.com

Michael Moore – is a case of success in his first films being followed by his producing one-sided biased manure to feed left wing taste.

Left-Wing Fascism

The Left is looking more and more like the Right. The Left has always had a fascist totalitarian side that does not tolerate multiplicity of ideas, yet the fractionalized left is so diverse no one can find its claim to legitimacy. There are areas of common interest. The Left is anti-fascist but not necessarily anti-war. The radical Left requires taking up arms to overcome oppression. Therefore, they have had no problem supporting the Russian or Cuban revolution.

They compare President George W. Bush to Hitler (or as singer Harry Bellefonte did when he called the President "the world's worst terrorist," as he praised Latin America's dangerous Left-wing radicals, while labeling the conservatives and libertarians Fascists. In fact, the opposite is true. The American Right stands for limited government, individual rights, morality, personal responsibility, and capitalism. While like fascism, the Left wing is anti-capitalistic, anti-Semitic and promotes national programs to control education, healthcare, and Welfare.

A 2003 Anti-Defamation League survey of university faculty in the US, which traditionally identify themselves as Left wing, found that 5% are strong anti-Semites and 65% are against current Israeli policies. Moreover, across the country, Jewish students who want to study in Israel face unfair barriers and restrictions. In some cases, students must forego college credit and financial aid to discover their Jewish homeland. This is because college and university administrators have suspended or placed significant restrictions on study abroad programs in Israel. Yet students are free to study in other Middle East countries, even though Israel is the only democratic nation in the region.

As expected, two of the largest state university systems in the country – the University of California and California State University – are among the worst offenders. These systems have been the dark stars of Left-wing culture for so long that it will require a sustained public out roar to dismantle their sick culture that brainwashes students to hate America and Israel, while promoting the agenda of terrorists, minority racists, and Left-wing radicals.

The brainwashing by the Left wing and Islamists is beginning at young ages in California. Middle school students study Islam for several weeks as part of world history. Their textbooks devote 55 pages to Islam – far more than to any other religion. Islam is presented in a wholly positive way, with Muslim religious beliefs as factual and Mohammed as a hero. By contrast, Judaism and Christianity are given little space, and nothing positive is said about Christianity.

Furthermore, the schools use handouts supplied by Saudi Arabia to give teachers ideas for activities. At one school, the teacher asked students to fast, at another to dress like Muslims, learn the Five Pillars of Islam, and memorize an Islamic prayer that extols the greatness of Allah. At another school, the front grounds of the school featured a banner for the day that read, "There is one God, Allah, and Mohammed is his prophet." Can you imagine what the ACLU would do if a teacher taught Christianity this way?

107

Left-Wing Europe

The psychotic language and behavior of the Left has spilled across the pond. In Britain, the Oxford don Tom Paulin exposed only the verbal tip of a dagger when he said that the "Jewish settlers on the West Bank should be shot dead," and that "I feel nothing but hatred for them." All sides of the political spectrum supported Lech Walesa and his Solidarity Movement against the Communist led Polish Government. But the Left found reason to stand by Solidarity when President Walesa turned openly anti-Semitic and, along with the Polish Catholic church, decreed that all Polish Jews had three months to leave the country before facing violent opposition.

European governments and elitists lend powerful diplomatic, economic, and political support to Israel's mortal enemies, while increasingly holding Israel to standards seldom obtainable by nations operating in perfect peace. As in the US, at the forefront of these assaults is Europe's academic community, with universities in England, France, Germany, and elsewhere becoming hotbeds of hostility and hatred of the Jewish State.

Take the recent boycott that occurred when 48,000 members of the British Association of University Teachers (BAUT) of Haifa and Bar-Ilan Universities, "investigated" Hebrew University. The goal of this boycott effort was to isolate Israeli universities, academics, and even students, eliminate funding for projects, and prevent participation in scientific and scholarly research and forums.

These backward academic institutions and their brainwashed faculties have a long history of anti-Semitism and academic jealousy of the Jewish people, because the Jewish people consistently win a disproportionate number of Nobel prizes and have academic success in spite of the extra hurdles they are required to jump. Rather then dealing with genocide in Sudan, repression of religious freedom in Saudi Arabia, and honor killings in Pakistan, these self-anointed pompous asses try instead to turn Israel into an international pariah, harming not only its international standing, but also its economy and national security.

The brazenness of this act alarmed even the British press, who, as we will see in later chapters, is not normally known for its pro-Israel sentiments. *The Times* of London described the boycott effort as being "ill timed as it is perverse" and warned what BAUT already knew – that it could provide an excuse for increased anti-Semitism.

The Left wing virus has seriously infected the brains of our former European allies. Signs of the danger caused by having Left wing majorities in Germany, Greece, and Sweden has shown itself in the debate regarding Iraq, where these countries have seriously equated George W. Bush and Tony Blair with Sodamn Insane and Osama bin Laden.

They have bought the big lie that the US is a hegemonic power that is trying to control as much of the world as it can. Though the US spends more than any other country in the world to fight AIDS and poverty, the Left wing believes that the US is indifferent to global poverty.

The political correctness of the Left is never balanced; they can dish out extreme abuse but cannot take it when they are criticized. They never condemn Muslims who say the most extreme things about Christian, Jews, and America.
So how come Americans are prosecuted by the media for hate speech when they return the compliment?

They did, however, get one thing correct when they learned that government is afraid of public opinion. Therefore, the Left wing remains a tire that is over-inflated, noisy, difficult to pull to the Right, and will likely put Western values on a collision course with Islamic and Left-wing extremists.

The European Left, who would be slaves or more likely dead if the Americans had not stopped Hitler, still prefer the failed approaches of Neville Chamberlain, who learned too late that you couldn't compromise with evil or negotiate with madmen. Today's Left still believes that you can compromise and negotiate peace with North Korea and Muslim terrorists. Unfortunately, history continually proves that such madmen only respond to military force.

It is a good thing that no Left-wing candidates were running for President in 1944. If they had been, instead of defeating Hitler and Tojo, we might have ended up with an exit strategy that saved American lives in the short run but cost us our freedom and way of life.

Honoring Left-Wing Losers

We have always honored people who have built our country. Great men like Washington, Lincoln, Jefferson, and Franklin are the fathers of our country. The Left uses masturbatory anger to force respect where it hasn't been earned, and tries to make heroes out of history's losers. Why should anti-American losers be put on pedestals, and the names of those who tried to destroy America engraved on our buildings?

The fact is that there is a lack of real, pro-American, positive minority or Left-wing role models. Indeed, Amherst named its 26-story library in honor of WEB Dubois. Dubois already has hundreds of schools across the nation named after him. What kind of world would honor this controversial founder of the NAACP, who was eventually kicked out of the NAACP for his advocacy of racial separation? How sick is it for America to memorialize Dubois, who eventually renounced his American citizenship, went to Kwame Nkrumah's Ghana, and lived there the last few years of his life? Furthermore, he joined the Communist Party, and when Stalin, who murdered thousands, died, Dubois eulogized him as a "great and courageous man."

The Left would like all leaders to be like Castro, to strive for the ideals Castro vomits for hours in his speeches. Leave it to the Left to idolize a man who, according to *Forbes* magazine, has twice the fortune of the Queen of England squirreled away in Swiss banks. Even the fist-raising Black power athletes that so embarrassed their country during the Mexico Olympics had a $300,000 monument built to them in my hometown of San Jose, California.

I have shown in this chapter that the ideals of the Left have been corrupted. In the next chapter, we learn that the Right does not have the right answers either.

Chapter 3
THE RIGHT IS RIGHT

By wrapping themselves in the mantle of religion, the GOP leadership has become the vehicle that the religious Right uses to carry their agenda. The religious Right pays for its ride by assuring GOP election victories and representing an amazing one-third of all Republicans.

Having God on your side means that you are always right, no matter what other people might think. The hot topic today is how and when the true believers are all going to fly off to paradise together, leaving behind their earthly possessions, clothes, false teeth, cell phones, and all the unsaved sinners like me.

Many on the Left pray that they will leave soon. True, the Redemption has always been a hot topic amongst evangelical religious groups. It's just that with increased access to people via TV, radio, and the Internet, these denominations are appealing now to more people than ever before.

Watching televangelists doing their healing act is, to me, like seeing an instant replay of the players in the Scopes Monkey Trial trying to disprove evolution. But as a management consultant, I realize that the Right is not a laughing matter. I'm continually amazed at how effective the high priests of the Right are in communicating, coordinating, and convincing their unquestioning flock to support their excessive lifestyles and political agenda. We must be aware of the damage that this vocal Right wing, Christian soldier voting block is causing in our country and in the world of rational thought.

In this chapter, false idols with names like the Reverend Louis Sheldon, Andrea Sheldon Lafferty, Reverend Pat Robinson, Ed Crane, Joseph Coors, John Ashcroft, Wanda Franz, Howard Ahmanson Jr., David Koch, Jerry Falwell, Wayne La Pierre, Ted Nugent, Al Mohler, Robert Reccord, Richard Land, and James Draper are heaped into the dustbin of history to join their Left-wing counterparts. My son, Brett Minkin, is the major contributor to this chapter.

Background

The changes that made the religious Right into a powerful society-changing force were subtle and slow going enough to remain unnoticed as they were happening. For most of this century, the Christian Right lived in rural areas and was below average in socio-economic factors like income, education, and occupational status. This group has achieved dramatic gains in the last half-century. This is especially true of younger evangelicals, who represent a large share of the new Christian Right. Their gains in education, white-collar occupations, and higher income brackets signaled their migration into urban and suburban settings. Upward mobility, in turn, undercut evangelical traditions of political apathy and Democratic partisanship.

As evangelicals moved into the middle class, they acquired resources that included available leisure time, money, communication networks, contacts with government officials, and greater exposure to information. They, like other upwardly mobile and highly taxed families, tended to migrate toward the policies of limited government, as advocated by the Republicans. According to a Gallup poll, 41% of Americans identify themselves as conservatives, 38% identify themselves as moderates, and only 18% identify themselves as liberals. The so-called "red state" conservatives from the Midwest, West, and South provide the base of Right-wing support, which is what brought George W. Bush to the White House.

The social transformation of evangelicals also produced an emphasis on what was called "church planting." So-called super churches, like Jerry Farwell's Thomas Road Baptist Church, took on a wide range of functions, and developed into the religious equivalents of major corporations. Local churches also began to provide a wide array of services for their members. As the ministry became more professional, seminaries produced clerical leaders who expanded church influence into such fields as education, counseling, and day care.

The evolution of churches from places of worship to social service centers brought them under government authority for regulations concerning zoning, educational practices, day-care facilities, minimum wage laws, and other working conditions. Churches felt the heavy hand of government in the 1970's and 1980's, and considered them to be an assault on their values. Ironically, religious conservatives were accused of "imposing their views" and "forcing their beliefs" on the public. But was this really the case?

Nathan Glazer made several observations about situations like this almost 20 years ago. Freedom for religious schools became an issue not because of any legal effort to expand their scope, but because the IRS and various state authorities had tried to impose new restrictions on private schools. Abortion became a national issue in 1973 not because evangelicals and fundamentalists wanted to strengthen prohibitions against abortion, but because liberals wanted them abolished, and the Supreme Court set national standards for state laws. Pornography in the 1980's did not become an issue because evangelicals and fundamentalists wanted to ban D.H. Lawrence, James Joyce, or even Henry Miller, but because in the 1960's and 1970's, under-the-table pornography moved to the top of the newsstands. Prayer in the schools did not become an issue because evangelicals and fundamentalists wanted to introduce new prayers or sectarian prayers, but because the Supreme Court ruled against all prayers.

This imposition of a liberal ethos by what many social scientists call the "new class elites" (made up of newspaper journalists, television producers, commentators, and the "knowledge class" from the universities) aroused to action many previously apolitical and socially indifferent religious conservatives. While many of them had always found plenty to complain about in the wider culture, the rapid changes in American society during the 60's and 70's sent shock waves through their community, and provided many new points of contention. As sociologist Steve Bruce has pointed out, "Conservative Protestants of the 1950's were offended by girls smoking in public," but by the late 1960's, "girls were to be seen on news film dancing naked at open-air rock concerts." In short, the era of Eisenhower's America was far different than the America of the 1960's and 1970's.

The result was a series of confrontations between the state's interest in regulation of the private provisions of social services and the church's claims of immunity under the free exercise clause.

In order to protect those rights, the Christian Right clergy became politically active, but social movements cannot convert grievances into political action unless they have access to political clout and other organizational resources. **Another subtle history mover for the Right occurred, as churches became powerful political forces in their local environment, aligning themselves with central organizations that could coordinate nationwide political action.**

The birth of television evangelists, who had direct access to viewers, and the ability to tap into mailing lists containing millions of names, solidified the base of the Religious Right. Farwell had his "Old Time Gospel Hour." The Christian Voice was connected to Pat Robertson's Christian Broadcast Network, and the Roundtable's leading spokesman, James Robison, had a nationally syndicated program.

Computer abilities to construct databases and send endless religious and political messages allowed conservatives to quickly progress in taking control of the Republican Party and in influencing US foreign and domestic policy during the Reagan years. The linkage of politics and religion grew. We had an influx of preachers, and even an astrologist in government halls, as it became politically correct to defer to religious pronouncements and to avoid alienating religious sensibilities.

The Right Issues

116

As the Christian Right moved to the suburbs and cities, they came face to face with direct assaults on the social values, customs, and habits dominant in the rural and small town strongholds where they grew up. The Christian Right has had a long tradition of fighting back against perceived assaults from public authority on their favored social issues. In the past, this tendency surfaced mostly in local and state conflicts over issues such as guns, liquor licensing, education, and pornography.

Today the Christian Right criticizes the federal government for taking over a number of tasks that were once reserved for the family. Medicaid has been condemned for encouraging people to shirk family obligations, Welfare for encouraging promiscuity, higher forms of taxation for forcing women from the household to the workplace, and the Supreme Court for decisions restricting government action in support of religion and hampering the expression of evangelical faith in public schools. Other "Right" issues follow.

Right to Life

With the international danger of unchecked population growth looming, the Right wing and their anti-abortion, pro-life supporters are sowing the seeds for future global disaster. Of all demographic trends, population growth and shifts are the most crucial in determining our future on this planet. These shifts offer startling insights into the social, political, and economic problems and potentials that will shape life and work in the next century. A global struggle currently exists between production and reproduction. While production has long been predominant in industrialized countries, three-quarters of the world's people live and reproduce in developing nations, and reproduction is winning over production.

Indeed, world population is likely to exceed 7.8 billion by 2020. Nearly 95% of this growth will occur in less developed nations, where the Right wing has successfully blocked family planning funding. To understand the enormous implications of the global population reaching 7.8 billion by 2020, here is some prospective. This staggering increase of nearly 2 billion people is twice the population of China and eight times that of the US. The point is that the earth's finite resources are just that: finite.

Women's Right to Choose
"Feminism was established so as to allow unattractive women easier access to the mainstream of society."
– Rush Limbaugh

After Hillary Clinton used the phrase "vast Right-wing conspiracy" in the 1990's, conservative websites soon appeared mocking her dress, hair, clothes, and speech, and even spreading rumors that she was a lesbian. The Right feels that the woman's place is in the home, and she should have no say in the matter of whether or not to carry a baby to term. This assumption is contrary to the Christian church's historical position, as enunciated by St. Augustine, that life does **not** begin at conception because "ensoulment" cannot occur in a formless body. The Right's mind-set has also caused severe restrictions on stem-cell research, the potential cure for a large number of diseases such as Parkinson's. Conservatives also blocked approval of the so-called "morning-after pill," which prevents pregnancy from occurring even before fertilization of the egg occurs. The Right appears to be very concerned with human life between the moment of conception and the moment of birth. After that, however, their concern wanes considerably.

Most of the Right's attitudes towards abortion, contraception, sex education, censorship, homosexuality, pornography, etc. are held over from the Puritans, who were some of the most sexually repressed people on the planet. Any sexual thoughts were thought to be shameful and evil. Sex was not to be enjoyed, and sex for anything other than procreation was considered dirty and sinful. A woman who became pregnant outside marriage was considered a whore, and became a social outcast. The man, of course, was not to blame. Hundreds of years later, many of these same attitudes prevail today in the form of the Religious Right.

An example of blatant Right-wing interference with a woman's right to choose is the decision by Browning Construction Company, one of Texas' largest construction companies, to back out of a project to build a clinic for Planned

Parenthood. A Right-wing coalition of religious activists and Republican Party faithful stopped construction 30 days after it began. Leading the effort was a newly created group called the Austin Area Pro-Life Concrete Contractors and Suppliers Association. The Association's chairman, Chris Danze, labeled Planned Parenthood "a social movement that promotes sexual chaos, especially of our youth." The association's boycott of the project was completely successful. Every concrete supplier within 60 miles of Austin refused to supply materials, and construction stopped. This kind of small-minded thinking leads to the continuing problem of unwanted babies, teen pregnancies, increased Welfare populations, and the AIDS epidemic.

Right to Die

The decision by the Florida legislature to overturn the courts by ordering the hospital to reconnect Terri Schiavo's feeding tube is a good example of interference in right-to-die matters. Mrs. Schiavo had been in a vegetative state for 13 years. After spending eight years by her hospital bed, her husband decided to abide by what he said Terri had told him before her seizure: she didn't want to live in that state. He asked the hospital to stop force-feeding her. A five-year battle ensued. On October 15, 2003, after having exhausted all judicial appeals, the hospital was ordered to abide by his wishes.

A combination of leading Republicans, conservative television hosts, and activists sprang into action. Within days, the Florida legislature passed a bill that gave Governor Jeb Bush, a man who had never met Mrs. Schiavo, the authority to override the wishes of her husband and those previously expressed by Mrs. Schiavo. An hour later the Governor exercised that authority; she was again being force-fed. Mercifully, after she died and after more battling (this time over where she should be buried) ended, the media circus moved on.

My son Brett is troubled by several far Right beliefs, including the issues surrounding the right to die. Brett's insights are:

Having spent over 15 years working in an intensive care unit, and having personally had to disconnect people of all ages from life-support, I can tell you there are definitely worse things than dying. On the other hand, end-of-life issues are very personal decisions, and there are no easy answers. Two years ago, I was faced with a similar situation involving my grandmother, Martha Simon, a wonderful woman who I loved dearly. I wish I could say that my years of clinical experience and strong opinions on the subject made the choice an easy one, but they didn't. All of that pretty much flew right out the window. What we, as a family, decided to do is immaterial to this book. As I write this, I still don't know if we made the right decision, but I certainly wouldn't want some grand-standing, Right winger like Rick Santorum or Jeb Bush to decide for me, or use my loved one to further their political cause. I know my grandmother (rest her soul) would agree with me on that.

Bible-ize Public Education

Part of the Right-wing strategy is to undermine the entire system of public education and to Bibile-ize the curriculum. School prayer, pledges under God, and bible study at or around public schools, along with the Ten Commandments, religious slogans, and dogma were passed into legislation by senators with an eye for assuring votes.

Intelligent design is a view of "creationism" that adheres more closely to biblical explanations of the origins of man and other species on our planet. Christian conservatives have launched an effort to give intelligent design equal standing with the theory of evolution in our nation's schools. Here is what the debate is about. Scientists have established the fact of evolution, with thousands of lines of evidence and the work of hundreds of thousands of researchers. The idea is based on material evidence, repeated experiments, and extensive documentation in the scientific literature.

This evidence flatly contradicts literal religious accounts. Religious conservatives have mounted a long-running social and political campaign to get their falsified dogma treated as truth, despite the absence of any material or logical support for their position. According to the Gallup Poll in 2004, 45% of Americans believe that "God created human beings much in their present form about 10,000 years ago." More then 50 years after the Scopes trial, such thinking is a national embarrassment. The debate is not about assessing the evidence, but about getting faith-based dogma into our schools.

In addition, religious conservatives have been trying to force public school systems into teaching "abstinence-only" sex education curriculums. Students are taught little or nothing about safe sex or contraception, leading to more teenage pregnancies and sexually transmitted diseases. Of course, if the Right wing has their way, the ability of these girls to have an abortion would be severely limited or taken away completely. Already over-burdened foster care systems and Child Welfare departments be unable to handle the massive influx of unwanted children. Slashed budgets for Welfare programs such as job training, childcare, etc. will make it increasingly difficult for the girls who decide to keep their babies to do so.

Moral Values
Fear Factor
My son also believes that the Right wing has successfully parleyed people's fears about sin, hell, heaven, morality, sodomy, and fellatio into the idea that the country is losing traditional values. The strategy of the Right wing appeals to fear, not to reason. Homophobia, women's rights, and other intolerances appeal to the conservative masses of true believers, who think that they are helping God by their contributions and votes. Playing on people's fears of further domestic terrorism after 9/11, the Bush Administration has nurtured, sustained, and manipulated that fear, using 24-hour news channels to pound their messages home on a near-constant basis to build support for the invasion of Iraq, the Patriot Act, and other controversial programs.

121

Since September 11th, Americans have been relentlessly assaulted with news stories of what turned out to be non-existent weapons of mass destruction, anthrax, smallpox, dirty bombs, nerve gas, and "orange alerts." Worried citizens stocked up on antibiotics, gas masks, and duct tape, and were constantly told that something bad could happen at any moment, although no one knew exactly what, where, or when. The public was scared and angry (a dangerous combination of emotions). They wanted the illusion of safety again, and Bush gave them that. People saw their President strutting around in a flight suit on the deck of an aircraft carrier, proclaiming "mission accomplished," and they bought into it.

Nearly every speech the President or Vice President makes has one or more September 11th reference included to once again play on that fear. The Right understands that if you repeat a lie often enough, eventually, it becomes the truth. One poll, taken just before the start of the war in Iraq, showed that the majority of Americans thought falsely that the United States had been attacked by Iraq on September 11th.

Onward Christian Airmen

Brett has noted that the Air Force recently released new guidelines for religious expression that no longer caution top officers about promoting their personal religious views. Conservative Christians, who said that the previous rules were too strict and lobbied the White House to change them, welcomed these revisions. Tom Minnery, vice president for Focus on the Family, applauded the new guidelines.

The original guidelines were created after allegations that evangelical Christians at the Air Force Academy in Colorado Springs were imposing their views on others. Some Christian chaplains were accused of telling cadets to warn non-believers that they would go to hell if they were not born again. Indeed, Mikey Weinstein, an academy graduate, sued the Air Force, claiming that evangelicals are allowed to push their faith on others at the academy. The case is in Federal court in New Mexico.

The revised guidelines specifically say that nothing should be understood to limit the substance of voluntary

122

discussions of religion, where it is reasonably clear that the discussions are personal, not official, and can be reasonably free of potential coercion. They also omit an earlier statement that chaplains should respect the rights of others to their own religious beliefs, including the right to hold no beliefs.

Censorship
The Boob Tube

When Janet Jackson showed a bit of nipple during a football halftime show, an outraged parson had his followers send 300,000 messages nearly overnight to FCC chairman Michael Powell, asking him to take immediate action concerning this inappropriate act. Powell yielded to pressure and began levying massive fines against TV networks, radio stations, and even talk show hosts themselves for airing material that conservative groups found offensive or "indecent."

Fearing more fines from the FCC, many of the networks folded under pressure and material that had been deemed acceptable only months before was now considered indecent. As a result, network TV viewing continues to plummet in favor of pay cable channels such as HBO, which offers higher-quality programming without commercials, and is not subject to censorship by the FCC. Broadcast radio listening has also dropped significantly, and the satellite radio market recently exploded. Satellite radio providers XM and Sirius (now featuring Powell's nemesis Howard Stern as the star of their network) are uncensored and have little or no commercials.

With well over 10 million subscribers nationwide, satellite radio is growing exponentially. Conservative members of Congress, backed by large conventional broadcast TV and radio networks hoping to regain their audience, are now trying to pass legislation to control the content of cable TV and satellite radio as well.

At a time when "sowing the seeds of freedom" in Iraq costs hundreds of billions of dollars as well as the lives of thousands of US soldiers and tens of thousands of Iraqi civilians, our own freedoms are being increasingly eaten away by the Right. Under the guise of "decency," "morality," and

123

"protecting children," we are being subjected to levels of censorship unseen since the McCarthy era, affecting television shows, talk radio, music lyrics, literature, and movies.

ABC canceled comedian Bill Mahr's TV show, "Politically Incorrect," for its anti-war stance, despite its high ratings. Mahr's show was quickly picked up by HBO, re-named "Real Time With Bill Mahr," and has gone on to become one of HBO's most successful series.

Starting in the mid-1980's, the Parents Music Resource Council (PMRC), led by Tipper Gore, forced record companies to place "parental advisory" stickers on rock albums that contained any lyrics or subject matter that they found to be potentially offensive to anyone (something that is entirely subjective to the listener). The parental advisory sticker was actually seen as a compromise between the PMRC and the music industry, as the PMRC was initially demanding that legislation be passed banning the sale of music they felt was offensive. This prompted a circus-like congressional hearing, during which artists as diverse as Frank Zappa, John Denver, and Dee Snyder of the heavy metal band Twisted Sister testified. Ultimately, the PMRC got their way, and parental advisory stickers began appearing on albums. Many chain stores, such as K-Mart, refuse to sell any albums with parental advisory stickers on them. This practice continues to this day.

In the early 1990's, the censorship battle heated up even more when the rap group 2 Live Crew was actually arrested after a Florida concert and charged with indecency. Coincidently, Florida is the same state where Jim Morrison of The Doors was arrested and found guilty of felony indecency during a concert 20 years earlier. (Morrison was arrested for exposing his penis on stage. He was convicted, even though no one in the audience testified to have actually seen the offending member.) After their arrest, 2 Live Crew's album was banned, and a record storeowner was arrested for selling it. The case made it all the way to the Supreme Court, and was eventually overturned. The album, initially largely ignored, began selling millions of copies after being banned in Florida. After the recent stacking of the Supreme Court with extremely conservative judges, however, the same case, if heard now, would have quite a different outcome.

Agenda of Right-Wing Government

Intoxicated by their success in electing a Right-leaning President and Congress, the Right wing was ready to redouble their efforts to implement other aspects of their agenda.

Change the Role of Government

The Right would like to strip government of all social and welfare functions, and all economic regulatory activity. They prefer for government to revert to the sole role of protecting property and sovereignty through the use of its military power. The change, they hope, will occur in all three branches of government. The Judiciary branch would be stacked with pro-life and pro-gun conservatives; the Legislative branch would dutifully pass the appropriate laws; and the Executive branch would become more centralized and autocratic.

Shift the Burden of Taxation from Capital to Consumption

The Right's goal is to eliminate all capital gains, inheritance, and corporate taxes, as well as the entire income tax system. Radical and repeated tax cuts translate into endless deficits. Instead of having to argue against social programs, the Right wing can simply say that they are acting realistically and dealing honestly, considering the lack of funds. The deficit, moreover, pushes the fiscal crises down to the state and local levels, where governments are often constitutionally prevented from running deficits.

Privatize

Under the Right's ideal plan, functions that simply cannot be eliminated will be privatized as much as possible. The Cato Institute, a libertarian public policy organization, led the Right wing's push for privatization of government services. In 2001, it was reported that the Cato Institute has spent about $3 million over the past six years to run a virtual war room, promoting Social Security privatization.

Eliminate Government Organizations

Some Right-wing ideas do make sense. The Cato Institute's support for the elimination of eight wasteful, bureaucratic cabinet agencies, Commerce, Education, Energy, Labor, Agriculture, Interior, Transportation, and Veterans Affairs, and the privatization of many government services except for Social Security makes sense to me. However, I quickly leave the room when Ed Crane, a key executive, states, "I think Franklin Roosevelt was a lousy President. What he did, which is, impose this great nanny state on America – was a great mistake."

Capitalistic Agenda

The Right worships the mythical American free-market capitalist motto "government should keep its hands off the private sector." But the reality that big business has its hands deep into the pockets of the government is ignored by the Right-wing capitalists. Today's "free [loading] capitalists" receive tens off billions of dollars in annual protectionist subsidies. In my own state of California, prime stomping ground of the free market entrepreneur, our giant agricultural industry meets under government sponsorship to control the prices of their major produce through market boards.

States' Rights

The Right believes that the US Constitution fundamentally designates the states as the basic units of the Federal union; that while the states, under the Constitution, surrender certain specified rights to the Federal government, they retain all other rights not explicitly surrendered, as guaranteed in the Ninth and Tenth Amendments to the Constitution. Therefore, Washington, and the Federal government, in any of its Executive, Legislative, or Judicial branches, has no rights or powers whatsoever except what the states under the Constitution have explicitly granted it. The rallying cry of "states' rights" was used to justify slavery and Jim Crow laws, and more recently, the Right has tried to use it to ban abortions, force the teaching of creationism in public schools, and pass anti-gay legislation. The Right seemed to forget all about their states' rights stance, however, when states like California passed medical marijuana legislation, Oregon passed Right-To-Die legislation, and Massachusetts passed gay marriage legislation.

Fiscal Responsibility
"How to Run the World's Largest Economy into the Ground in Under Four Years" by G.W. Bush

(My son Brett, who is 40, wrote the next six sections of this chapter). One of the basic precepts of conservatism has always been cutting government spending. Yet somehow, even while slashing budgets for Welfare, after-school programs, job training programs, education, health care, child care, social security, veteran's benefits (during a war), levee repair in New Orleans and elsewhere, unemployment benefits, and virtually every other social program (as one would expect a Republican president would try to do), George Bush, the "Hero Of The Republican Party," still managed to take the largest budget surplus in our country's history and turn it into the largest budget deficit in our country's history in under four years. **Bush's budget deficit is now larger than the budget deficits of all US Presidents … COMBINED!!!** We now have the largest trade deficit in our history, but to hear President Bush tell it, our economy is "on the march."

Despite record profits by the oil companies, gas prices are at record highs. What is the use in having a President and Vice President who are "good friends" of the oil industry if we can't even get cheap gas out of the deal?

Worse yet, the administration has been giving huge tax breaks to corporations, actually encouraging them to "outsource" American jobs to other countries where labor is cheaper. They even had the gall to put "experts" on talk shows, saying that the outsourcing of American jobs is actually *good* for the economy! What kind of idiots do they think we are?

The administration has also made it easy for US corporations to further avoid taxes by basing themselves (on paper) in places like the Cayman Islands. They have given billions of Federal dollars to large corporations in the form of economic stimulus packages, and billions more in tax breaks to the wealthiest 1% of Americans. Bush now wants to make these tax breaks (originally "sold" to Congress as a temporary refund that would jump-start the failing economy) permanent. The cost of the Iraq war is well over $200 billion, and rising, with no end in sight. To borrow from comedian Lewis Black, "I would go into more detail, but my nurse is on a break, and I don't know where she keeps the shots." Despite repeated warnings from both the Left and the Right that our economy is in serious trouble, Bush has chosen to "stay the course" … right into a wall.

Gay Wrongs
Getting the Government Out of Our Bedrooms
"Oh, you're one of those sodomites. You should only get AIDS and die, you pig."- Michael Savage

No group stirs up the white-hot Puritan rage of the Right as much as homosexuals. Apparently, the sight of two men holding hands in public is causing the downfall of Western Civilization, as we know it. Who knew? Conservatives truly believe that the "gay agenda" is to somehow recruit as many young heterosexuals as possible, and "turn" them gay. They also use this logic to defend their opposition to gay couples adopting children (even children of the opposite sex), and some conservatives oppose gay people working as teachers for the same reason. Perhaps gay fairy dust does make some hypocrites into homosexuals. Indeed, anti-gay preacher Reverend Haggard, president of the National Association of Evangelicals, recently confessed to having a multi-year relationship with a homosexual prostitute. Once again, Uncle Tony's "You don't believe this shit, do you?" comes to mind, as it increasingly has over the last several years.

In the 1950's, the famed Kinsey report on human sexuality stated that gays and bisexuals make up 10% to 15%

of the population (roughly the same percentage of the population as blacks and left-handed people). Yet the Right seems to think that it's acceptable to treat them as 2nd class citizens, and conservatives continue to do all they can to prevent gays (as well as unmarried heterosexual couples) from obtaining any of the legal rights that are given to all heterosexual married couples (tax benefits, power of attorney, healthcare decision making, insurance coverage, etc.). Indeed, Bush is currently trying to get a constitutional amendment banning gay marriage. Apparently, the "life, liberty, and the pursuit of happiness" stuff only applies to heterosexuals.

In 2003, prior to the Supreme Court's decision striking down a Texas law that banned sodomy between homosexual couples (as well as heterosexual couples), former Pennsylvania Senator Rick Sanctorum warned that if you have the right to gay sex within your home, then you have the right to bigamy, and you then have the right to incest and adultery, etc. Coincidently, at the same time, the state of Texas also repealed a law banning sex with farm animals. Apparently, in Texas, it is OK to have sex with a goat, as long as the goat is of the opposite sex … otherwise, you are considered a pervert. But it's not OK to have gay sex within your own home.

Understandably, Santorum's remarks caused a wave of condemnation, but they also rallied the Right to his defense. Right-wing groups commended Sanctorum for maintaining dignity under fire and sticking to his principles. They argued that his views about homosexuality were in line with the position of the Catholic Church, and therefore rooted in his Catholic faith. In this way, the Right sought to equate any criticism of his views with bigotry against his religion and the Catholic Church.

The Reverend Jerry Falwell has made a number of statements attacking the gay community over the years, but one of the most bizarre would have to be when he came out against the children's TV show, "The Teletubbies," stating that one of its characters, Tinkie Winkie, is gay. Tinkie Winkie is one of four characters dressed in different color costumes with various shapes sticking out of their heads. The show, aimed at

129

infants and toddlers, has dialog consisting primarily of baby talk. According to the good reverend, Tinkie Winkie is gay because he is purple, has an upside down triangle shape on his head, and carries what looked like a purse. Reverend Falwell did not elaborate on the sexual orientations of the other characters on the show, Dipsy, La-La, and Po. It seems to many that the only real outcome of Falwell's statement was to make him look like an idiot, and begin a huge increase in sales of Tinkie Winkie merchandise to gay people.

If there ever is a "Jackass of the Century Award," Another of Falwell's comments really puts him in strong contention as the winner. As a guest on Pat Robertson's show, "The 700 Club," and two days after the attacks of September 11th, Falwell said, "I really believe that the pagans, and the abortionists, and the feminists, and the gays, and the lesbians who are actively trying to make that an alternative lifestyle, the ACLU, People For The American Way, all of them who have tried to secularize America – I point the finger in their face, and say, 'You helped make this happen.'" Robertson's response: "Well, I totally concur."

More recently, when Israeli Prime Minister, Ariel Sharon, suffered a massive inter-cranial hemorrhage, leaving him in a coma, Robertson told his viewers that this was divine retribution for Sharon pulling out of Gaza as part of the Middle East peace process. Nice guy. So much for "Compassionate Conservatism."

I've heard it said that possibly the only man alive who could beat Falwell and Robertson for the "Jackass of the Century Award" is the Reverend Fred Phelps. Phelps and his supporters have such an intense hatred of gays that they went so far as to demonstrate at the funeral of Matthew Sheppard, a 21-year-old Wyoming college student who was brutally beaten, tied to a fence, and while he begged for his life, was left to die. Why? Only because he was gay. Phelps and his supporters held signs at the funeral that had such "Christian" sayings as, "Fags burn in hell," and "God hates fags." They then berated Sheppard's grieving parents as they arrived at the funeral to bury their only son.

130

More recently, Phelps and his supporters have begun demonstrating at the funerals of soldiers who were killed in Iraq. Even though most, or all, of the dead soldiers were heterosexual, Phelps stated that their deaths are God's punishment for fighting for a country that tolerates homosexuality. How someone can consider himself a man of God and do such a thing is beyond my comprehension. If there is a hell, its fires burn for men like Fred Phelps.

Hyper-Patriotism
Super-Size Those Freedom Fries

While there is nothing wrong with having a sense of pride in your country, the Right takes patriotism to new and sometimes alarming levels. Hyper-patriotism gives rise to the idea that our country is somehow special in the eyes of God, that we are more deserving of His blessings than lesser countries, and that we are actually doing God's will. This removes any accountability for our actions. One need only watch the often-ridiculed footage of John Ashcroft, almost misty-eyed, singing "Let The Eagle Soar" (a song he composed himself) to understand the extent to which the Right truly believes in this stuff. Believing in something does not necessarily make it so, however. Hitler thought he was doing God's will too. In fact, on the belts of the S.S. soldiers' uniforms was the German inscription, "God is with us."

The prevailing attitude of the Bush Administration and the Right seems to be "my country, wrong or right." I used to see bumper stickers with that statement when I was growing up in the 70's and 80's, and even as a young child, I found it profoundly disturbing, even chilling. It was at odds with everything I believed then, and believe now. My father would probably attribute this to some kind of liberal "brainwashing" (and I would probably respectfully, and with great love, respond that this is nonsense). On the contrary, I wonder what kind of Right-wing brainwashing would make someone believe that, and put it on his car.

This thought process (hyper-patriotism) creates a sort of mob mentality, and implies that blind patriotism is somehow more important than real morality or truth. It creates an environment where anyone who dares to question anything the government does, no matter how wrong, is immediately branded unpatriotic or a traitor. Make no mistake, I love this country, and more importantly, I love the ideas upon which it was built. I wouldn't want to live anywhere else.

That being said, however, there are times (like now) when the leaders of this country lose sight of many of the ideas that are the foundation of this country. Liberals are frequently accused of "hating America," when I believe that just the opposite is true. Which parent loves his child more – the one who chastises the child when he misbehaves, or the one who ignores or tries to make excuses for the behavior? ("Look how cute! Tyler's practicing brain surgery on the dog again!") To me, a true patriot is someone who is willing to stand up and call bullshit what it is, especially when it is unpopular to do so.

Hyper-patriotism also creates an arrogance that seems to permeate nearly every decision the Bush Administration makes, both domestically and abroad. They seem to feel that the ends always justify the means, no matter what, even if they lie, cheat, or steal to do it, and no matter whom it hurts. Many of the core principles on which our country was founded are pushed aside by this administration if they are inconvenient or block goals. Unfortunately, many people in this country are willing to look the other way. Ben Franklin said it best when he said that those who are willing to give up some of their liberty for a small measure of safety deserve neither liberty nor safety.

Corporate Feeding Frenzy
The Sacred Cows of the Right

The Right always looks out for the interests of their "sacred cow" industries, and the Bush Administration has taken this idea to new levels. These include big oil, the timber industry, the mining industry, big pharmacology, chemical manufacturing, real estate developers, and big tobacco; basically, those industries that have the most to lose from environmental protection legislation, and health and safety regulations. These are the industries, along with the Christian

Right (itself a multi-million dollar industry with tax-exempt status) that are responsible for putting George W. Bush into office, and they expect to see results from their investment ... and Bush has delivered in spades. Upon taking office in 2000, Bush began appointing dozens of former top executives and lobbyists (many of whom still had personal financial interests in their respective industries) to posts directly responsible for regulating these very same industries. He also put unqualified cronies in vital positions. ("Brownie, you're doing a heck of a job.")

As a result, environmental regulations were weakened or removed completely, anti-trust laws were virtually ignored, pensions were raided, corporations received massive tax breaks and billions more in cash, and shady back-room deals of all kinds were made at the highest levels of government. The inmates were now running the asylum. The industries were trusted to regulate themselves. This is like trusting wolves to guard sheep. A corporate feeding frenzy on a scale never before seen ensued, and continues unabated to this day. Like glutens at a buffet, these modern-day robber barons seem insatiable, feeding off the country for all it is worth, consuming everything in their path. They will continue to do so for as long as possible, until nothing is left.

Anti-Environmentalism
Clearing the Air
"God says, 'Earth is yours. Take it. Rape it. It's yours.'"
– Ann Coulter

Several years ago, I was talking to a conservative uncle of mine, and he was telling me about a recent trip to the jungles of Costa Rica. He told me that it was one of the most beautiful places he had ever seen, but he would be just as happy to see it paved over and built up. When I asked why he would say such a thing, he simply replied that both of his sons are in the construction business, and they might benefit from that. I could hardly contain my horror. I did, however, suddenly understand the true scope of the cultural divide that exists in our country. Living in California, at times it seems to me that conservatives live in some bizarre parallel universe that is completely alien to me, and probably vice-versa. Perhaps nowhere are our universes further apart than in our attitudes toward the environment.

The Right often seems to be openly hostile towards the environment, and anyone who tries to protect it. To them, every forest is potential timber, every river is a potential dam, every lake could be filled with sewage, and every open space is potential real estate development. Every coastline could be dotted with oilrigs, and every hill is a potential open-pit mine.

A lot of this mentality, like many of the Right's attitudes, is biblical in origin. James Watt, former Secretary of the Interior under Ronald Reagan, once said that it didn't matter what we did to the environment because when Jesus comes back it will all be restored. This was the man in charge of our environmental policy! Evangelical Christians, such as George Bush and James Watt, operate on the belief that Earth and everything on it – animals, trees, water, mountains, soil, and oceans – was given to humans by God and is ours to do with as we choose. Conservation is not needed, because God will provide us with all we need, so we will never run out of anything.

Match this with the Right's fatalistic belief that the apocalypse is right around the corner. At this time, the souls of believers will fly off to heaven, leaving Jews, Moslems, Buddhists, gays, liberals, and other assorted non-believers behind. You can see why the environment is a low-priority for Evangelicals. They see any granola-eatin', sandal-wearin', tree-huggin', evolution-believin', import-drivin', blue-state liberal as a threat to their entire way of life. They have the same attitude toward any science having to do with evolution or dinosaurs, warnings of global warming, greenhouse gasses, ozone depletion, melting polar ice caps, climate changes, acid rain, and anything else that does not fit into their rigid political / religious / corporate belief system.

The Right wing's apparent contempt for science exists because science, religion, and the Right's political agenda don't always jibe. As a result, we're told that occurrences of global warming, acid rain, and huge holes in the ozone layer don't really exist. (Dan Quayle once actually remarked that recent "studies" pointed out that global warming might actually be *good* for the environment.) Nicotine, of course, is not really addictive. Kansas for a time stopped teaching evolution in science classes. Public schools get funding for abstinence-only sex education programs. The classic book **Animal Farm** was banned from one school district for being "anti-meat." Many schools have begun banning costumes and decorations on Halloween because they believe it is a "satanic" celebration.

Our President, and many like him, believes that the earth is 5,000 years old, was created in seven days, and that dinosaurs never really existed.

Republican administrations, including the current Bush Administration, often downplay their reactionary environmental views by giving their environmental policies nice sounding names like "Clear Skies," but the reality is often just the opposite. During a press conference held at the edge of the Grand Canyon, the President's father, George H.W. Bush spoke glowingly of his concern for the environment so as to pitch his environmental policy. Al Gore later commented that anyone who believed that the President cared about the environment should look closely, to see Elvis, alive and well, floating down the Colorado River on a raft behind the President.

The War on Intellect

Brett's final grievance is his belief that the Right wing seems to have an open contempt for higher education in general, so it is no surprise that their leader is George W. Bush. Despite having attended Yale and Harvard (lots of people get into Yale with a "C" average, right?), few people, even Bush's biggest supporters, would go as far as to call him an intellectual. He often says that he's not "book smart," but the Right insists that he is smart in other ways. Many would not be so kind. Interesting how the Right painted Bush's 2004 Presidential challenger, John Kerry, as a member of the "academic elite," even though the two went to college together.

135

A conservative acquaintance of mine recently defended Bush by pointing out that he got a masters degree from Harvard. I responded by pointing out that Elvis was given a black belt in karate, but that didn't mean he earned it. The twice-elected President of the United States, the leader of the free world, the man with his finger on the button, has proudly proclaimed that he's "not much of a reader." He also said, "The majority of our imports come from other countries," "when it comes to evolution, the jury is still out," and uses words like "strategery." Our country is in the hands of a man who once waved at Stevie Wonder. In a country of 200 million people, is this man the best leader we could find?

Since Bush's election, education budgets have been slashed, and conservatives have proposed abolishing the Education Department completely. Is it any wonder that our students' test scores are so much lower than those of other countries?

Right-Wing Organizations

The reactionaries in the Right wing have built a broad and powerful coalition. They have become a big tent for the anti-abortionists, conservative churches (including the Catholic Right wing), anti-feminists, homophobes, anti-immigrants, anti-affirmative action groups, gun advocates, property rights advocates, free enterprise, big business advocates, and more. Let's look at some of the key Right-wing constituents in the US.

The Christian Coalition

The Christian Coalition controls the agenda of the Republican Party by training and electing pro-family Christian candidates to public office. These candidates always remember who is pulling their strings. At an awards ceremony for Friends of the Family, the Christian coalition showered praise on 31 elected Alabama officials who had a 100% voting record on specific "pro-family" conservative issues. Out of the 31 receiving the award, 30 of them were Republicans.

The Coalition, founded and once headed by their former president, the charismatic Pat Robertson, has 30 chapters listed on their website. In 2000, the group launched their biggest election year campaign ever, distributing 70 million voter guides to their members and conservative churches in every state. Robertson is given credit for throwing his support behind Bush very early in his candidacy, and gaining the support of the Religious Right, who make up one-third of the GOP base.

The Christian Coalition's principal contribution to electoral politics is the distribution of election eve voter guides. Normally non-partisan, but plainly directive, the guides outline a candidate's position on a variety of issues. The Coalition's descriptions, however, often use manipulative and stealth tactics to influence voters. They describe a supporter of the National Endowment for the Arts, for example, as a proponent of "tax-funded obscene art."

I (Barry Minkin) do support Pat Robertson's direct "either you are with us or against us" view of foreign policy, and I agree with his strong support for the necessary war against terrorism. I also agree with his position regarding the unacceptability of Blacks' demands for compensation, and their residual hatred for Whites and slavery – something that happened generations ago.

Talking about Black leaders who stir up the divisions and hatred, Robertson has said, "to play on the hatred of people for your own personal gain is abhorrent." Perhaps Jessie Jackson took that personally, since he was quick to condemn Robertson when Pat give his perceptive but too frank opinion about the need to eliminate Hugo Chavez, the pro-Castro Venezuelan dictator, who is an arch enemy of the US, and is determined to damage US interests at home and abroad.

Robertson's Christian Broadcasting Network (CBN) also deserves praise for having the guts to speak up about the litigious Council on American-Islamic Relations (CAIR). CAIR, according to US Senator Charles Schumer, has been known to "[have] ties to terrorists." CBN's unwavering support for Israel is also refreshing given the strong anti-Israel bias of most Left-wing media.

I do not, however, support Robertson's continuing attempts to undermine a basic tenant of the American constitution – the separation of church and state. Robertson believes,

> We have a court that has essentially stuck its finger in God's eye and said we are going to legislate you out of our schools. We're going to take your commandments from off the courthouse steps in various states. We are not going to let little children read the commandments of God. We are not going to let the bible be read, no prayer in our schools. We have insulted God at the highest levels of our government.

I believe that all religious study and expression, regardless of the denomination, should remain private, and also decry Robertson's anti-abortion stand and his negative views regarding homosexuality.

The National Right to Life Council (NRLC)

The NRLC is the largest anti-abortion, grassroots organization, with over 3000 thousand Right To Life chapters in all 50 states. One of the organization's central goals is a constitutional amendment that bans all abortion. Led by President Wanda Franz, the NRLC was #8 on *Fortune* magazine's Poor 25 List, which ranks the most influential lobbying groups in Washington DC.

Besides denying abortions to women, the NRLC contributes to the many problems in our society caused by teen pregnancy, AIDS, overpopulation, back-alley abortions, lack of choice, and harassment of desperate pregnant women and their doctors. Also negatively impacted by the NRLC are people who want to die with dignity, research into spinal and other injuries, global overpopulation, and the explosion in Welfare and crime.

The Traditional Values Coalition (TVC)

Founded by the Reverend Louis Sheldon in 1980, TVC is the largest church lobby group in the US, claiming over 43,000 churches nationwide, and represents 12 dominations. Their goal is to restore America's cultural heritage by opposing gay and lesbian civil rights. They usually refer to gays and lesbians as sexual predators and pedophiles. The TVC is also against reproductive freedom, the teaching of evolution, and sex education criteria that does not stress abstinence, to the exclusion of information on birth control and disease prevention. Moreover, the TVC also promotes prayer in schools and supports the use of filters in public libraries to prevent the dangers of pornography.

The TVC actively lobbies against anti-hate crime legislation because this legislation, according to Sheldon, will be "used by homosexual activists to punish any person who has the courage to speak out against the recruitment of children by homosexuals." They oppose rules prohibiting churches from directly supporting political candidates either through endorsement or campaign contributions.

The God-loving Reverend Sheldon believes that

> Americans should understand that their attitudes about homosexuality have been deliberately and deceitfully changed by a masterful propaganda / marketing campaign that rivals that of Adolph Hitler. In fact, many of the strategies used by homosexuals to bring about cultural change in America are taken from Hitler's writings and propaganda welfare manuals.

Shelton must be proud of his daughter, Andrea Shelton Lafferty, who, in reference to fetal tissue research said, "I think we're going to have to apologize to the Nazis for this."

Far Right-Wing Extremists
Neo Nazis / Skinheads

The Oklahoma bombing brought home to the American people our vulnerability to threats from Right-wing extremists, neo-Nazi skinheads, and White supremacists in our own communities.

When you think about skinheads, you probably visualize angry young men wearing big black boots and Nazi symbols. These happen to be a few of their trademarks, but across the world, "Skinhead" actually refers to a diverse cult of young people. The origins of the cult go back to the 60's in England. At that time, menacing-looking, shaven-headed, and tattooed youth in combat boots began to be seen on the streets. This cult has now evolved into a large collection of smaller gangs across 33 countries. The members' ages range from 13 to 25; about half are hard-core activists, and the rest supporters.

The cult has ties with political and other violent and nonviolent groups such as the White Aryan Resistance, KKK, and several others. They get support from so-called punks. Being a skinhead is not a hobby for the weekends, but a lifestyle full of violence and hatred.

When FBI agents searched a rented storage locker in a small East Texas town in 2003, they were alarmed to discover a huge cache of weapons and the ingredients to make a cyanide bomb capable of killing thousands. This was not a foreign terrorist with ties to al-Qaeda but a 63-year-old Texan with an affinity for anti-government militias and White supremacist views.

According to the ADL (Anti-Defamation League), the number of crimes committed by the far-Right neo-Nazis and skinheads continues at a high level in the US. Racist skinhead activity occurs in every state of the country, with groups now totaling over 100, most of which did not exist five years ago. In large part, the growth of the Internet has fueled this resurgence. Racist skinheads connect and reconnect online through a multitude of websites like Stormfront and Jew Watch, which are deep reservoirs of hate, and powerful recruitment vehicles for these perverts. They keep their movement afloat with profits from the booming "White power" music industry that propels their ugly message and effectively woos alienated youth. Indeed, Orange County, California is now the center of the active hate music scene, while liberal Sweden is now the number one producer of racist music. Perhaps we can put all the rappers and White power music idiots on an island together and destroy them all by forcing each to listen to the other's malicious noise called music.

The Southern Baptist Convention (SBC)

Always a bastion of Right-wing fundamentalist intolerance, the SBC leaders have directed a successful two-decade campaign to root out liberalism within the SBC, thereby making that organization even more of a threat to our Constitution. For example, Robert Reccord, Richard Lamb, and James Draper, heads of three SBC entities, felt compelled to alert the Convention "about a critical matter the Lord has placed in our hearts." These leaders want to put prayer onto our public high school campuses. They want students to act as missionaries to break the separation of church and state through student-led prayer and bible study.

They have ensured that their assault on the separation of church and state be seen rather as an assault on their student pawns' religious freedom. Strategies include "see you at the pole," where high school students gather around the flag pole and pray, which shows a complete lack of respect for the Constitutional separation of church and state. To be even more confrontational, they invite parents in a prayer walk prior to "see you at the pole" events.

Evangelists should not have free reign to proselytize other students in our public schools. With the percentage of baptisms in the 12 to 17-year-old group the lowest in Southern Baptist recorded history, the SBC decided, "In light of these statistics, it is clear that we cannot continue doing business as usual on our high school campuses or bow to the pressure to allow continued secularization of our schools."

The SBC is even fighting with and splitting from the World Baptist Council (WBC), a fellowship of 43 million Baptists, to create a more conservative body. These fundamentalists, like the Islam fundamentalists we're fighting in our war on terrorism, believe that only their perverted interpretation of religion is correct.

Conversion and schism is the goal of these sick bigots. How about the chutzpah of Al Mohler, president of the

Southern Baptist Theological Seminary in Louisville, Kentucky, comparing Judaism to a deadly tumor? Pointing to Scripture as mandating Jewish conversion, he said that the act of warning Jews about the danger of their beliefs was "the ultimate act of Christian love." When these Jews for Jesus loonies sent out by the SBC approach me, I simply remind them that Jews and others that decide to follow Jesus are called Christians.

The National Rifle Association (NRA)

If we need another organization to highlight the extremist, racist Right and their bizarre world of illogic and inflexibility, it would be the NRA. The members of the NRA, like much of the Right wing, distort our Constitution to support their Right-wing agenda. The NRA's main agenda is the deregulation of guns. The NRA decided that the Second Amendment to the Constitution, giving colonial militias the right to bear arms, could be distorted to free gun dealers from common sense gun control regulation. Over a five-year period, one such dealer supplied 2,370 guns linked to crime, yet no criminal charges have been brought against this dealer or any others on the list of the top 25 most negligent gun dealers. Charles Schumer, a Senator from New York, wants to prosecute the dealers, but the NRA wants to immunize them. The NRA is out of control. It bullies Congress into outrageous favors, while trying to intimidate opponents with a 19-page blacklist that includes authors, celebrities, sports teams, religious organizations, and businesses.

The NRA seems least interested in the use of guns by sportsmen, as evidenced by their support of assault weapons. In a recent incident, a Florida man was charged with attempted first-degree murder of a law enforcement officer. He told a witness that he was "hunting sheriffs." The AR-15 assault weapon he used was the same weapon that the DC snipers used in their reign of terror. In 1998 alone, AR-15's were used to kill American law-enforcement officers in six separate incidents. One in five law enforcement officers who died in the line of duty was killed with assault weapons. These guns are not designed for hunting deer or target shooting, but they are

142

effective if you are hunting people. Unless deer have learned to drive tanks (it would make for a fairer fight, if they did), why should hunters be allowed to purchase armor-piercing bullets? Doesn't it make sense to ban all assault weapons so that our law enforcement officers don't risk being outgunned? To anyone with common sense it does, but not to the gun industry that got around a ban by producing civilian versions of these assault weapons.

The influence of the NRA is so far-reaching that many of George W. Bush's successful political races in the so-called red states were based on whether the NRA endorsed or derided a candidacy. The organization's support comes with puppet-like strings made of steel cable, permanently attached to the people they endorse. The impact of flexed political muscle caught the attention of Frank Lautenberg (D-NJ) when he said, "The NRA and its cohorts are trying to deregulate us into a society where guns overrule judgment and order."

Looking at some recent legislation, guns seem to already overrule judgment and order. Just try to follow the twisted logic of the legislation passed by two committees (and supported by Governor Jeb Bush of Florida) that give gun range owners immunity from Florida's pollution laws. It goes like this: Florida residents need to practice their gun skills, so ranges are a necessary component (the bill's language) of the constitutional right to bear arms, yet if ranges are forced to clean up the lead and arsenic pollution that they cause, they will go out of business and deny Floridians that right. The bill would actually punish state regulators who try to address the serious public health threat from shooters littering the landscape with lead.

Senator Durell Peaden, a Republican and bill sponsor, took the argument one illogical step further by denying that lead contamination is even a problem. "Pea brain" Peaden concluded, "It is hard for me to consider us having the two highest performing school districts if birdshot and lead cause brain damage."

After reading some quotes from the NRA leadership, I'm convinced that lead causes brain damage. NRA Board Member Ted Nugent explains on the website, www.NRAleaders.com, how apartheid in South Africa isn't that cut and dry. NRA CEO Wayne La Pierre calls gun control advocates political terrorists, and NRA researcher John Lott suggests that teachers carry concealed weapons in schools.

Americans are strong supporters of gun ownership; 66% are in favor and only 20% against. The NRA has done a masterful job of selling the public their propaganda. Indeed almost 58% of Americans believe the ditty "If guns are outlawed only outlaws will have guns." And almost twice as many believe a ban on guns would make the country more dangerous then safe. Guess who the big gun owners are? People age 65 and older are most likely to own guns. Thirty-seven percent of all Americans age 65 and older personally own a gun.

Right Foundations
The Heritage Foundation

Trying not to take a far Right turn, but keeping well Right of center, is the influential Heritage Foundation. Founded by Joseph Coors (of Coors Beer) in 1973, the Heritage Foundation's mission is to formulate and promote conservative public policies based on the principles of free enterprise, limited government, individual freedom, traditional American values, and a strong national defense.

The Heritage Foundation is the biggest conservative think tank in Washington, DC. The Foundation takes credit for much of President Bush's policy, both foreign and domestic. They support faith-based initiatives, school vouchers, a ban on abortion, and overturning affirmative action.

Corporate sponsors of the organization have included General Motors, Ford Motors, Proctor and Gamble, Chase Manhattan Bank, Dow Chemical, the Readers Digest Association, and Mobil Oil. The *Wall Street Journal* says, "No policy shop has more clout then the conservative Heritage Foundation." John Ashcroft, head of the Justice Department, said, "Keep up the wonderful work of truth that emanates from Heritage."

In the mid-70's, conservatives created several foundations by pouring millions of dollars into the New Right coffers. In the mid-1990's, the most active foundations were Lynde and Harry Bradley Foundation, Cathage Foundation, Earhardt Foundation, Koch Foundations, JM Foundation, Henry Salvation Foundation, Phillip McKenna, and Smith Richardson Foundations.

In the next chapter, Islamic myths are revealed and the hypocrisy of the United Nations is laid bare.

Chapter 4
THE UN IS NOT UNFAIR,
AND OTHER ARABIAN FABLES

Our Left-wing teachers, politicians, churches, and media have made an idol of the United Nations (UN), and have taught our children to respect its decisions because they represent the views of a majority of the world's countries and global consensus. They hold that the UN is always right, and that this is a good thing. In reality, however, the positions and actions of the UN often go against the values of our country, lessons of history, the good of the future world, and rational thought. This chapter is a lesson plan based on facts rather than myths and fables. I will objectively highlight why the UN is not an organization worthy of our praise or respect, but rather a threat to our way of life.

We previously learned that lies are often perceived as truth, if they are told often enough. Nowhere is there a better example than with the lies the UN has perpetuated about the Middle East conflict. When lies come from a respected organization that is thought to be fair and impartial like the UN, they are more readily accepted by the naïve, brainwashed masses. **The world's misplaced trust in the UN is a subtle threat to Western values.** Let's take our heads out of the sand and dismantle the big UN tent that's been placed over the Arab bazaar.

I would like to thank Gerardo Joffe's organization, Facts and Logic About the Middle East (FLAME), for being a major contributor to this chapter. For those interested in more fact-filled material that demolishes the propaganda war and the myths against Israel, a must read is David Meir Levi's *Big Lies,* a publication of the Daniel Horowitz Freedom Center.

Myth – The UN Is a Fair and Impartial Body
Israel is indeed an outcast in the UN, and thus by extension a pariah in the world community. Founded in 1948,

over 50 years ago – about the same time as many other countries – Israel's legitimacy and right to exist is still questioned and debated in the UN.

After the Six Day War, the hostility of the UN toward Israel expanded out of all proportion. The UN Security Council passed 88 resolutions against Israel, and the UN General Assembly passed 400. Notably, the General Assembly adopted some 20 blatantly anti-Israel resolutions that hinder rather then advance peace.

In 1974, Yassir Arafat addressed the General Assembly with a holstered pistol on his hip and received a standing ovation from that body. Then in 1975, the General Assembly increased their hostility toward Israel by passing a resolution declaring Zionism a form of racism. This infamous resolution remained in effect for 16 years, until it was finally repealed under pressure from the US (one of Israel's only allies).

The very structure of the UN explains this collective hostility. In the General Assembly, 130 members always automatically vote against Israel. In the inner circle of hatred is a core of 20 Arab nations, part of a 56-member Muslim group, that present the harshest condemnations of Israel. These countries consistently join the Arab block in their anti-Israel resolutions. Another non-aligned group, made up essentially of the underdeveloped countries of the world, supports the Arab countries. Though they have their differences, the non-aligned group is aligned in their hatred of the US, and considers Israel this nation's surrogate.

Though America generously funds 25% of the UN budget, each country's vote in the General Assembly counts for the same amount. The vote of the US counts for nothing more than those of Libya, Panama, Iran, Syria, Cuba, North Korea, or Communist China. These countries provide very little of the UN funding, but they use their equal votes to attack the United States. Below are the actual voting records of various Islamic / Arabic states as recorded by both the US State Department, and United Nations:

- Kuwait votes **against** the US **67%** of the time
- Qatar votes **against** the US **67%** of the time

148

- United Arab Emirates votes **against** the US **70%** of the time
- Jordan votes **against** the US **71%** of the time
- Tunisia votes **against** the US **71%** of the time
- Saudi Arabia votes **against** the US **73%** of the time
- Yemen votes **against** the US **74%** of the time
- Algeria votes **against** the US **74%** of the time
- Oman votes **against** the US **74%** of the time
- Sudan votes **against** the US **75%** of the time
- Libya votes **against** the US **76%** of the time
- Egypt votes **against** the US **79%** of the time
- Lebanon votes **against** the US **80%** of the time
- India votes **against** the US **81%** of the time
- Syria votes **against** the US **84%** of the time

The greatest outrage is that of the 190 members of the UN, Israel is the only country that cannot be a member of the Security Council, the most important body of the UN. Syria, classified as a terrorist state, has been elected to a two-year term on that Council. Such outlaw countries as North Korea, and even Iraq under Saddam Hussein, were eligible for membership. Israel is not.

The General Assembly has repeatedly convened emergency sessions dedicated to condemning the Jewish State, but has held no such session on the Rwandan massacres, Indonesian crimes in East Timor, ethnic cleansing in the former Yugoslavia, Iraqi killing of the Kurds, Vietnamese mass murder of ethnic Chinese, or genocide in the Sudan. Sudan, a member of the Arab League, has been protected at the UN by Arab states despite the Sudanese government's genocide against Christians and non-Arab Muslims.

Sodamn Insane was not alone in buying influence at the UN, where corruption goes far beyond the Iraq Oil for Food program. For more then 30 years, Arab states have used their oil wealth, and threats of withholding oil, to guarantee an automatic anti-Israel majority.

The Human Rights Commission

The most virulent center of anti-Israel activities has been the pus-filled pimple close to the head of the UN, laughingly called the Human Rights Commission (UNCHR). This collection of misfits has, with a straight face, declared the democracy of Israel "the principal human rights violator in the world today." Since its inception, about 25% percent of its resolutions condemn Israel. Indeed, a whole agenda item at the Commission is devoted to Israel, while the other 190 member states are all considered in less than one agenda.

Such egregious human rights violations as those of China in Tibet, or Russia in Chechnya, have never come to the UN floor for discussion. The genocide in Rwanda, the ethnic cleansing in Yugoslavia, the horrors in Indonesia's East Timor, the disappearance of a few hundred thousand refugees in the Congo, and the killing of Christians are not found worthy of the attention of the Human Rights Commission. However, such canards as the old blood libel that has Jews using the blood of Muslims and Christians for their Passover baking or that the Israelis inject Arab children with the AIDS virus are earnestly discussed in the forum.

Instead of focusing on the question of human rights, the UNCHR used their 60th session in Geneva to focus on the killing of Sheikh Ahmed Yassin, the founder of the terrorist organization Hamas. Keep in mind that the UNCHR has never before called a special session to decry and deplore Hamas, though that organization is responsible for the murder of about 1000 Israelis. At the special session, the UN passed a resolution condemning Israel for the killing of Yassin, with a final vote of 31-3, with 18 abstentions.

Nabil Ramlawi, the delegate from the Palestinian Authority to the UN Human Rights Commission, was forced publicly to apologize to the Commission for filing a false complaint in which he accused Israel of having "injected the AIDS virus into 300 Palestinian children." This "human rights" member also said, "When Israel was established, it was established on Zionist ideology and its practices were even worse then those used by the Nazis."

The UN Office of the High Commissioner for Human Rights is now involving itself in bias issues that impact terrorists (a probable stakeholder group), and recently demanded "that measures taken in the struggle against terrorism do not discriminate in purpose or effect on grounds of race, color, descent, or national or ethnic origin." This logic is biased, since most terrorists apprehended are Arabs, and because there is not a more representative mix of nationalities.

Other UN entities, including the Division for Palestinian Rights of the Secretariat, the Committee on the Exercise of the Inalienable Rights of the Palestinians, and the Special Committee to Investigate Israeli Practices Affecting the Human Rights of the Palestinian People, daily expend precious resources to promote the Palestinian cause, to the detriment of Israel's fair treatment and any possible progress toward a negotiated two-state solution.

Finally, there is the United Nations Relief and Works Agency (UNRWA), established in 1949. For more then 50 years, UNRWA has funded and administered the so-called refugee camps involved in murderous anti-Israel activity. Included is the notorious Jenin camp, which is a source of terrorists who have killed over 600 Israeli civilians and wounded thousands more. The UNRWA landlords have been criminally negligent in allowing terrorist recruiting, training, organizing, weapons storing, and bomb development activities to be carried out under their noses.

Obviously, the pressure that the Arab and other Muslim countries exert via direct economic power is the main cause of anti-Israel activities and anti-Semitism in the UN. But most disturbing is the many European nations acquiescence to such activity, just as their actions or inactions were complicit in the Holocaust.

Created after WWII and mostly in Africa, the underdeveloped nations of the world, though represented in the General Assembly, have regressed socially, politically, economically, and in virtually all other aspects since freeing themselves from their colonial condition. Millions have died in fratricidal wars. Millions have died from starvation and disease. Rather than spending energy condemning and hating

151

Israel, other countries should use that country as an example of how to build an advanced and prosperous democracy.

The UN Hates the United States

It is not only our ally Israel that the UN hates; it is also the US. A delegate from the US to the United Nations Commission on Human Rights, Eileen Sauerbrey, was astonished at the level of hatred directed at the United States.

> We were frequently attacked as decadent fat cats who exploit the less privileged. We are accused of consuming almost everything that is produced, squandering, polluting, and wanting to dominate an increasingly less democratic world. **I did not recognize the country that others perceive. Nor could I anticipate the hostility fermenting in that United Nations body would be manifested in terrorist attacks against innocent Americans.**

Oil for Food Corruption

A Nevada Senator said that money received for the Oil for Food Program was illegally used to rearm Iraq, and is in essence now being used to kill US troops. Part of the money went to pay $25,000 bonuses to the families of Palestinian suicide bombers, according to US investigators. These incentive bonuses give Palestinian parents support for their restocking efforts, and should help insure the supply of disposable human robots and insure a major market share for the only export from the Palestinians to the global market.

Yet a yearlong investigation of the UN's Oil for Food Program issued an overly cautious wrist slapping; if the UN did not address its management shortcomings, the world's premier international organization could lose what legitimacy it has in addressing global security. What legitimacy? While the Left was praising the French and Russians for their votes not to go to war in Iraq, and pinning a "lone wolf aggressor" label on the US, our "allies," these immoral bandits, were selling their

Security Council votes for the $11 billion their companies received from the oil for food scam.

The report blames former Secretary General Annan for poor management of the program. "One more time, the secretary-general is out to lunch. He doesn't understand the process," says Edward Luck, a UN expert at Columbia University in New York. To comprehend how far down the toilet the UN resides, one must think about Kofi Annan's, "I know nothing," reaction to this scam, called "the largest corruption scandal in the history of the human race." Perhaps the reason is that many of his associates and his son were involved in it (to the tune of $750,000). Kofi's motives for speaking out against a confrontation in Iran just before he left office are also suspect.

The demand for Annan to step down came from Senator Norm Coleman (R-Minn). That demand came when his subcommittee said that it had evidence that Sodamn Insane's government had raised more then $21.3 billion in illegal revenue by subverting UN sanctions and the Oil for Food Program.

Any public or private leader would, if faced with the facts, resign, be fired, or be removed from office. But Kofi knows he can ride it out and survive, even if it came to a majority vote of the General Assembly (which won't happen). Regardless of the transgressions, the African ambassadors won't vote Kofi Annan out because he is the guy who highlights the never-ending problems of that always dark continent. The Arab, socialist, communist, and a fair number of Left-wing European ambassadors won't fire Kofi, because they are always looking for ways to embarrass the US and take it down a peg.

Frequently throughout its history, the UN has been under attack. But the UN, with its 191 member nations and its sprawling network of sixty-odd offices and agencies, keeps rolling along, hatching new schemes to change the world and expand its bureaucratic reach. These schemes are almost always political, even when labeled social or scientific.

The UN Pushes For Global Taxes

A United Nations conference is asking world leaders, including President Bush, to consider global taxes to finance increased foreign aid spending.

This is a renewed effort to force American taxpayers to pay the UN directly, without American oversight or approval. Richard Rahn wrote in the *Washington Times* that UN bureaucrats and others…

> Have proposed an international tax on aviation fuel, a tax on airline tickets, taxes on international currency transactions, carbon use taxes, a 4.8-cent tax on each gallon of gasoline, and other taxes on an extensive range of transactions, goods, and services.

The UN needs more reform, not more tax dollars, and the US should oppose all efforts to create a global tax regime. To this end, the House passed a bill last month that now awaits action in the Senate. The legislation, S. 3633, the "Protection Against United Nations Taxation Act of 2006," would stop US dues payments to the UN if it attempts to implement or impose any kind of tax on US citizens.

Palestinian UN Status

There are numerous occupied people around the world seeking statehood or national liberation, including Kurds, Tibetans, and Turkish Armenians. The only group that has received official recognition by the UN, including observer status and the right to speak and participate in committee work, is the same group that invented modern international terrorism – namely the Palestinians.

These rewards were first granted in the 1970's, when the PLO, committed to the destruction of a UN member state, was invited to speak before the UN General Assembly. By rewarding the PLO for such policies, the UN made it permissible to adopt terrorism as a means of protest. The Tibetans, whose land was brutally stolen from them and occupied for a longer period then the Palestinians, never practiced terrorism and cannot even get a hearing with the UN.

The UN has refused to condemn terrorism unequivocally, and has instead upheld "the legitimacy of the struggle for national liberation movements" against occupiers. In other words, the use of terrorism against innocent civilians to resist occupation is legitimate.

The UN routinely allows Palestinian and Hezbollah terrorists to use UN-sponsored refugee camps as terrorist bases. Major Paeta Hess-von Kruedemer, a Canadian UN peacekeeper killed in Lebanon by an IAF missile strike on his post, wrote an e-mail only six days before he was killed to his former commander in the Canadian army. He said that Hezbollah was using the UN post as a human shield. Kruedener added in the email that the Israeli Defense Forces (IDF) strikes near the UN post prior to his death were "necessary," and that the IDF fire was not intentionally targeting the post. In the past, a UN vehicle was used as cover to capture an Israeli soldier who was then tortured to death.

Arabian Fables
Myth – The Palestinians

The concept of a Palestinian people is a fundamental lie and the most successful manipulation of the media in modern history. This lie that caused the deaths of thousands of innocent people is continually and libelously spread by a media that is malicious, naïve, and uniformed, and by anti-Semitic Left-wing groups and churches, Jimmy "toxic peanut syndrome" Carter, revisionist Middle East professors, and PLO propagandists.

Until 1948, the Jews Were the Palestinians! In reality, the concept of Palestinians is one that did not exist until about 1948, when the Arab inhabitants of what was to become Palestine wanted to differentiate themselves from the Jews.

The soldiers in the Palestinian Brigade of the British World War II Army were all Jews. (At that time, the Palestine Arabs were in Berlin hatching plans with Adolph Hitler, called "The Conquest and How to Kill All Jews.") The Palestine

Symphony Orchestra members were all Jews, and what was then *The Palestine Post* is now the *Jerusalem Post*. What's more, many of the Palestinians, or their immediate ancestors, came to the area attracted by the prosperity created by the Jews in what had previously been a wasteland.

"Palestinian" Identity as Propaganda Device

A prime example of propaganda masquerading as fact can be found in the modern assertion by "Palestinian" Arabs and other revisionist historians that even before the dawn of Christianity there existed an ancient nation-state known as "Palestine." Further, they claim that the nation, inhabited by "Palestinians," continued to exist even under the yoke of successive conquering empires, until the creation of modern Israel brutally usurped it in 1948. Today's "Palestinian" Arabs imply that they are the descendants of those ancient "Palestinians."

As a result of the successful Jewish revolt against the Hellenic-Syrian Seleucid Empire in the second century BC (commemorated as the Jewish holiday of Chanukah) prior to the Christian era, the geographic area identified by revisionist historians as "Palestine" *instead* hosted the independent nation-state known as *Judea*. This was the successor entity to the northern biblical kingdom of Israel and to the south, the biblical kingdom of Judah was inhabited *not* by Arabs, but by *Jews*. Several hundred years later, in 135 AD, after having become a province of the Roman Empire, Judea revolted a third and final time against Rome, and was crushed by Emperor Hadrian. Rome's army also suffered devastating losses in the battle, including the complete annihilation of its illustrious XXII Legion. In furtherance of Rome's costly victory, Hadrian – in a blatant propaganda effort to de-legitimize further national Jewish claims to the land – renamed the province Palestina (Palestine) after the Philistines, a long-extinct Aegean people. They had disappeared from history more than 700 years earlier, after being extirpated by the Babylonian Empire.

Even though the province had been converted from Judea ("Land of the Jews") into Palestina ("Land of the

Philistines"), and a vengeful Rome had massacred and expelled much of the land's inhabitants, it still continued to be populated by Jews, along with substantial minority populations of Christians and Samaritans. There were, in fact, hardly any Arabs until the great Arab invasion of 638 AD. Even under the rule of the Arabs and all subsequently superseding empires, the Jewish people *nevertheless* maintained a *continuous* national presence in "Palestine" –
right up until the resurrection therein of the Jewish nation-state of Israel in 1948.

In contrast, the ersatz people identified nowadays as the "Palestinians" are a collection of diverse Arab clans plus a smattering of other ethnic groups such as Serbs (these are the so-called Bosnian Muslims who were Serbian Orthodox Christians before their forced conversion to Islam), as well as Circassians and Chechens. All were transported from their lands of origin to the Middle East, including to the land of Israel, by the Ottoman Empire several centuries ago, for reasons *virtually identical* to those of the Roman Empire. They have, since Israel's Six Day War of 1967, publicly declared themselves to be a distinct ethnic nation named after those *very same* defunct Philistines, despite the fact that the ancient Philistines were *not even* Arabs. The fact that the "Palestinian" Arabs constitute a faux people is hardly surprising, due to the fact that by 1948 a substantial portion of the "Palestinian" Arab population, who resided in the British-administered mandate of Palestine, originated not *from* that territory, but rather from the *surrounding Arab lands*, which now comprise the modern states of Lebanon, Syria, Jordan, Iraq, and Egypt.

In this regard, it is noteworthy that *none* of the foundational international instruments dealing with the Middle East conflict ever referred to the Arab inhabitants of Mandatory Palestine as the *"Palestinian"* people. Prior to Israel's resurrection as a Jewish nation-state in 1948, only the *Jewish* inhabitants of Mandatory Palestine called themselves and were known to the world as "Palestinians." Moreover, during the 19 years (from 1948 to 1967) that Judea, Samaria, the eastern portion of Jerusalem, and Gaza were illegally occupied, respectively, by Jordan and Egypt, *neither* the Arab inhabitants of those areas *nor* the larger Arab and Muslim worlds *ever* asserted the existence therein of either an *ethnically distinct* "Palestinian" people or a *historical nation-state* of "Palestine." Consequently, during this same period, there was never *any* demand from any quarter for the establishment in Judea, Samaria, the eastern portion of Jerusalem, and Gaza of a "Palestinian" state. In fact, the Arabs of Judea, Samaria, and the eastern portion of Jerusalem emphatically insisted that they were *"southern Syrians"* prior to Israel's 1948 War of Independence. In deference to this *non-assertion* of "Palestinian" Arab *ethnic* identity, the League of Nations' Mandate for Palestine of 1922 referred to the local Arab population collectively as *"existing non-Jewish communities."* Furthermore, the United Nations Security Council Resolution No. 242 of 1967 referred to them collectively as *"the refugee problem."* **In other words, the *very language* of these international instruments confirms that the concept of a "Palestinian" ethnic identity is a recent fabrication.**

Indeed, this hapless band of troublemakers accepted that they were "Jordanians" from 1948 to 1967, only to assert their identity as "Palestinians" after the Jewish people's reacquisition of these territories in the Six Day War. Moreover, the leadership of the "Palestinian" people even went so far as to *publicly disavow* any claim to these very areas during those 19 years of illegal occupation by Jordan and Egypt, per Article 24 of the National Covenant of the Palestine Liberation Organization, enacted May 28, 1964.

Myth – The Nationhood of the Palestinians

The Arabs who now call themselves Palestinians do so to persuade a misinformed world that Palestine is their ancestral homeland. But of course, they have no distinct national identity. They are entirely the same in language, custom, tribal ties, and family ties as the Arabs of Syria and Jordan. There is no more difference between the Palestinians and other Arabs of those countries than there is between citizens of Minnesota and citizens of Wisconsin.

Myth – The West Bank

Again this is a concept that did not exist until 1948, when the army of the Kingdom of Trans-Jordan, together with five other Arab armies, invaded the Jewish state of Israel on the very day of its creation.

In what can be described as a biblical miracle, the ragtag Jewish forces defeated the combined Arab might during that invasion. But Trans-Jordan stayed in possession of the territories of Judea and Samaria and the eastern part of the city of Jerusalem. The Jordanians promptly expelled all Jews from the area occupied, destroyed all Jewish institutions and houses of worship, used Jewish cemetery headstones to build military latrines. In the aftermath of the Six Day War, they also renamed and popularized the territories with the nouveau appellation "West Bank," a de-Judaizing substitution for the historical names Judea and Samaria, as they had been called since time immemorial.

The attempts were quite successful in persuading a uniformed world that these territories were ancestral parts of the Jordanian Arab Kingdom, itself a recent creation of British power diplomacy. Even after the total rout of the Arabs in the 1967 Six Day War, in which the Jordanians were driven out of Judea, Samaria, and Jerusalem, they continued to call this territory the West Bank – a geographical and political concept that cannot be found on any except the most recent maps. The concept of the West Bank is yet another example of how a big lie told long enough can change history.

Myth – The Occupied Territories
A Brief History

Most of the area now called the Middle East was part of the Ottoman (Turkish) Empire. Germany lost WWI, and so did its ally Turkey. With that, the Ottoman Empire ceased to exist, and the League of Nations assigned Britain and France as the mandatory powers. France assumed mandatory control over what is now Syria and Lebanon. Britain assumed mandatory control of the rest, including

159

Palestine (now Jordan and Israel), the West Bank, and the Golan Heights (claimed by Syria as its age-old patrimony).

In 1917, the British issued the Balfour Declaration, under which Palestine was to become the homeland for the Jewish people. In 1921, Winston Churchill, who was then Colonial Secretary of Great Britain, separated all the land east of the Jordan River from the territory designated to be the Jewish homeland, and awarded it to the Hashemites, rulers of the Kingdom of Trans-Jordan.

The Arabs, whipped up by their fanatic clergy, were fiercely opposed to the presence of Jews on what they called sacred Moslem territory. The British tried to arbitrate constant warfare between the two groups, always favoring the Arabs, who they considered more important to their imperial interests.

In 1947, the British decided that they'd had enough, and resigned the mandate. They left the Arab and Jewish antagonists to their own devices and turned it over to the United Nations, who partitioned Palestine into a Jewish and Arab state. The area west of the Jordan River (the West Bank) and the Gaza strip were allotted to the Arabs. Jerusalem was to be an international zone. After much soul searching, the Jews accepted the partition, and in April 1948, declared an independent state in the area allotted to them by the partition. The Arabs rejected the partition out of hand, and on the day of Israel's birth five armies attacked the Jewish State, killing 6,000 people: about 1% of its population. The Jewish forces, however, decisively defeated the combined Arab might.

Myth – Israel is an Occupier

Israel is not an occupier. In fact, Israel has always stayed in control of most of the area east of the Jordan River, except for the Gaza strip, which stayed under Egyptian control. The West Bank and the eastern part of Jerusalem stayed under Trans-Jordan, which promptly renamed itself Jordan and proceeded to ruthlessly expel all Jews and destroy the remaining vestiges of over 2,000 years of Jewish presence in that land.

In the Six Day War, Israel recovered the West Bank, the eastern part of Jerusalem, the Gaza Strip, and Egypt's Sinai Peninsula, and conquered and annexed the Golan Heights. During the 19 years that Jordan was in possession of the West Bank and the Gaza Strip, it didn't occur to them or anybody else, including the "Palestinians," that they should have a state or even that they were a distinct nationality. The claim for that didn't arise until after the war.

Jews have been living in Judea and Samaria since biblical times. The area was made "Jude rein" (a Nazi term meaning free of Jews) by Jordan when it came into procession of the territory. After 1967, Jews moved back into the area, and a great hullabaloo began concerning the 200,000 settlers who occupy less then 2% of the land. But there is no concern about the hundreds of thousands of Arabs who, lured by the prosperity of Israel, have flooded into the area, nor the more then 1 million Arabs who live in Israel and enjoy full rights of citizenship.

Remarkably, not a word is heard about the hundreds of thousands of Jewish refugees from Arab countries who been forced out of their homes and businesses, their property confiscated. Israel acquired the territories (the West Bank and Gaza Strip) in defense of an aggressive war waged against it. No country in history has ever been asked to return territories acquired in this way. Did the Poles return the huge chunk of Germany acquired in the wake of World War II? Did the Czechs return the Sudetenland? Did the French return Alsace-Lorraine? Only Israel is being asked to return such territories. The last sovereign of the West Bank and the Gaza Strip was the Ottomans, since then the West Bank and the Gaza Strip are unallocated territories.

To speak of Israel as an occupier is preposterous. To speak of it as former UN Secretary General Kofi Annan did, as illegal occupiers, is poisonous slander. He knows better. **But unfortunately, the big lie of Israel's occupation has been repeated so long and so often that even people of good faith have come to believe and accept it.**

Myth – Arab East Jerusalem

The city of Jerusalem, divided for 19 years, has been reunited for more than 30 years since Israel's victory in the Six Day War. But there is still much talk, and many people believe that solving the Middle East problem will not be possible until Israeli Jews relinquish their occupation and return Jerusalem, or at the very minimum its eastern part, to its rightful owners, the Moslem Arabs.

The Facts – A city of Many Nationalities

Before the end of the 1967 Six Day War, when the Israeli Defense Forces conquered Jerusalem and took it from the Jordanians, references to Jerusalem being a Moslem holy city were rarely heard. Jerusalem had always been a city in which many religions and nationalities lived side by side. It was only when the city was in Jewish hands that the Moslem Arabs declared their willingness to wage jihad (holy war) to bring the city back into Arab possession.

The notion of calling Jerusalem an Islamic holy city has only come about in modern times, especially after Jordan lost the city to Israel in the Six Day War. The concept gained currency by the dint of constant repetition. The basis for the claim is an Islamic holy site, namely the Temple Mount (sacred to Moslems and Jews) with its two mosques, El Aksa and the Dome of the Rock, which are both located in Jerusalem. The site is believed to be the place from which Mohammed ascended to heaven.

The Truth is, Mohammed Never Set Foot in Jerusalem

Aware that Jerusalem was the holy city of Christians and Jews, Mohammed wished to convert them to his new religion. So he commanded his followers to build a mosque in Jerusalem. But never in Moslem history did this mosque compare in significance to the Moslem holy cities of Mecca and Medina, where no infidel may visit.

With this being the basis of the tenuous Moslem claim, they demand the entire Temple Mount to be their holy site. The Israeli Government, in its constant spirit of accommodation to Moslem sensibilities, largely acceded to the tradition, placing the area in and around the two mosques in Moslem control. But how would the Christians feel if instead of the Temple Mount, Moslem tradition believed Mohammed made his ascent from the Church of the Holy Sepulcher, so Moslem Arabs claimed that site as their property? The Christian world, often too ready to consent to Moslem claims against Jews and Israelis, would be greatly astonished and would certainly resist such a claim.

Moslem Arab assertiveness and illogic doesn't end there. On the tenuous claim of the Temple Mount, they have construed a claim to the entire city of Jerusalem (or at least to its eastern part), declaring it to be their third holiest city. If the city stayed in the hands of the infidel Jews, it would be an insult to all Moslems and Arabs, according to the Moslems.

But the city of Jerusalem, in contrast to Baghdad, Cairo, and Damascus, never played any major role in the political and religious lives of the Moslem Arabs. **It was never a political, a national, or even a provincial or sub-provincial capital of any country since biblical times, only the site of one Muslim holy place, and otherwise a backwater to the Arabs. Muslims did not discover their passion for Jerusalem until very recent history.**

In contrast, Jerusalem has stood at the center of the Jewish people's national life since King David made it the capital of his kingdom in 1003 BCE. The city remained the capital until the Babylonians conquered the kingdom 400 years later. After the return from Babylonian exile, Jerusalem again served as the capital of the Jewish people for five and a half centuries. They have been living there since biblical times, and have been the majority population there since the 19th Century.

Jews have synagogues and other holy sites in most of the cities of the world. Can they claim sovereignty over those cites because of it? Of course not! It would be preposterous, and people would not accept it. And the Moslem Arab claim to Jerusalem, based on the mosques on the Temple Mount, is just as untenable. Jerusalem has been the center of Jewish life, of Jewish learning, and of Jewish thinking for over 3000

163

years. That is why the State of Israel has rededicated the Jewish holy city to be its indivisible capital.

Myth – Occupation Is the Cause of Terrorism
Israel's "Intransigence" Stands in the Way of Peace in the Holy Land

This is typical of anti-Zionist propaganda. What is shocking is that this naïve one-sided position is contained in a resolution of the Presbyterian Church leadership. The church is thereby suggesting that Israel has only itself to blame for the atrocities inflicted upon thousands of innocent Israeli men, women, and children by the likes of Hamas, Hezbollah, and Islamic Jihad. On October 17, 2004, a delegation of the church's openly anti-Israel members met on TV in Lebanon with what a US government spokesman described as "the A-team of global terrorism."

We are talking about Hezbollah, the ultra-violent Islamic group, funded and dominated by Iran – an organization that has a whole lot of blood on its hands. It was a Hezbollah bomb, probably made in Iran, that took the lives of 241 Marines in Beirut, and just recently started a devastating war with Israel, destroying much of Lebanon, and killing many Israelis. The group's leader called for more suicide bombings in Israel. Murder, he said, is "the only way to root out the Zionists." (His sponsor in Iran has mentioned that he has 40,000 homicide bombers ready to go against the West.)

Did this matter to the Presbyterian delegation? Apparently not. "We treasure the precious words of Hezbollah," said the Reverend Ronald Stone, "and your expression of goodwill towards the American People."

To further their outrageous, misguided, hateful anti-Israel agenda, the church then declared that Jews should be the targets of Presbyterian missionary activities. They also stated that Israel's security fence, designed to protect Israelis from suicide bombers, somehow made the country a racist state, and that economic war should be authorized by establishing a task force to consider divestment of church stock

164

holdings in multinational corporations doing business in Israel. The Presbyterian General Assembly compared Israel to South Africa during apartheid.

The Presbyterians are not the only ones who routinely vilify and libel Israel. To many South Americans and Eastern Europeans, the knee-jerk reaction to most any evil is that there is a Jewish connection. For example, Cardinal Oscar Andres Rodriguez Meridiaga, the archbishop of Honduras, has the gall to blame the "Jewish media" for the scandal involving Catholic priests with young parishioners.

What are the facts?

The myth that Israel's "occupation of Arab lands" is the cause of the conflict is just that – a myth! Arabs have been slaughtering Jews long before the "occupation," began, and long before the creation of the State of Israel in 1948. In 1929, for example, Arabs killed 133 Jews and wounded 399 in Hebron. Those who were not killed fled, making this city, where Jews had lived for centuries, "Jude rein." The Mufti of Jerusalem met in 1941 with Hitler and declared his kinship with Nazi Germany, because "we have the same enemy as Germany, namely the Jews."

Palestine incorporated what is now the Kingdom of Jordan and was previously part of the Ottoman (Turkish) Empire. After World War 1, Britain was given the Mandate, in accordance to the Balfour Declaration, in which the area was designated to be a homeland for the Jews. This was formalized by the League of Nations and the 52 nations comprising the League. In violation of the Mandate, the British severed all the lands east of the Jordan River, giving them to the Arabs who, under the Hashemite rulers, created Jordan. The Jews acquiesced to this betrayal. Britain finally relinquished its Mandate, turning its responsibility over to the United Nations, who partitioned the area into a contiguous land mass for the Arab sector and three discontinuous pieces for the Jewish sector. Jerusalem, located in the very center of the Arab sector, was to be "internationalized." The Jewish sector was made up mostly of the desolate Negev desert. The Jews accepted this plan. However, the Arabs, who "never miss an opportunity to miss an opportunity" rejected it out of hand, and invaded the nascent Jewish state with the armies of six nations. The war cost thousands of lives and caused over 650,000 Arabs to flee. If the Arabs had compromised, they would have had their own state since 1948.

Unending Arab Aggression

In the Six Day War of 1967, Israel again defeated the combined Arab might, maintaining possession and administration of the Golan Heights, Gaza, Judea / Samaria (the "West Bank"), and of the entire city of Jerusalem. Israel had no intention of staying in possession of these territories. It waited for the Arabs to make proposals for peace, which were not forthcoming. Instead, the Arab League met in Khartoum and promulgated their "three no's" ... no peace with Israel, no negotiation with Israel, and no recognition of Israel.

On Yom Kippur of 1973, Egypt and Syria once again attacked Israel. Again, the heroic people of Israel defeated the combined Arab armies, and drove them across the Suez Canal to within miles of Cairo. In the aftermath of that war, Egypt's president, Anwar Sadat, came to Jerusalem and spoke to the Knesset, Israel's parliament. He offered a peace treaty imposing very tough conditions: among others, the return of the entire Sinai, along with cities that Israel built, the return of oil fields Israel had developed (which would have made the country energy independent in the foreseeable future), and a relinquishing of the strategic mountain passes and early warning systems that protected Israel against future attacks. This was the first time in recorded history that the vanquished imposed conditions on the victor. In what was obviously a major act of folly, and, once again, an incessant quest for peace, Israel agreed to recognize the murderous PLO, invited it back into Palestine from exile in Tunis, and signed the Oslo Accord, by which governmental authority was to be bestowed on the Palestinians. But instead of accepting the outstretched hand of peace, the Palestinians launched their "intifadas," which cost thousands of lives and left the Palestinians themselves impoverished, with their economy in a shambles.

166

The above is a mere outline of the "peace process." In 2000, under the stewardship of President Clinton, Israeli Prime Minister Ehud Barak made unprecedented concessions for the sake of peace, giving away 98% of the land that the Palestinians requested, control over most areas of eastern Jerusalem, and authority over the Temple Mount. To the dismay of Clinton, Arafat curtly rejected this dramatic offer under the pretext that Israel would not accept the return of refugees.

Myth – Israel's "Intransigence?"
Fact: No way!

At every turn in this almost 100-year strife, Israel has offered compromises and concessions. The current folly, withdrawing from Gaza, is the latest example. **Arabs, whose almost exclusive concern is the destruction of Israel, are the cause of this ongoing bloodletting and unending war. Unless and until their mind set changes, things will not improve, but such a change of mindset does not seem likely**. Even the current leader of Hamas and the Palestinians has admitted in a newspaper article that his people have developed a "culture of violence."

Some clear thinkers like Walid Shoebat, an Arab, clearly understand that the Israeli Arab conflict is not about geography but about hatred of the Jews. Throughout Islamic and Christendom's history, Jews have been persecuted. The persecution of Israel is just the same as the old anti-Semitism. The Arab refugees are being used as pawns, to create a terrorist breeding ground as a form of aggression against Israel. The Arab refugee problem was caused by Arab aggression, and not by Israel. Why should Israel be responsible for their fate, which has been brought on by the attitudes of others?

Shoebat believes that no one, be they Arab or Jew, has a "right of return." Jews who fled Arab persecution from 1948 to 1956 should have no right of return to Arab lands, and Arabs who ran away in 1948 and 1967 should likewise lose the right of return either. This should end all argument. The Jews accept this judgment, while the Arabs reject EVERYTHING.

Myth – Israel Is A Racist Country
Facts – Racism, Bigotry and Hate are the "Fundamentals" in the Islamic World, not in Israel

In one of the most astonishing propaganda coups ever, a United Nations conference on racism, which took place in Durban, South Africa in 2001, declared that Zionism was actually racism. No wonder the US and Israel walked out of the conference, which was dominated by representatives of Islamic and Arab countries, and other anti-Israel forces, whose conclusions were predictable from the start.

The supreme irony of this conference was that it accused no other nation of racism – only Israel. In truth, Israel should have been given accolades as **perhaps the most ethnically diverse and tolerant country in the world.** More then half of Israel's Jewish population consists of people of color – Blacks from Ethiopia and Yemen, as well as brown-skinned people from Morocco, Iran, Yemen, Syria, Egypt, and Israel itself. In addition, Israel's population includes more then 1 million Arabs, who enjoy the same civil rights as Jewish Israelis. In Israel, hate speech is banned and discrimination based on race and religion is against the law.

In contrast, anti-Semitism – a poisonous form of racism directed specifically against the Jewish people – is rampant in most Muslim societies. Not only is anti-Semitism commonplace in Muslim nations, but is propagated shamelessly by their leaders in state-sponsored media and by Muslim clergy. For example, the small-minded, spineless, lying pervert who currently runs Iran supports the inbred homicidal maniacs called Hezbollah, and has held several conferences where he calls for the destruction of the Jewish state. He has even sponsored a contest for cartoons denying the Holocaust.

Furthermore, Iran recently hosted a conference of prominent Holocaust deniers, saying that it planned to examine whether the World War II genocide of Jews actually took place, drawing condemnation from both Israel and Germany. The conference, initiated by President Mahmoud Amadman, was an apparent attempt to burnish his status at home and abroad as the world's ultimate Islamic asshole. Organizers touted the conference as a "scholarly gathering," but the 67 participant ass wipes, hailing from 30 countries, were predominantly Holocaust deniers rather than academics. This collection of bottom-feeding low lives included David Duke, the former Louisiana state representative and Ku Klux Klan leader, France's Robert Faurisson, and Australian Frederick Toben, who was jailed in Germany in 1999 for questioning the Holocaust.

The slime that is running Iran even sponsored a law that would require non-Muslims to wear an insignia. Human rights groups are raising alarms over this new law, which requires the country's Jews, Christians, and other religious minorities to wear colored badges to identify them as non-Muslims. "This is reminiscent of the Holocaust," said Rabbi Marvin Hier, the dean of the Simon Wiesenthal Center in Los Angeles. "Iran is moving closer and closer to the ideology of the Nazis." How about presenting "The Most Naïve Award" to current-day Neville Chamberlains in the US Congress, who recommend talking with the current Iranian Hitler.

Malaysian Prime Minister Mahathir Mohammed declared in a 2003 speech to the Organization of Islamic Conference that "today Jews rule the world by proxy. They get others to fight and die for them." Imagine if an American President made that kind of sweeping and bigoted statement about Blacks, Latinos, or any other race. A justifiable uproar, and perhaps even an impeachment, would inevitably ensue. Yet there was no condemnation by the Muslim world for Mohamed's comments. Rather, virtually all of the conference's Muslim leaders actually voiced their approval.

In response to a terrorist attack in Saudi Arabia in May 2004, crown Prince Abdullah declared, "Zionism is behind (the) terrorist attacks in the Kingdom." Zionism is the code word often used by Islamic anti-Semites for Jews. US Congressman Tom Lantos called the Prince's assertion "an outrage… Blatant hypocrisy," but Islamic leaders were silent. In fact, millions of

Muslims still insist that Zionists were behind the September 11 attacks on the World Trade Center.

Anti-Semitism is expressed so freely and ubiquitously in most Islamic societies that no citizen can escape it. During Ramadan in 2002, Egypt's state-controlled TV aired "Horseman without a Horse," a program based on the notorious forgery, "The Protocols of Zion," in which Jews allegedly use the blood of non-Jews to make Passover matzos. In Iran, a TV series, "Zahra's Blue Eyes," portrays "Zionists" kidnapping Palestinian children and harvesting their organs.

Perhaps nowhere is the hatred of Jews more virulent than among the Palestinians. Most perniciously, Palestinian children are taught in school (and in UN refuge camps) that Jews are descended from apes and pigs, and that the noblest thing they can do is to kill Jews. "The Jews are wickedness in its very essence" is a quote from *Facilitating the Rules of the Arabic Language*, Grade 9, part 2 (1999), p.24.

Muslim clerics encourage this racism. Imam Ibrahim Madiras, an employee of the Palestinian Authority, declared in a 2005 television sermon, "Jews are a cancer." And later, that "Muslims must kill the Jews ... [and] rejoice in Allah's victory." It is no surprise, then, that the 1982 doctoral dissertation of Palestinian president Mahmoud Abbas, the "moderate" leader the US and Israel are working with for peace, made the astounding claim that "Zionists" collaborated with the Nazis to annihilate the Jewish people in order to drive the survivors to Palestine.

Anti-Semitism and the Prospects for Peace

Islamic anti-Semitism permeates the Arab Middle East and creates an atmosphere in which Jews are reviled and represented as subhuman. How can the Palestinian people embrace peace with a people represented by religious and political leaders as dehumanized veil beings? Even more importantly, how can Israel be expected to trust a so-called partner in peace when that partner is expressing abject hatred and murderous intent toward Jews on a daily basis? Yet the US and many European nations continue to demand that Israel make one-sided sacrifices for peace with a people steeped in racism and committed to its destruction.

Until Islamic leaders muster the integrity to condemn anti-Semitism (and anti-Zionism), we can't expect Israel to accept a forced peace with the Palestinians. Likewise, **until moderate Muslims reject racism in all forms, they can't expect Islam to enjoy full respect as a political and spiritual force among the world's people. Their attempted use of demonstrations and coercion to force respect of their religion is a failed strategy.**

Myth – Suicide Bombers Kill Innocent Civilians Because They Seek Freedom and Peace
Facts

It is easy to sympathize with Arabs in the disputed Israeli territories and Gaza. They live in squalid conditions and economic hopelessness. Indeed, many Westerners believe it's the desperate poverty, plus strict Israeli security measures, that provoke suicide bombers to blow themselves up in pizza parlors, buses, and college cafeterias. Unfortunately, this romanticized image of the suicide bomber doesn't square with the facts.

Who are the Suicide Bombers?

Study after study shows that the primary motivation of suicide bombers is neither desperation, nor depression, nor hopelessness. Indeed, most suicide bombers are middle class, educated, and emotionally stable. Noted psychologist Dr. Irwin Mansdorf observed,

> While [suicide bombers] many feel oppressed, the stimulus for the act is nationalistic and political, not psychopathological and clinical. In the case of Islamic terror, [there is] the additional variable of becoming a shahid [martyr] with all its attendant religious rewards.

In fact, terrorist groups known for their outspoken religious and political agendas like Hamas, Islamic Jihad, Hezbollah, and al-Qaeda, claim credit for nearly every suicide bombing in Israel and around the world.

What Do They Say They Want?

Hamas and Islamic Jihad, as well as the young men and women they recruit as human bombs, make no secret of their goals. Indeed, Hamas' charter says, "Israel will exist … until Islam will obliterate it." **Make no mistake: when well-meaning Westerners speak of Israeli "occupation," they are generally referring to the disputed territories in the West Bank. When Hamas and Islamic Jihad speak of occupation, they refer to all the land between the Mediterranean Sea and the Jordan River, including all of present-day Israel.** Even the official symbol of the Palestinian Authority depicts a map of the region, in which there is no Israel.

It is telling that Palestinian bombers never claim that they are killing to achieve peace with Israel. Rather, they murder as a matter of honor, as a religious and political imperative, to rid the region of a people they see as infidels. Ultimately, of course, all jihadists, whether in Israel, Iraq, Saudi Arabia, or Iran, seek to make the world, including the US, a fundamentalist Islamic dictatorship.

Can Killing Innocent People Lead to Peace?

What is the military objective of randomly killing unarmed men, women, and children as they dine, dance, or celebrate religious events? It can only be to strike terror into the hearts of its victims, their families, and their communities. I must ask: when has this barbaric tactic ever worked? When has it led to peace and freedom for its perpetrators? The answer is never ever in human history has terrorism succeeded as a military strategy. Yet the suicide bombings continue, even as Israel withdraws from Gaza and places more territory in the hands of Palestinians.

Why do Palestinian Poverty and Security Restrictions Continue?

Suicide bombers never claim that they kill innocents to solve Palestinians' economic plight, but there is no doubt that Arabs in Gaza and the disputed territories suffer from heart-rending poverty, corruption, and political oppression. UN refugee camps have helped make the Palestinians perpetual dependents on global handouts. Unlimited UN charity and lack of personal and societal responsibility contributed to the Palestinians having the highest birthrate in the world. Poverty, high birthrates, and cash incentives all contribute to suicide attacks. Billions of dollars have poured into the Palestinian Authority from the US, the UN, and European nations, but virtually none of this money has found its way to economic development. In fact, most landed in the bank accounts of corrupt Palestinian politicians or went to support terror operations. Indeed, **to this day, the Palestinian Authority still makes reward payments to the families of suicide bombers.** Now that the avowedly terrorist group Hamas has taken control of the Palestinian Authority, the world community has cut off funding to the group, and has limited aid strictly to humanitarian purposes.

Don't believe that suicide bombers kill civilians to rid Israel of security fences and checkpoints, though they are an inconvenience, and frustrating for many Palestinians. Indeed, these stringent security measures were instituted by Israel precisely to prevent murder by suicide bombers. The good news is that they work.

What is the Next Step Toward Arab-Israeli Peace?

Above all, **Muslims must**, as *New York Times* writer Anne Applebaum asserts, **change the culture that celebrates self-immolation and that sick form of honor and pride.** How completely screwed up has the world's moral compass become when Israel, a country where most people live the Jewish principles of L'chayim, meaning to live, and tekun olem, meaning make the world better, is faulted? There are so many Israeli and Jewish citizen heroes, like Holocaust survivor and esteemed professor Liviu Librescu of Virginia Tech, who gave his life to save his students from a deranged gunman. Why should these people and their country be branded with the world's worst image? How can their Palestinian neighbors, who celebrate death and dance in the street after their children blow themselves up and kill as many innocent people as possible, be the darlings of so much of the brainwashed world? Instead of glorifying suicide bombers, the Muslim world, on whose behalf these terrorists claim they are acting, should scorn their barbaric acts. Only then can we hope for peace in Israel, Iraq, Iran, and in the rest of the world.

In the next chapter, "Economists and Other Pundits: Why the Experts are Missing it," we are again confronted with how removed the academic world is from the real world. We learn how cult-like figures have brainwashed generations of students into checking common sense at the door as they enter their Economics classrooms.

Chapter 5
ECONOMISTS AND OTHER PUNDITS:
WHY THE EXPERTS ARE MISSING IT

"He's naked!"
The Emperor's New Clothes – Hans Christian Andersen

"An economist is someone who wanted to be an accountant but didn't have the personality for it." **– Barry Minkin**

In this chapter, we learn how the economic wizards' tools and theories, invalid "econo-babble," but accepted nevertheless, have blinded our leaders into using inadequate measures and outdated techniques to chart the country's future direction. Indeed, we will soon realize that a license to operate a crystal ball is as useful as a degree in Economics from our leading universities.

In the near future, today's economists, along with their theories and tools, will be shown to be as wrong as those experts who believed the Earth was flat during Columbus' time. Until that day, however, our strong reliance on invalid economic thought and the charlatans who continue to promote it will persist as another subtle force undermining Western society.

Economists love to go on programs like the "Lehrer News Hour" and debate ferociously the potential effect of proposals like President Bush's tax cut package. One says that the small one-time rebate stimulated economy back into the happiest of times, while the other will smirk and suggest that tax cuts were not needed since the downturn was a normal part of the economic cycle, making a rebound inevitable.

The casual viewer might think that these people have few beliefs in common, but nothing could be farther from the truth. Virtually all leading economists share one unifying belief: they make their living predicting how tomorrow will be like yesterday. Because they are forever looking backward and studying the past, they do not and cannot see our economic future.

Let me demystify and challenge the basic economic belief systems, methodology, and tools espoused by wizards with names like Bernanke, Greenspan, Friedman, Kemp, and Reagan. If we keep relying on conjurers to cure our economic woes, unpleasant economic surprises will threaten global stability.

Recycling Business Cycles

Most economists and business forecasters believe in what is called the business cycle and the ability of monetary policy to control its effects. They view a downturn as a natural and expected event, part of the boom and bust pattern that has characterized US economic activity for more than a century. Economists believe that they can predict the path of these cycles, and thereby predict our economic direction. Indeed, we hear them every night on TV, with their latest predictions on when the economy will rebound and how strong that recovery will be.

Let me now present a simple and clear summary of the business cycle dogma. First comes an expansion phase usually lasting three to four years. This phase is believed to start when interest rates and inflation are low. At this point, the experts would expect consumers to borrow money to make purchases of big-ticket items such as cars, homes, furniture, and appliances. Corporations, predicting increased consumer demand and greater profits, also borrow money so that they can increase production to meet that anticipated heightened consumer demand. Institutional and individual investors buy stock, anticipating corporate profits. The service and high-tech sectors typically expand, as the manufacturing sector requires more products and services.

As the demand for credit increases and more borrowers compete for loans, interest rates start to rise. Inflation increases, as the rising demand for goods and services sparks price and wage increases. A decline in spending occurs as tightened credit cuts back on the demand for the more expensive products. This decline is a signal that the contraction phase in the business cycle is underway. Factories and the service sector cut back production and lower prices to move their inventory. Consumer and business borrowing declines, while investors, anticipating lower corporate profits, sell their stock. Layoffs increase, and consumer spending decreases. After some months at this point, we are in a recession.

Why These Fluctuations?

Wave-like expansion and contractions in business can be traced almost back to the founding of the United States. Economists have continually seen cyclical movements in employment, factory output, interest rates, and bank credit, as well as in such far removed phenomenon as marriage, birth, and divorce rates. By studying many economic times series, The National Bureau of Economic Research (NBER) believes that it identified 30 complete business cycles between 1834 and 1958, each having an average duration of just over four years. Cycles of three to five years are called the Kitchin cycle, named for Joseph Kitchin, who first wrote about them. The Kitchin cycle, which the government and the mass media most frequently cite, tracks inventories, wholesale prices, interest rates, and bank clearings.

Over the decades, Kitchin cycles have differed markedly in amplitude. Every second or third cycle has been more violent than the intervening one. Peaks that cumulated in about 1899, 1907, 1913, 1920, 1929, and 1944 seemed to have ended in major booms that proceeded severe declines in business. These six peaks are considered to enclose five such major cycles, with an average duration of nine years, lasting 45 years altogether. These major cycles, averaging 8 to 11 years in length, have been called Juglar cycles, for a Frenchman who wrote about them over 130 years ago.

Nicolai Kondratieff, a Russian economist, found statistical evidence of cycles of even longer duration, at least in the case of commodity prices and interest rates. These cycles are purported to have an average duration of between 40 and 50 years.

177

Do These Cycles Really Exist?

Mainstream economists rely so much on the business cycle theory that they no longer question its existence or value as a predictor of economic events, such as the next recovery. I question its existence, and so have some others in the past.

W. Allen Wallis, former professor of Statistics in Economics at the University of Chicago, said flatly that the business cycles don't exist. He believes that these so-called business cycles are not cycles with the rigid periodicity implied by the term, but oscillations of variable, and unpredictable duration and amplitude. **Almost any series, if stared at long enough, begins to shape up into patterns and cycles,** he says. An enterprising new Rorschach (founder of the famous inkblot test in psychology) might someday develop a test of statistical personality based on a standard set of random correlated times series.

Two other respected observers believed that the business cycle, which forms the basis of current economic forecasting, is a psychological rather than a real-world tool. They are Arthur F. Burns and Wesley C. Mitchell, former experts with the NBER, who first identified the short cycle that today's economists and politicians are so patiently waiting to rebound. Burns and Mitchell warned that when we speak of observing business cycles, we use figurative language. **Like other concepts, business cycles can be seen only in the mind's eye.** Some cyclical theories fall because of their own weight, or lack thereof. British economist William Jevons (1834 - 1882) found a correlation between 11-year sunspot cycles, the cycle of rainfall in the Ohio and Mississippi Valleys, and a cycle of the same length in business conditions. A recalculation of sunspot data and a decline in the relative importance of the Ohio and Mississippi Valleys killed that theory.

Harold Barger, a former professor of Money and Banking at Columbia University, noted that no two cycles are exactly alike in duration, amplitude, or even in the area of the economy principally affected. No two Kitchin cycles, which average only four years, are alike. Their peaks and valleys vary considerably; some peaks were followed by severe financial crisis, while others were succeeded by declines so gradual that nobody even recognized the decline until many months later. Barger asked the obvious question: **"If individual business cycles display so many differences from each other, how can we say anything useful about business cycles in general?"** I completely agree with these writers, who have denied the existence of cycles in economics. The fluctuations we observe are essentially random in nature.

Reliance on Macro Measures

Most of what we hear in the media these days consists of economists discussing such indicators as Gross Domestic Product (GDP), changes in money aggregates, and so on. Supposedly, these tell us about the health and direction of the economy.

But these measures are so macro in nature that observing them produces little in the way of knowledge of what's going on in the real world. For example, we have been told many times in the past of great GDP numbers, supposedly an indicator of a great economic expansion. Yet at the same time, everyone, from top-level managers to department store clerks, had to worry about their jobs, as many businesses were subsisting hand-to-mouth, waiting for a recovery that never got going in earnest.

We ought to be extremely cautious about the value of economic data received and used by economists, futurists, government, and other pundits. Robert Eisner of Northwestern University said in an address to the American Economic Association, "Economic statistics often do not measure what economic theory pretends they do." Somehow, econometricians, theorists, and economic analysts of all stripes have lost essential communication with the compilers and synthesizers of their data. He wrote, **"to put it bluntly, many of us have literally not known what we are talking about**, or have confused our listeners, and ourselves, into thinking that what we are talking about is directly relevant to the matters with which we are concerned."

As Burns and Mitchell noted, **"What we have seen over the last century and a half is not uniform rising or**

179

falling economic activities. Instead, we have seen changed readings taken from many recording instruments of varying reliability." These readings have to be decoded for our purpose: one set of components must be put together in a new fashion. The whole procedure is far removed from what actually happens in the real world. Whether its results will be worth having cannot be assured in advance, and can be determined only by pragmatic tests after the results have been attained.

We can all observe economic activities as easily and directly as we can observe the weather. We merely need to watch our associates and ourselves as we work and spend. What we observe has a wealth of meanings, which no symbols can convey. We know, more or less, the plans and problems, successes and failures of the people we observe through direct contact, but we also realize that what happens to us and our narrow circle is determined largely by what is being done by millions of unidentified strangers. What these unknowns are doing is important to us, but we cannot observe them directly.

Someone tending an open-hearth furnace has a close-up view of steel production, but seeing is only a tiny segment of that vast process. They might work at one furnace, but cannot see the hundreds of other furnaces in operation in the country. Further, the smelting is only one stage in a process that includes mining iron, limestone, and coal, transporting raw resources, raising capital to build plants, hiring and training workers, setting prices, and selling goods in markets, to give rise to demand so that the whole process begins again.

No one can personally watch all these activities, but the people dependent on the steel industry need an overall view of what is happening. They attempt to use symbols, which actually bear no semblance to the actual processes. The complex steel-making and marketing process is reduced to a column of numbers purporting to show how many tons of units have been turned out in a given area for successive days or weeks.

In this example, we can readily see that the tonnage reports in the complex steel operation have little connection with the real world. Yet GDP and most of the economic indicators used to forecast our economic weather are the cumulative results of combined output reports like this, collected in many widely diverse businesses, from steel to beef. The price fluctuations and their effects on the supply and demand of beef, and the time it takes to breed cattle and get them to market, are just a few factors that determine the health of the beef business. **Think of the scores of other industries, each with its own complex processes, being combined with the cattle business to provide an economic measure called GDP, and you'll have to agree that economists can't tell cow manure from knowledge.**

The View from the Top Down – How the 1970's and 1980's Crushed the Idols of Economics
Keynesian – The Classics

Maynard Keynes was born in the 1880's. Though not a highly trained economist, he dominated economic policy until the 1970's. This economic idol thought that you could spend your way out of recession and increase employment by cutting taxes and boosting government spending.

The centerpiece of Keynesian economics was the multiplier. By running a deficit, the government injected money into the economy, and as this injection rippled through the economy, it would produce a far larger boost in gross national product. The question, of course, is where does the government get the money it injects into the economy? Well, it borrows it. But if you borrow from Peter to pay Paul, what is there to be multiplied?

The Keynesians also believed in the so-called Phillips curve. Simply put, they believed that there was a tradeoff between unemployment and inflation. In other words, the cure for unemployment was a little more inflation. **But when the 1970's were dealt more inflation and more unemployment simultaneously, the whole Keynesian universe imploded.**

The stagflation of the 1970's upset the political universe as well as economic orthodoxy. The simultaneous stagnation and inflation of the 1970's not only bewildered policymakers, but also ruptured the prevailing consensus of the economics profession. Prime Minister Callaghan, a former head of Britain's labor government, said about Keynesian economics,

> I tell you, in all candor, that option [Keynesian economics] no longer exists, and that insofar as it ever did exist, it only worked by injecting bigger doses of inflation into the economy followed by higher levels of unemployment as the next step. That is the history of the last 20 years.

The important point to remember is that as late as the 1970's, generations of economists were being taught a failed theory, which is still being advocated by some of them today.

The Monetarists

The late Milton Friedman led the modern assault on Keynes from the University of Chicago. Friedman's centerpiece was controlling the money supply. As a simple example, draw a small circle in the middle of a piece of paper and call it M-1. This represents the total of all the US currency and checking deposits. A concentric circle overlaying M-1, M-2, includes what was in M-1 plus savings and deposits. A large concentric circle overlaying the M-1 and M-2 circles is called utilized trade credit, or a total of the maximum chargeable on all issued credit cards.

The monetarists believed that they can control domestic inflation and the money available to businesses by simply controlling M-1 and M-2 through the interest rates they charge member banks. **Like the Keynes theory that failed in the 1970's, the monetarists took their blows around 1981, when M-1 signaled that money growth was too slow, and M-2 said it was too fast.**

As 1981 developed, inflation headed down, but interest rates refused to follow, and correspondingly, bond prices plunged. The falling bond prices would normally be a sign to economists of expected future inflation, but the signal was confounded by disinflation in other markets such as gold, and the strength of the dollar being in foreign exchange markets. In his *Newsweek* column, Milton Friedman, the monetarist guru, ruled out the obvious answers to this unexpected confusion ("Hey guys, I was wrong"), and concluded that perhaps this bubble would burst. If it did not, back to the computer.

Unfortunately, these discredited, unproven, fiscal and monetary theories and policies are still the major tools that the Fed uses to control interest rates and inflation.

The Supply Siders

The premise of supply-side economics, as explained by a small elite group of supporters who carp at both the Keynesians and the Monetarists, was to fight inflation with a tight monetary policy, and to offset the possible reversionary impact of tight monetary policy with the incentive effects of marginal tax rate reductions.

This policy, also called Reaganomics, was blamed for one of the most costly recessions since the Great Depression, with unemployment hitting 11%. Bush senior, you might remember, called Reaganomics "voodoo economics," and others have said that it is nothing but smoke and mirrors.

Irving Kristol, however, stated in November of 1982 that the reason for the collapse was not Reaganomics, but a collision between the swollen Carter budget for 1981 and the tight money policies of the Fed. The supply-siders would not take blame for the 1982 recession, but continue to take credit for the seven fat years that followed, beginning in 1983 and ending in the 1990 recession. These proponents are behind some of the current Bush junior economic policy that includes targeted tax cuts to promote rebirth of entrepreneurial vigor.

Looking Up – My Real-World View of the Economy 1970- 80

My basic premise states that you must get "into it to understand it." You cannot expect to stay on Wall Street or among the eucalyptus groves at Stanford University and talk meaningfully about the US economy if you think you're going to do so based only on what you've read, analyzed, or viewed from the latest M1 or other figures. Nor can one hearken back to unproven economic strategies, whose outcomes are a continual surprise to economists. Astrology has more meaning. You would not ask your doctor to fix your plumbing, so why would you ask an economist, who spends his life in academia and has never been involved with running a business, to understand the complexities of business in the real world? They don't understand!

If you truly understand what makes the economy work, your outcomes should be predictable. In the 1970's, I was the first to predict a major decline in the US manufacturing sector, which had been growing steadily until then. My dissonance with economic thought evolved not because I am smarter or claim some special gift. It was simply a matter of being at the right place at the right time. In my case, I was working as a project leader for Stanford Research Institute (SRI) as consultant to America's auto industry, the economic heart of our country, and to Japanese auto manufacturers.

During the 1970's and 1980's, I interviewed scores of companies in the two-digit standard industrial classifications (SIC) codes about factors that would determine their economic success or failure in the not-to-distant future. In the 1970's, the real economic engine of the US was the manufacturing sector, based on a strong auto industry. As I listened, I learned what really made the US economy tick.

> **Now we reach the halfway house; half the world's economies are auto related; half the world resources are auto devoted; and half the world will be involved in an auto accident at some time in their lives.**
> **"Autogeddon," a fact based poem – Heathcote Williams**

The 1950's were the happy days for the US automakers and their blue-collar union employees. US manufacturers built three out of every four cars produced in the world, and US imports represented less than 1% of domestic sales. When the foreign cars appeared on the scene, Detroit could have built better, smaller cars, but instead US automobiles grew even bigger and gaudier, sporting absolutely useless tail fins.

By the time Eisenhower left office in 1960, the US accounted for just 50% of the world automobile market, and imports captured a 10% share of American sales. Ironically, the Cold War played a minor role in the foreign auto invasion, but a peculiar fringe benefit that was allowed to hundreds of thousands of US troops stationed in Europe mattered. They could ship home, free of charge, one foreign-purchased automobile. While the total number actually shipped was probably fewer than 100,000 autos, the presence of foreign cars on US highways served as rolling advertisements for Volkswagen, Austin Healy, and other European manufacturers, whose postwar factories were producing record numbers of vehicles. Volkswagen advertising was catching the imagination of Americans, and soon the VW Beetle became an anti-snobbery status symbol.

The End of the Golden Age

1950 to 1973 was called the Golden Age in an OECD Study of the Century. Then in 1973, the oil embargo came along, and all across the country, millions of Americans waited in long gas lines. The longer they waited, the more they calculated, for the first time, just how precious few miles their guzzlers could go on a gallon of gas. Suddenly, Americans were interested in small cars in a big way!

The US auto manufacturers, however, continued to ignore the sales charts. They did not have the products the market demanded, and sales of domestically produced cars fell sharply. Honda, on the other hand, had the right product, and its growth was dramatic.

By 1977 and 1978, memories of gas lines had faded and domestic car sales rose to new heights. Detroit executives popped champagne corks and toasted their own wisdom. Unfortunately, Detroit's success in 1977 and 1978 led to the dangerous and erroneous misperception that without high energy prices, consumers felt no need to economize or buy fuel-efficient cars.

In the years between 1979 and 1982, the party ended. The second gas crunch accompanied the Iranian revolution in the spring of 1979. But unlike the sequence of events that followed the oil embargo of 1973, this time buyers failed to return to larger vehicles after the initial fuel shock wore off. Domestic manufacturers found themselves selling all the small cars they could produce, and fewer larger models. Detroit was forced to wait for new generations of small fuel-efficient cars that were still only on the drawing boards. In fact, **Detroit committed to spend more money on massive redesign programs then it cost to send the Apollo mission to the moon. In other words, our "can't do" management was spending $1 billion for every half-mile improvement in average, fleet fuel economy**.

While Detroit was trying to make a U-turn, domestic car sales plummeted for four years, from 1979 to 1982, making it easy for me to predict that a recession was coming. **This was the longest period of falling car sales in US history**. Sales in 1982 were an incredible 45% lower than 1978 sales had been. Instead of meeting the challenge head-on, with vaunted Yankee ingenuity, Detroit instead began waving the white flag. Plant after domestic plant closed, and over 55,000 workers lost their jobs. As a result, the small-car fever that gripped the nation was a boon for foreign manufacturers, who had long concentrated their attention on the small car segment of the marketplace.

My SRI experience taught me not to believe the still-accepted econo-babble of economists, academics, Washington, and Wall Street. Robert Bartley, editor of the *Wall Street Journal*, ascribed the decline to the usual economic nonsense when he said,

> **The 1982 recession was caused by monetary policy**, for better or for worse. Or, to view it more instructively, it was caused by a timing mismatch. The tight money part of the policy mix was put in place as early as October 1979 and especially in the fall of 1980. The tax cuts didn't start until October 1981, and were not effective on a net basis until January 1983. In between there was a recession.

The economic elite completely ignored the fact that the engine running the US economy (the automobile business) had stopped, for reasons having nothing to do with the intellectual masturbation being practiced by our leading economists.

University of Maryland Professor of Economics Melville Ulmer more eloquently summed up my thinking about economics and the practitioners of this black art:

> Since mainstream economics is by nature dogmatic, and most often ideological to boot, experience has proved to be an ineffective teacher. **Facts do not disturb deductive reason based on arbitrary assumptions. Moreover, professional reputations, including Nobel prizes, continue to rest on faithful devotion to sacred mysteries of mainstream methodology.** The weight of such personal investments has calcified into a self-perpetuating cult, with guild-like restrictions on apprenticeships and approved research procedures. This is why no perspective turnabout appears to be in the offing, at least not one generated within the professional mainstream itself.
>
> The prestige of no professional group, doctors, lawyers or politicians, can plummet indefinitely without courting the complete rejection of its consuming public. Economics cannot be exempted. Competition in the world of ideas seems certain to enforce a return to standards that will ensure its ultimate survival: Plain speaking, testable theories, and verifiable evidence, whether inspired by present or future dissidents in the prevailing mainstream. Until the counter-revolution arises, as it must in time, the authority of economics and economists, which is already fallen so far, will no doubt fall even lower.

We must develop a practical valid economics and economic forecasting technique. I have tried to show that the problems of the auto industry and the ripple effect through the country, including the high-tech sector, were the real cause of the 1982 recession. It was not the machinations of economists and politicians, whose efforts still have little or no impact on the scores of companies in all economic sectors, that were the real engines of the economy, even then.

If we looked at the recovery from 1983 to 1987, the 1990 recession, or our current economy, we must learn that contrary to popular beliefs, recessions are not caused, nor cured, nor even significantly impacted, by the actions of the Wizards of Oz, Alan Greenspan, current federal reserve chairman Ben Bernanke, or their predecessors. Indeed, the numerous interest rates cuts and hikes initiated by the Federal Reserve System, as well as President Bush's tax cut, have had little or no impact on the economy.

Economists and politicians are always surprised by the impact, or lack thereof, made on the economy by their tax policy and rate adjustments. Once again, most of the actions taken by the Federal Reserve Bank to raise our lower rates by a quarter of one percent make little or no difference to the economy. Indeed, think of the Federal Reserve Chairman as a puppeteer, without the strings that would attach him to the real world of business.

Moreover, the few hundred dollars in a tax cut given by the Bush administration did nothing to solve our economic problems. Most Americans have limited disposable income, and used this money to pay rent and buy food, not to buy the durable big-ticket items like cars and appliances needed to stimulate the economy.

In truth, low interest rates actually hurt seniors, and the other members of our society who want to safely save money in CD's or other fixed-rate accounts, instead of gambling in the stock market. "Gambling?" I can here you say. "No way, look at the long-term growth in the stock market." Remember that today's world is nothing like the world of yesterday, and that tomorrow will be very different from today. Looking at past performances to predict the future is a fool's game, where only the stockbrokers win.

Yes, the low rates help homebuilders, but over the years I have asked thousands of people the following question, "If the interest rate went up or down 3% either way, would it impact your business?" I always get a couple of yes responses from people connected to homebuilding. However, well over 95% of the group reported that interest rates have little or no impact on their businesses.

The moral of the story is that the economy is too important to trust to the economists. We need a new economics that is based on how the real world works, not controlled by the entrenched economists who continue to fail us. We must customize programs to meet company-specific needs. We can no longer afford to trickle down money into the economy through Washington. As the late Paul Tsongas noted, this is the equivalent of feeding oats to the horses to feed the birds.

What Real Factors Will Impact the Economy?

I've learned firsthand that organizations are as individual as people. The factors that affect the success or failure of companies, even within the same industry, can be quite different. Therefore, a one-size-fits-all, top-down approach is of little value.

I have also observed that most of the determinants of organizational success were not the type of data collected and analyzed by economists or others charged with determining economic direction. Economic forecasting must be based on factors that impact organizations and propel economic growth. Therefore, a bottom-up, company-specific approach will always produce more accurate forecasts than top-down macroeconomic tools and theories.

In this section, I am going to point out 14 economic trends that I have been watching. After you sail through the Fourteen C's, you will understand why I see economic trouble ahead, despite the glowing forecasts of the economic establishment.

C1: Connectivity

Remember when your stockbroker recommended foreign investment as a hedge against problems in the US economy? As global markets connected, they tended to mimic each other. We first learned from the Mexican peso fiasco and similar problems in Thailand, South Korea, Hong Kong, Indonesia, and Russia. Economic problems elsewhere in the world can cause serious economic problems in the US. In the future, this pattern will continue and worsen because the US is the largest net investor in these emerging markets.

The problem stretches both ways. Just as the US cushions potential downturns in its domestic economy with foreign investment, foreign banks invest in the US as a hedge against problems that could develop in their own countries. But when the US experiences a cataclysm such as the October 1997 market crash, investors panic. In fact, foreign central banks liquidated $7 billion in US government securities during the crash, dragging our markets even lower. Bear in mind that things could get worse. Foreign holdings of Federal Government T- bill and T-bond debt reached 46% in 2005. Japan holds 31% and China 12% of the $2.2 trillion total.

C2: Complexity

Not long ago, investors could profit from foreign exchange transactions simply by learning about and acting on news likely to impact financial markets. Today, with the world watching CNN and other international media sites, everyone learns what is happening at the same time; the result is that foreign exchange is a far less profitable pursuit.

Consequently, in order to make money, investment houses have developed complex strategies such as the use of derivatives, a major cause for hedge fund collapse. Complexity has caused a breakdown of our early warning systems, and at this point no one can possibly understand what is happening in the economy! For example, what if principals in a couple of large investment houses decided over lunch in Geneva to quietly buy a huge quantity of copper as a hedge against winter wheat or some other commodity? I doubt that any economist would understand that fluctuations in the price of copper the next day were traceable to that transaction, unless they're privy to the information of the purchase. Not even with the assistance of powerful computer programs could

190

an economist possibly understand the impact of over $3 trillion a day of such cross-border financial transactions.

Complexity adds the element of surprise to economic scenarios, with the result that economic predictions are way off the mark. Indeed, the Asian Development Bank's predictions of growth in Asia have been off by 50%. Coin flips are just as accurate!

C3: Capacity

This is the first time in many years that global over-capacity exists in most industries. The excess supply will only grow as Asia tries to export itself out of trouble. Take the automobile industry, for example. An oversupply of autos forced Toyota to close two new plants in Thailand, further hurting the ailing Japanese and Thai economies. At the same time, China, Korea, Indonesia, and Malaysia are developing national car programs, adding to the difficulty of car companies trying to survive in the price-competitive Asian economy.

It is not just in the automobile sector that over-capacity is happening. Take semiconductors: Taiwan is building a dozen new billion-dollar plants, despite an 82% crash in prices for the basic D-RAM chip. Moreover, chemicals are also at over-capacity, with prices for petrochemicals down 36%. Yet Indonesia, Thailand, South Korea, China, and Taiwan are blindly sinking billions into sprawling petrochemical complexes.

C4: Corporate Profits

The ripple effect of Asian over-capacity impacts other regions of the world. An example is the Mexican garment industry, which got trade breaks with NAFTA but cannot raise prices because it still competes with Asia. Prices for goods and services are also stagnating in the US, because they are forced to compete with goods and services from parts of the world where labor is considerably cheaper. Indeed, falling or stable prices currently characterize two-thirds of US manufacturing production.

My optimistic colleagues would argue that keeping prices down is good for consumers. That's true, and car buyers were pleased when the cost of a new car came down

somewhat last year. But a lower price means less profit.
Indeed, a 1% drop in price will cause a 12.3% drop in profits in
the average Standard and Poor 1000 company. Drops of this
magnitude can provoke serious economic havoc. No wonder
we are seeing record bankruptcies and debt!

In the Great Depression of the 1930's, a deflation spiral
sank prices 10% annually. Moderately leveraged companies
went belly up, unemployment soared, and the stock market
plunged.

C5: Consolidation

To keep profits up, companies are going through a
record round of merger and acquisition (M&A) activity. Average
corporate profits are inflated by 20%, simply because of M&A
activity. Moreover, a major contributing factor to the growing
army of unemployed is the unprecedented rash of corporate
mergers, acquisitions, consolidations, and bankruptcies. A
significant part of my consulting practice involves identifying
acquisition candidates for companies worldwide. The practice
has presented me with a broad perspective on the rapidly
narrowing industrial landscape.

Consolidation, in essence, means fewer jobs. And the
segment hit hardest by this trend is the middle class. For the
first time, there is no relationship between the growth in
corporate profits and the growth in salaried jobs. Indeed, the
inverse is true: salaried workers representing about 40% of the
workforce suffered about 62% of recent layoffs. Even the high-
tech sector, the new engine of the US economy after we
shipped most of our manufacturing jobs oversea, continues to
unravel.

That is not just an economic pothole. It is a chasm,
because for every job eliminated in manufacturing or high
technology, 6.2 jobs in the service sector are reduced or
eliminated. The service sector in Silicon Valley is currently
suffering the ripple effect of recent high-tech layoffs. Together,
these consolidations present a serious and long-range problem
that will become an icy downhill slope for US employment for
years to come.

C6: Costs

Labor costs are not as attractive as they once were. In Korea, for example, thanks to their unions, labor cost is no longer lower than in most Western countries. Because of its loss of competitive edge, Pohang Steel was forced to lay off 20,000 employees. With the weak yen and other economic problems, Japan is bringing manufacturing projects back home, causing problems for the less-developed countries that relied on that business. Seventy percent of Japan's investment in Asia went into the manufacturing sector.

C7: China

Moving from Mao to McDonalds in one decade is quite dramatic, but China has serious imbalances behind their spectacular trade performance, high investment flows, and high GDP growth. For example, there is raising inequality between the more developed coastal provinces and the less developed, poorer, inland regions. According to World Bank estimates, more than 152 million people in China still lived in poverty in 2003, consuming less than one US dollar a day. In addition, most of China's growth has been based on foreign investment rather than domestic growth. Foreign investment is responsible for the Asian miracle. Asia's developing countries received $916 billion in capital investment, a sum slightly larger than foreign investment into the US. Furthermore, 70% of China's bank loans go to state-owned enterprises (SOE's), though many of the 100,000 SOE's are spilling red ink, making it difficult for small entrepreneurs to get capital.

To make matters worse, China lacks infrastructure. Poor highways and ports plus pollution and population problems will continue to make China a hellish place to live and work, no matter their economic growth.

C8: Corporate Planning

Long-term planning, that gaze into the future to spot potential threats and maximize future opportunities, has fallen out of fashion. Once the most glamorous and richly rewarded occupation in corporate America, long-term planning now commands little attention among top management.

Many management consultants, formerly godlike in their ability to shape corporate future, have been demoted, both symbolically and actually. By forcing vision to refocus on the short term – next quarter – consultants did their bit to re-engineer strategy. By chipping away at operational inefficiencies or hacking off bureaucratic flab, consultants became the masters of corporate liposuction.

The result of the bloody deed was record profits for corporations, and the cutting of expenditures essential for future growth. R&D, as a percentage of GDP, continues to drop, as do investment in new plants and equipment. For all the rhetoric about wanting skilled workers, spending on training is at its lowest levels since the 1980's. Unfortunately, a lean-and-mean company can lack the muscle and stamina required for long-range success and survival.

C9: Competition

The US is having difficulty competing internationally. Indeed, the Council on Competitiveness estimates that the US is lagging behind in one-third of its cutting edge technologies. One technology that particularly troubles me is LCD's, the liquid crystal displays that are found in our lap top computers and power high definition televisions. Even now, companies like IBM are forced to buy these displays offshore, further increasing our negative trade balance with Asia. Speaking of IBM, it seems only yesterday that IBM was the only game in town. Now more than 300 IBM clones compete for the PC business.

C10: Confused Investors

There is little correlation between declining corporate performance and stock prices. The percentage of our money tied up in the market is currently at record levels. But people's expectations of making it big in the market are clearly unrealistic. As a result of the low interest rates on savings, money market accounts, and certificates of deposit, investors have been forced to hold on to declining stock portfolios.

C11: Cash Out

Most of us have enough clothes in our closets, and computers that are fast enough to satisfy our on line needs. Without a major breakthrough, there may be a movement toward both income poles, shrinking the middle class consumer as a percentage of the population. This phenomenon, particularly evident in the US, is a distressing fact for business to contemplate. The proportion of low wage earners in the global work force will continue to rise, creating an underclass in a two-tier wage structure. Already, a sizeable proportion of US workers are paid markedly less then comparable workers in other, advanced countries. However, highly paid US workers still earn more then their counterparts in most nations.

The affluent control most of the discretionary income (DI) in the US. Only one-third of US households have DI, with an average amount of $12,300.00. Not surprisingly, the rich have most of the DI. Just over one-quarter of US households earn more than $40,000 a year, but they comprise about two-thirds of the households in the DI group, and control almost 90% of the nation's DI.

The outlook for the poor and middle class is bleak. The world does very little to reduce the poor population, and nothing on the horizon will pull any significant percentage of them into middle class ranks.

C12: Conspicuously Absent Consumption

With less discretionary income due to declining wages and increasing unemployment, we should expect more shopping but less buying, further shrinking our bloated service sector.

We are entering a world where more of us will have less money to make discretionary purchases. Particularly hard hit will be non-essential high-tech firms that provide increased productivity tools. The problem for companies is not one of productivity, but one of simply needing more work. Also hurt will be commercial construction companies and their financial service backers. Those firms that did not learn the lessons of excessive overbuilding in the 1980's are about to learn them now. As companies continue to run out of capital, we will see more vacancy signs all over the country.

C13: Capitalism Crumbles

Our economy is in a pivotal period, changing from a market-driven position to one that requires increased government spending. Already, about one-third of our GDP is affected by government, whether at the Federal, state, or local level, and more than 16% of us are employed by the government. With massive expenditures for the war on terrorism and other programs, the percentage of GDP controlled by the government will continue to increase.

Another economic fault-line will occur as state and local governments receive more obligations and less cash from the federal government. Growing budget deficits at the state and local level will force many program cutbacks and add to the growing legion of the unemployed.

C14: Capital Crunch

Small businesses employ the most people nationally, but they are the least likely to benefit from low interest loans. In the high-tech sector, the publicized explosion of venture capital and favorable bank rates does little to help startup companies. Indeed, more then seven out of every ten Americans starting a business rely on personal savings and loans from relatives and friends. Also, venture capitalists (VC's), after having backed so many losers, are risk adverse, making it almost impossible for a new firm to get VC financing. Even the pension funds and institutions that provide most of the VC funds are looking for safe opportunities with good short-term profit possibilities.

No Bounce Back

The recent problems of international business failures and the stagnation and consolidation of the US manufacturing, high-tech, and service sectors will create situations that are not cyclical in nature, but structural. The economy is not simply weak or sick. It has been stricken with profound, fundamental internal problems that no amount of economic pump priming by the Fed can ever cure. The layoffs will not be temporary; these jobs will be permanently lost, many to foreign workers. Foreign ownership of US businesses is virtually irreversible. The record number of mergers and bankruptcies has dug economic holes that no upturn can ever fill.

The list of economic woes is a long one: intense global competition, record government employment and regulations, global over-capacity, unbridled consumer debt, stagnating incomes, bad bank loans, declining educational levels, and insufficient corporate and government planning. These issues will paralyze our economic, social, and political environment for years to come.

We expect our government officials to be on top of the many problems, exposed by the "Ten Great Lies," and at least begin to address these long-range troubles. In the next chapter, we will see that government is the continuing cause of problems, and rarely the solution.

Chapter 6
GOVERNMENT IS FOR THE PEOPLE

In this chapter, I will push many of our government leaders, and their army of bureaucrats, off the big fat marble pedestals they built for themselves with our tax money. In our media-driven world, where image has more value then substance, we listen to our elected representatives speak populist sound bites through pearly white teeth. (They have the free health and dental plans that we only dream about.) Our leaders believe in government for the people, but in many cases "the people" are increasingly becoming special interests, friends, and family, in addition to themselves.

Let's take a helicopter trip so that we can look down at the political landscape of our country and observe the terrible blight growing upon our land. Special interests, with aid from their government accomplices, are taking ever more control of the federal presses that print our money, using these very funds for their narrow agendas. Mediocre, overpaid, self-serving bureaucrats and politicians squander our resources on the Federal, State, and local levels. If we do not pay attention, these parasites will continue to sap our treasury, destroy our moral fiber, and devastate our country's future.

What is the Federal Government, Anyway?
Answer

Our government is made up of dozens of special interest groups with the same zip code. If you share the widespread view that our government exists to serve the best interests of the nation as a whole, it will of course sound like treason to suggest dismantling the Federal government. However, the public has little appreciation of the special interest groups that control our government. I'm not only talking about the political action committees (PACs). I'm thinking about the federal agencies themselves – the people and institutions our tax dollars are supporting.

In the legislative branch for example, the Agriculture Department represents farmers; the Department of Housing, Education, and Welfare, the professionals who provide welfare and education services; the Department of the Interior, Western interests only; and the Armed Services Committee, military contractors. According to George Schultz, who has held several top-level cabinet posts, the chief danger to society is collusion among the various representatives from interest groups, departments, legislative committees, and organized special interest groups.

Not surprisingly, the special interest advocacy system has become our government, and subverts the concept of a single executive branch, usurping its power. This includes the creation of so-called independent agencies that make policy without the direction or influence of the President, and the subversion of the Presidential budget. Instead, independent agencies submit their own budgets directly to Congress.

Why is Government so Inefficient?

The very system of constitutional checks and laws that help preserve our liberties impede efficient operation. Government, as we often forget, is chiefly what agencies do. James Q. Wilson, an expert on government bureaucracy, observes, **"owing to putting process over outcome, equity over efficiency, we get more or less the government we desire."** Government in the United States is not designed to be efficient or powerful, but tolerable and malleable. Government can't say yes. Government is constrained. Where do the constraints come from? "Americans," believes Wilson, "distrust anyone who wields power and sought to prevent abuse by surrounding all power wielders with constitutional checks and laws."

But as George Schultz and Kenneth Dam point out, equity arguments are all too often used as a kind of camouflage to provide support for narrow self-interest. True, the notion of the "fair shake" still holds a basic appeal to Americans today, as Teddy Roosevelt's slogan the "square deal" for all citizens did in his time.

200

Certainly, a key problem in formulating public policy is how to recognize the legitimacy of a concern for the poor and disadvantaged while avoiding the rhetoric of poverty or minority becoming the servant of well-placed interests. Happily, with certain exceptions, America has not generally experienced flagrant oppression of a minority by the majority. Indeed, we are now operating from what Robert Dahl calls **a system of "minorities rule," in which public policies are the result of opinions and interests of neither a majority nor a minority, but rather are arrived at through compromises of various organized and vocal minorities. The old squeaky wheel syndrome is the oil that moves politicians.**

At any rate, it is common to see economists and financially oriented government officials lined up behind a relatively efficient solution. The more politically inclined officials support what they believe – or at least what they believe Congress and the people believe – is the equitable solution. In the opinion of R. Joseph Monsen Jr. and Mark Cannon, this system of

> Making public policy by minorities rule through a political brokerage system of negotiation and compromise, though imperfect, represents the most effective democratic system yet devised for a large bureaucratic society comprising rival economic interests.

The High Cost of Over-Regulation

"Detailed regulation," says James Wilson, "is rarely compatible with energy, pride, exercise of initiative." But how can government delegate trust? He concludes that it can't. We've all heard the story of the $600 Pentagon ashtray. The ashtray was a consequence of adhering to regulations set forth in an acquisition rulebook of several thousand pages. The pertinent rule states that when an aircraft is turned over from active duty to the reserves, it must come with a complete inventory.

Statutory Deadlines

The so-called "statutory deadlines" are popularly thought of as a management tool for curbing unnecessary delay and firmly establishing priorities for recalcitrant bureaucrats. Such deadlines require that Federal and State agencies accomplish specific actions by a certain date. But too often there is no valid rationale for the date chosen. Members of Congress lack an incentive for assigning deadlines based on cost-benefit analysis in the way businesses set deadlines if they hope to continue. Politicians tend to set deadlines in ways that generate the greatest amount of press coverage and constituent concern or support, another example of planning for the short term, with negative consequences for the longer term.

Expertise and the Nature of Work

People tend to do what they know how to do, rather than do the job for which they've been hired. This seems a matter of common sense, but has a profound influence on what actually gets done in this country. Too often, this influence is deeply damaging.

For example, diplomats, as Wilson notes, "principally deliver, respond to, and comment on written reports." The Foreign Service, therefore, "prizes drafting ability above all other skills." One result of this expertise is that everything is heavily, though cautiously, documented.

When the Occupational Safety and Health Administration (OSHA) was formed, its field inspectors found it easier to address safety rather than health hazards. As Tom Peters explained, "counting the number of missing rungs from a ladder is a lot less difficult, ambiguous, and risky then dealing with the carcinogenic potentials of various substances a worker might encounter."

Staffers at the Federal Trade Commission (FTC) are trained as lawyers, so they tend to seek out instances where the law is broken and emphasize the pursuit of "winnable" cases. This keeps them busy, and they feel good when they win a case, but it doesn't necessarily mean that they're tackling the real tough problems – the ones that promise no easy victories.

Agency Culture

Government agencies, like corporate America, have their own cultures. For example, the culture of the National Aeronautics and Space Administration (NASA) could be called "macho." Above all, NASA prided itself on its "we can do anything" ethos. Such excessive can-doism was a major contributor to the Challenger disaster. It ran counter to NASA culture to admit that they were having difficulties. But ignoring problems instead of solving them set the stage for tragedy.

One way to ensure success is never to risk failure. For this reason, agencies rarely take a stand that will be opposed or unpopular. Of course, given the power of inertia, change – even positive change – is more likely to generate opposition than a posture that doesn't rock the boat.

For whom are these agencies working? An agency like the Federal Drug Administration (FDA) is going to sue states and prevent seniors from getting lower-cost drugs from Canada and other countries. In this case, one must seriously wonder if the drug companies and HMO's have the FDA in their pocket.

The rules for these agencies aren't any more logical than the actions. Usually the rules, which require the red tape that we all hate so much, were not generated by the bureaucracies themselves, but have been imposed on the agencies by well-intentioned politicians, to ensure "procedural fairness." The Federal Acquisition Rule Book, which runs over 6,000 pages, contains dozens of provisions that mandate giving special attention to women, small businesses, minorities, handicapped workers, and veterans. These rules are often absurd, and are a known cause of the nightmares of those forced to comply.

Civil Service

Almost everyone has a favorite story or two about the legendary inefficiencies in our Federal civil service. Usually, attention to nit-picking detail takes precedence over getting the job done. James Wilson recounts this with a vignette I'd like to share with you.

> One day, a personnel specialist at the United States Ocean Systems Center in San Diego visited an electronics engineer working on torpedo designs. "I'm here to classify your job. What do you do?" The engineer was irked by this unwelcome intrusion, muttered that he "invented things." The personnel specialist wrote down this fact and returned to the office. She took from the shelf the volume entitled "Position Classification Standards Form Electronics Engineering" published by the US Civil Service Commission. She decided that inventing things was not part of the job description of a GS-15 engineer, but it might be part of an assignment of a GS-13. She advised the engineer's supervisor that the job should be downgraded to the lower level. The supervisor erupted in anger. The engineer, as it turned out, was the world's leading expert on the logic system of torpedo guidance.

A Committee Of Lawyers
Most of the people in Congress are lawyers, always near the top of surveys of the most despised groups in America. How would you expect anything to get done in a committee consisting of hundreds of lawyers? Judging by the results, or lack thereof, obviously you can't get things done unless it directly impacts the special interests of the representatives and their backers.

The Western Outlaws
Fifty-one percent of Senators represent only 17% of the population. This gives the less-populous Western states disproportionate power in the Senate. These Western outlaws believe in government for the people, but the people they are interested in, too often, are not the American public. Western senators and congressmen, mostly Republicans, often with Executive Branch support, sell out the interests of Americans in

order to do the dirty work for corporations and businesses that engage in resource activities on publicly owned lands.

Land Leases

With self-assured arrogance and defiance, these outlaws help companies and developers, with whom they've had long, personal, and often professional ties, pay less-than-market rents for access to public lands. These companies did so well with the help of their Congressional sponsors that a large secondary market in public land leases developed. As an example, a lessee may pay the government $1 per acre, and then turn around and sublease it's the land rights to another company for $10 per acre.

Government Land Trade

Land trades between the federal government and private companies are usually not fair to the public. A *Seattle Times* investigation found that these transactions are routinely manipulated by special interests behind closed doors. The manipulators include not only large companies like Weyerhaeuser, but also land speculators, politicians, and even environmental groups.

For example, Crown Pacific got the land they desired, despite last-minute revelations that the US Forest Service had proposed trading 31,000 acres of national forest, including 4,000 acres of old growth, to the timber company.

Mining On Public Land

These Congressional outlaws also use the hard rock mining laws enacted in 1872 as their weapon of choice. Under a series of Nineteenth-Century variations on the Homestead Act, mineral-rich government-owned land is sold for as little as $2.50 per acre. In 1994, Interior Secretary Bruce Babbitt was forced under the Mining Law of 1872 to turn over the title to acres of public land that contained more then $100 billion in gold. In return, a Canadian-based company paid less then $10,000 in gold as the price for the land. Babbitt called it the greatest gold heist since the days of Butch Cassidy. Over the past 125 years, ownership of more than 3.2 million acres of government land has been handed over in a similar way.

The Homestead Act was originally intended for small-scale hard rock miners, to encourage family-sized homesteading in the American West. It is noteworthy that 23 of the top 40 companies who have used this act, and are now extracting minerals from public lands, are either subsidiaries of, or largely controlled by, foreign corporations. Again, I ask … government for *what* people?

Besides foreign corporations, major US corporations are also key beneficiaries of this particular legislation. For example, Chevron purchased the 2,036 acres that make up the Stillwater Mine, located in the Bear Tooth-Absaroka Wilderness, 40 miles from Yellowstone Park, for a total of $10,180 (i.e., $5 an acre). The value of the mine's reserves of palladium and platinum is estimated at a much higher $30 billion.

Timber

Timber offers another classic opportunity for the Congressional Western Outlaws to fleece America. In exchange for logging fees, the US Forest Service builds and maintains roads. Only rarely do the fees cover the costs. The US Forest Service routinely loses $1.2 billion annually, for services provided to private logging companies. This is over and above what they make from the sale of timber cut on public lands. In effect, the taxpayers pay private timber companies to remove our public trees. And the rip offs will continue. President Bush and Congress recently created the misnamed Healthy Forest Initiative, which targets the remaining 4% of our original forests for logging under the guise of forest fire management.

Public forest supply comprises less then 4% of the timber supply harvested from this country, and due to the government welfare given to the timber interests, half the trees cut in the US are exported as minimally processed wood, pulp, and chips.

Oilrigs On Public Lands

There are 46,000 oilrigs currently operating on American public lands. The Bush Administration has promoted oil interests both at home and abroad. The Bureau of Land Management is contemplating the eventual drilling of 50,000 oil and gas wells in the Powder River Basin of Wyoming. A current proposal would drill 5,000 wells, and would require building 2,500 miles of new roads, along with 2,500 miles of new pipelines. This plan would ravage 3,600 square miles of predominately public land in Wyoming. (The impacts of these activities are further discussed in Chapter 10: Man is Listening to Mother Nature).

Ranching on Public Land

Public lands ranchers have permanently destroyed millions of acres of land in the arid regions of the West, yet they provide only 3% of the nation's beef supply. The cost for a rancher to use public land for grazing is a mere $1.35 per month for a head of cattle, compared to approximately $10 per month on private lands. According to the Cato Institute, public land ranchers receive $200 million in direct subsidies yearly. These indirect subsidies and public assets liquidation cost the taxpayers billions per year.

Land exchanges between the Federal Government and private companies often aren't fair to the public. Indeed these transactions are others that are routinely manipulated by special interests, behind closed doors. The manipulators include large companies, land speculators, and Western Outlaw politicians. Good examples of Western Outlaw states offending in this way include Wyoming, Alaska, Idaho, and Montana.

Controlled by Church and Guns

Besides being controlled by the special interests of resource companies, many of these Western Senators and Representatives are also controlled by the Right wing Christian Coalition and the NRA. I estimate that over 50% of US senators rely on Christian Coalition voter support, and in turn vote the Coalition agenda, which continues to destroy another basic American tenant: the separation of church and state. Most of these Senators think that it is important for the public to know which church they belong to, and list them in online biographies. Both senators, in states such as Alabama, Colorado, Virginia, and Kansas, have received perfect scores for voting the Christian Coalition agenda during their time in office.

In many Southern, Western, and Midwest areas, the NRA hand picks candidates, destroys rivals, and then manipulates the puppet strings controlling elected representatives so that they vote the organization line. Bob Barnes, a Republican candidate for the Texas Senate, is one such narrowly focused poster boy for the NRA. Barnes is a proud member of the NRA, and a firm believer in the right to bear arms and the necessity of strengthening our concealed weapons laws. Barnes sees two big issues out there: first, to ensure that cities don't overstep their bounds by passing overbearing anti-gun owner ordinances against the spirit of our Right-to-Carry laws. The second is to allow people with a Texas CHL (Concealed Handgun License) to lawfully carry a firearm in another state. "Some other states already recognize our permit, but I will work to see that they all do." Thanks, Bob. It will make me feel safe at night knowing some redneck Texan is carrying a concealed weapon in my state.

Others who and are in the holster of the NRA for their political life, and who have received perfect 100% ratings from the organization include: Joe Wilson SC, Chris Cannon UT, Virgil Goode VA, Rick Boucher VA, Barbara Cubin WY, Don Young AK, Wally Herger CA, John Doolittle CA, Richard Pombo CA, Duncan Hunter CA, Cliff Stearns FL, Tom Feeney FL, Phil Gingrey GA, Mike Simpson ID, Mark Souder IN, Todd Tiahrt KS, Jim Bunning KY, John Dingell MI, Thomas Reynold NY, and Bob Ney OH. As expected, 90% of the above group is Republican and 42% use a nickname, though in all fairness there was not a "Billy Bob" among them.

On the other side, there are those in Congress who vote continually to support liberal domestic and foreign policies. They, in turn, receive the Americans for Democratic Action (ADA) highest ratings. This 100% group includes Lynn Woolsey CA,

Howard Berman CA, Jessie Jackson IL, Danny Davis IL, Jim McGovern MA, Michael Capuano MA, Martin Sabo MN, Stephanie Jones OH, and Russ Feingold WI. As expected, this group is made up of all Democrats.

It's Not Your Money!

Renowned statesman Henry Clay once said, "Government is a trust and the officers of the government are the trustees; and both the trust and the trustees are created for the benefit of the people." Our politicians echo these sentiments when they campaign for our votes, but the sad fact is that for many in our government, long-term public service is a forgotten concept. The concept of public service has evolved into a shortsighted, personal, special interest grab bag. A recently reported example is that of Representative James T. Walsh (R-NY), who spent taxpayer money to fund building renovations at his alma mater. Representative Walsh used his power as chairman of the House Appropriations Subcommittee on Veterans Affairs / Housing and Urban Development to secure a $4.5 million grant to fund a building renovation at St. Bonaventure University. This amount is 50% greater then the largest single private gift to the University.

While most private schools rely on alumni philanthropists for large donations, St Bonaventure has the benefit of having a "Cardinal" on the House Appropriations Committee. This big spender has no problem donating our tax dollars, and will probably expect the building to be named after him. "Cardinal James" is not alone; our public officials are being caught time and again with their hands in the proverbial cookie jar. When they are caught, they express no remorse, and in fact, many act as if what they are doing is proper. They are indignant when questioned, as if they believe that taking from the till or rewarding a contributor or friend is a perk of their job, rather than what it really is: a breach of public trust.

In this part of the chapter, I hope to raise the ire of the silent majority, "I'm not going to take it anymore," independent thinkers and voters looking for an alternative to the dirty business-as-usual crowd. Let's look at a few of the thousands of examples of how politicians squander the hard-earned money you pay in taxes. To begin with, Libertarian Party leader Steve Dasbach highlights some of the following rip-offs:

1. **A retirement program for chimpanzees** – To care for animals formerly used in government research, Congress created the Chimpanzee Health Improvement, Maintenance, and Protection Act (CHIMP), which spent about $45,000 per animal in 2001.

2. **Turning money into dung** – Congress voted to give $4 million to the International Fertilizer Development Center for waste research.

3. **Subsidizing Congressional erections** – The Congressional health insurance program actually covers Viagra, which, according to Dasbach, "demonstrates that the worst case of 'electile dysfunction' in the world can be found right here in Washington DC." These same hard-ons voted against Viagra benefits for Medicare.

4. **Trying to convince teenagers not to have sex** – An "emergency" spending provision in the 2001 military construction bill includes $20 million for a teenage abstinence program.

5. **Dr. Seuss memorial** – The HUD funding bill contains $400,000 to memorialize the author of **Green Eggs and Ham**, and other children's books; a classic case of Pork-I-Am.

6. **Trying to convince fat people to walk up stairs** – The Center for Disease Control spent $14,900 to redecorate a stairwell to encourage obese employees to walk rather then use the elevator.

7. **Welfare program in Chukotka, Russia** – The 2001 foreign aid bill contains $3 million for a University of Alaska program designed to "improve social conditions" in the eastern Russian province.

8. **Subsidizing a bug lab** – Republican Thad Cochran stung taxpayers for $5 million when he inserted money into an agriculture bill to build an insect laboratory in his home state of Mississippi.

9. **Paying medical schools not to train doctors** – In an attempt to relieve a doctor glut without reducing funding for

210

teaching hospitals, Congress agreed to pay medical schools $400 million to NOT train doctors.

10. Peanut Festival – Congress approved hundreds of thousands of our dollars for a National Peanut Festival in Alabama. Perhaps the nut festival was a congressional family reunion?

Not to be outdone, the Heritage Foundation provided these additional examples of government waste. As they say, a billion here, a billion there, could add up to more then pocket change.

The Federal government cannot account for **$24.5 billion** spent in 2003. A White House review of just a sample of the federal budget identified **$90 billion** spent on programs that were deemed either ineffective, marginally adequate, or operating under a flawed purpose or design. The Congressional Budget Office published a "Budget Options" book identifying **$140 billion** in potential spending cuts. The Federal government spends **$23 billion** annually on special interest pork projects such as grants to the Rock and Roll Hall of Fame, or funds to combat teenage "Goth" culture in Blue Springs, Missouri. Washington spends **tens of billions of dollars** on failed and outdated programs such as the Rural Utilities Service, US Geological Survey, and Economic Development Association.

The Federal government made **$20 billion** in overpayments in 2001. The Department of Housing and Urban Development overpaid by **$3.3 billion** in 2001. Over one recent 18-month period, Air Force and Navy personnel used government-funded credit cards to charge **$102,000** for admission to entertainment events, **$48,250** for gambling, **$69,300** for cruises, and **$73,950 for exotic dance clubs and prostitutes.** The Advanced Technology Program spends **$150 million** annually, subsidizing private businesses, with 40% going to Fortune 500 companies. The Defense Department wasted **$100 million** on unused flight tickets, and never bothered to collect refunds, even when the tickets were reimbursable.

The Conservation Reserve Program pays farmers **$2 billion** annually not to farm their land. Washington spends **$60**

billion annually on corporate welfare, versus **$43 billion** on homeland security. The Department of Agriculture spends **$12 billion to 30 billion** annually on farm subsidies, the vast majority of which goes to agribusinesses and farmers averaging $135,000 in annual income. **Massive farm subsidies** also go to several members of Congress, and celebrity hobby farmers such as **David Rockefeller**, **Ted Turner, Scottie Pippen,** and the late Enron CEO **Ken Lay.**

The Medicare Program pays as much as **eight times** the amount of other federal agencies for the same drugs and medical supplies. Congressional investigators were able to receive **$55,000** in Federal student loan funding for a fictional college they created to test the Department of Education. The Army Corps of Engineers has been accused of **illegally manipulating data** to justify expensive unnecessary public works projects.

Food stamp overpayments cost **$600 million** annually. School lunch program abuse costs **$120 million** annually. Veterans' program overpayments cost **$800 million** annually, and Earned Income Tax Credit (EITC) overpayments cost **$800 million** annually. Better tracking of student loan recipients would save **$1 billion** annually.

Preventing states from using accounting tricks to secure additional Medicaid funds would save **several billion dollars** annually. Medicare contractors owe the federal government **$7 billion.**

And then there are those unnecessary projects, given as presents to special interests from Congress to prove to the constituents that they still have the long sticky fingers needed to steal from the taxpayers' wallets. Citizens against Government Waste (CAGW) provided these 2005 examples of so-called "pork-barrel" projects:

- $10,000,000 for the International Fund for Ireland
- $3,000,000 for the Cal Ripken Sr. Foundation
- $1.7 million for the International Fertilizer Development Center (as if there wasn't enough fertilizer in Congress to supply the world)

212

- $1,430,000 for various Halls of Fame, including the Country Music Hall of Fame and Museum in Nashville, TN, and the Paper Industry International Hall of Fame in Appleton, WI
- $350,000 for the Inner Harmony Foundation and Wellness Center in Scranton, PA
- $100,000 for the Tiger Woods foundation
- $100,000 for the Back to School program

In 2005, Federal pork barrel spending tipped the scales at 19% "fatter" then 2004. CAGW noted at that time that **the total number of pork projects had increased by 49.5% in the last two years.** You would think alarm bells would have gone off all over Congress and the country.

But The Meat Goes On!

Congress continues to waste taxpayers' dollars to please the people back home, despite the soaring deficit and mounting bills for hurricane damage and the war in Iraq. Citizens Against Government Waste (CAGW) identified 375 projects – costing **$3.4 billion** – in its **"2006 Congressional Pig Book."** The 53 pages of pork barrel projects "symbolize the most egregious and blatant example of pork." The report also says that Congress approved a record $29 billion in earmarks for 2006: **a 6.2% increase over last year's $27.3 billion.**

Among the projects the group identified are:

- **$13.5** million for the International Fund for Ireland, which helped finance the **World Toilet Summit**
- **$6.4 million** for wood utilization research in 11 states
- **$1 million** for the Water Free Urinal Conservation Initiative in Michigan
- **$500,000** for the Sparta Teapot Museum in Sparta, NC

I won't even get into the cost of the Hurricane Katrina response caused by the Federal government 's hastily improvised $10 billion effort, which produced vast sums of waste and misspent funds, according to an array of government audits and outside analysts.

Hey, a few million here and a few million there is pocket change for these big spenders. It would be funny if it weren't our money. This is what happens when special interests get to the people who control the government's money press.

Double Trouble – Government Duplication of Programs and Services

Government layering of new programs over existing ones creates duplication. Having several agencies perform similar duties is wasteful, and confuses program beneficiaries, who must navigate each program's rules and requirements.

Part of the problem is a lack of organization design – a specialty of mine as a management consultant. Simply put, some overlap is inevitable because some agencies are defined by **whom they serve** (e.g., veterans, Native Americans, urbanites, and rural families), while others are defined by **what they provide** (e.g. housing, education, health care, and economic development). When these agencies' constituencies overlap, each relevant agency will often have its own program. With **342 separate economic development programs,** the Federal government needs to make consolidation a priority.

Consolidating duplicative programs would save many billions of dollars and streamline government services. In addition to the programs that should be eliminated completely, the Heritage Foundation suggests that Congress should consolidate the following sets of programs:

- 342 economic development programs
- 130 programs serving at-risk youth
- 90 early childhood development programs
- 75 programs funding international education, culture, and training
- 72 Federal programs dedicated to assuring water safety
- 130 programs serving the disabled
- 50 homeless assistance programs
- 45 Federal agencies investigating Federal criminals

- 40 separate employment and training programs
- 28 rural development programs
- 27 teen pregnancy programs
- 26 small, extraneous K-12 school grant programs
- 23 agencies providing aid to the former Soviet republics
- 19 programs fighting substance abuse
- 17 rural water and wastewater programs in eight agencies
- 17 trade agencies monitoring 400 international trade pacts
- 12 food safety programs
- 11 principal statistics agencies
- 4 overlapping land management agencies
- A partridge in a pear tree.

You might be thinking, "Pork barrel spending, duplication of effort, and mismanagement is a way of life, and so what's new? Why the threat now?" Like our society, our government is becoming fatter and unhealthier. Record budget deficits, and record amounts of government control over our economy and employment are quickly leading us down a dangerous path.

We need an independent group, which I call the "new untouchables," to stop the politicians from destroying our country. We have lost the common sense of the middle and have allowed both the Democrats and Republicans to squander our tax money. Before I present my concept for the new untouchables, let me highlight why it is time to force the current Congress out of the marble halls.

Garbage In, Garbage Out

Can you imagine working for a company that has little more then 500 employees with the following statistics?

- 29 accused of spousal abuse
- 7 arrested for fraud
- 19 accused of writing bad checks

- 117 who have either directly or indirectly bankrupted at least two businesses
- 3 have done time for assault
- 71 cannot get a credit card due to bad credit
- 14 arrested on drug-related charges
- 8 arrested for shoplifting
- 21 defendants in current lawsuits
- 84 arrested for drunk driving in the last year

That organization, as reported by Steve Dasbach, the Libertarian Party national director, **is the 535 members of the United States Congress**. This is the same group of losers that crank out hundreds of new laws each year to keep the rest of us in line. (His comments in a Libertarian publication were based on research in Capitol Hill Blue, an online publication that covers Federal politics. The research covers both past and present members of Congress, so the article is misleading in leaving the impression that the statistics are referring to the present Congress.)

How can you expect anything positive to come out of government, when so many losers are serving themselves at the Congressional trough? Politicians who routinely write bad checks and engage in fraudulent practices could explain why the country is more then $5 trillion in debt, why Federal programs are so wasteful, and why the cost of government keeps climbing. No wonder Mark Twain once said that Congress may be America's only "distinct criminal class." In China they hang corrupt politicians, while in America members of Congress receive their salaries even while in jail. Honestly, which of these methods will discourage corruption?

The Citizens Against Government Waste (CAGW) is a private, non-partisan, nonprofit organization that represents more than one million members and supporters nation wide. CAGW's mission is to eliminate waste, mismanagement, and inefficiency in the Federal government. Their ratings indicate the degree to which each elected official supported the interests of their organization in that year. For 2005, the average score for the House was 45%, with Republicans averaging 73% and Democrats 24%. From their data, I put together a list of some of the worst offenders. Allyson Schwartz scored 0% (D-PA). Close behind, with scores of 3%, were Chaka Fattah (Dem PA), Alcee Hastings (D-FLA), Sander Levin (D-MICH), John Lewis (D-GA), Nita Lowey (D-NY), Brad Miller (D-NC), Bobby Scott (D-VA), and Peter Visclosky (D-IND). The lowest-scoring Republicans, at 44%, were Sherwood Boehlert (R-NY), Jim Gerlach (R-PA), Tim Johnson (R-ILL), Robert Simmons (R-CONN), and Christopher Smith (R-NJ). The lowest score in the Senate was 4%, obtained by seven Democratic senators: Byron Dorgan (D-ND), Richard Durbin (D-ILL), Tom Harkin (D-IA), Frank Lautenberg (D-NJ), Pat Leahy (D-VT), Paul Sarbanes (D-MD), and Minority Leader Harry Reid (D-NEV). For the Republicans, the lowest Senate score went to Lincoln Chaffee (R-RI). Like others in Congress, many in this group also suffer from "con-junket-ites," and travel first class anywhere in the world with staff, family, and friends, with the taxpayers picking up the tab. What a country.

The Whiners – The Black And Hispanic Caucus

These groups never seem to bring anything to the party, but demand an ever-larger share of the pork pie. The Hispanic Caucus learned all the wrong lessons from the Black Caucus, who thoroughly acquired the skills and insights required to milk the system from Big Business and White Congressional porkers. Like the Black Caucus, the Hispanic platform uses government pressure to force industry into buying from Hispanic vendors, and to pressure business to put Hispanics into executive positions and on boards. As minorities become a majority in many districts, particularly in California and Texas, Congress' growing number of Hispanics will continue to exert even more political pressure on business, forcing it to supply money and jobs to solve the problems in their unmanageable states.

Meanwhile, Black communities profit from their confrontational style by electing agitators like Bobby Rush to represent them. Rush, a former leader of the Black Panthers and SNCC (organizations that preached the destruction of this country), is now sworn to protect it.

The West Coast Tea Party Liberals

In my personal opinion, this group of women illustrates the "Peter Principle," which states that people rise to the level of their incompetence. I put Peter "Principle" Stark among them, for unbelievably thinking that the Al Zarqawi killing was a publicity stunt to help Bush's falling poll numbers. People on my "Peter Principle" list include Lynn Woolsey, Zoë Lofgren, Jane Harmon, Anna Eschoo, Barbara Boxer, Tammy Baldwin, Barbara Lee, Nancy Pelosi, Susan Davis, Loretta Sanchez, and Grace Flores Napolitano. These women seem to support without question all the politically correct and Left-wing causes. They and their knee-jerk liberal congressional buddies sent billions of taxpayer dollars to help the Hurricane Katrina victims without proper oversight. The GAO reports that there has already been over a billion dollars worth of fraud in that area, including giving people funding for housing when they are already living rent-free on the government tab.

Furthermore, these tea party liberals threaten our security with their own paralysis by analysis and weak-on-defense approach. They support the UN and EU protection of rogue states by allowing non-productive stalling tactics, which they call diplomacy, but which countries like Iran view as a free pass to enrich uranium.

To give another example, Jane Harmon, misplaced on the intelligence committee, insists on ever more intelligence on the nuclear capabilities and intentions of Iran. While she waits for a notarized letter from the cowardly deviant midget eunuch, Iranians openly detonate rockets, calling for the destruction of the US and Israel almost daily. Even a Russian general is telling us that Iran is very close to developing WMD.

The Wax Museum of Politics

Congress seems like a private club for American royalty. By invoking obsolete rules and tradition, the members continue to lose relevance in the modern world. They are the now buggy whip manufacturers in a space-age world. Many of these old farts have indeed become caricatures of themselves. In my central casting company, Robert Bird of West Virginia would play the role of a mouthy old-time Southern gentleman.

Senator Ted Stevens of Alaska would play the "it's my Senate and the treasury is my personal piggybank, so don't cross me or else" type.

Senator Ted Kennedy, no Jack Kennedy, would of course be typecast as the rich tax-and-spend liberal, championing illegal immigrants and reverse discrimination more then the safety of Americans. In my very deep, much-discussed movie, the rich tax-and-spend actor would be so out of it that they wouldn't realize that the country's treasury they were sworn to protect has been stolen by a gang of civil rights conmen, who use the money to stomp on our country's values. Values like every person's right to be treated equally "without regard to race, color, or national origin."

These very liberals get help from the judicial activists on the US Supreme Court, who, with the stroke of a pen and ignorance of how the real world works, caused the equal protection clause of the Fourteenth Amendment and the Civil Rights Act of 1964 to be meaningless by making race-based preferences for the underprivileged necessary.

And then there is minority leader Harry Reid (D-NEV), who I envision as so tightly wrapped into the immigrant and diversity gang tortilla that he unbelievably denounced a proposed amendment to make English the national language as "racist" warning that the amendment could undercut a civil rights law. Of course, Dennis Kucinich appears to me as the "Alfred E. Newman" of Left-wing causes. He is always jumping on the anti-war bandwagon early, and will never miss a beat to drum our country out of Iraq before we have completed our mission.

Spineless Bureaucrats

Like the UN debating society, many Congressional leaders are the Chamberlains of our time. Neville Chamberlain was the British minister who thought that he could make a deal with Hitler. Bill Nelson of Florida and Darrel Issa of California are currently competing for my nomination for the Chamberlain Award by meeting with Bashara al Assad, terror master of Syria, and an accomplice to murder in Lebanon.

219

The Foreign Relations and Judicial committee have too many spineless bureaucrats who love the media spotlight. These political beavers and their media co-dependents dam up all attempts at improving our security at home and abroad.

Joe Bidden of Delaware and Dick Lugar of Indiana seem to me to be the prime examples of Senators who are too comfortable with the seniority mindset of government bureaucrats. They like to hear themselves talk, but don't have the will to stand up to our enemies. Senator Lugar suggested a "Grand Bargain" approach to Iran, including direct talks and concessions as an alternative to sanctions and force. Bidden will fight by sending additional forces to complete our mission in Iraq. Add Patrick Lehey of Vermont and Chuck Hegel of Nebraska to the soft-on-terrorism crowd that continues to undermine the NSA and our national security. Finally, there are the antics of the judicial committee, where backbiting egos that will tackle anything to stay in front of the TV camera make both the public and the serious people on the committee, like Jeff Sessions of Alabama, cringe.

Local government
Combining Municipal Services
The Federal government is not the only one wasting our money; the State and local governments are also poor stewards of financial resources. As a management consultant, I helped companies save millions of dollars by updating their organization structure. When looking at organizations, the early logic for the organization design is evident and no longer applies. Opportunities are usually apparent for eliminating duplication and improving efficiencies. In Northern California towns and cities, where I have done many studies, there is good cooperation on regional issues, but little support to share resources and eliminate duplication.

For example, every town on the peninsula in California has a costly police force and fire organization. Policemen and fireman with annual compensation of over $150,000 are emblematic of the inability and unwillingness of local governments to control costs. **In San Jose, police and fire**

officials make up a majority of the city's 100 highest-paid employees, while San Jose leads the state cities in disability claims from safety employees. When you look at the proximity of the facilities and the bloated size of departments, as well as the rarity of serious crime or major fires in this area, combining departments, and reducing bloated payrolls, **overtime, enormous pension obligations, and flexible work hours that allow for second jobs and businesses makes obvious sense.** But to all politicians, safety services are a sort of sacred cow that cannot be sacrificed, though the cost of such services makes up a large percentage of local budgets.

Another example is the US postal service (USPS), which has an army of unionized workers. These 700,000-plus workers make the mail service the fourth largest civilian employer in the world. With such a huge workforce lobbying for more goodies for themselves, real reform such as cutting bloated staffing levels is impossible. Furthermore, the power of local government unions, particularly the police and fire unions, keeps growing and hurting the communities they serve. A simple rule for independent voters would be not to vote for a candidate supported by police or firefighters, since that person probably doesn't have the balls to stand up to the insatiable greed of the unions.

Mayor's Dreams

A Camden, New Jersey mayor, Gwendolyn Faison, replaced his Chevy Impala with a Lincoln Continental, costing taxpayers $16,000. When questioned about her conduct, Mayor Faison told the *Courier-Post*, "I'm a fancy mayor. I need a fancy car." Such unbridled and blatant audacity is unfortunately commonplace in local politics across the country, and reflects an attitude shared by many. They seem to think that "serving the public" is a license to serve themselves at the public trough.

In San Jose, where I live, politicians rejoiced when a new City Hall was built to look like a cathedral. Like most government-controlled construction jobs, the City Hall came in millions over budget. These same bureaucrats were thrilled when the city of San Jose became the 10th-largest city in the US. Most of the residents could care less, since they understand that bigger cities mean more problems and compensation due bureaucrats.

Empire-building development officials with inflated egos, social engineering city planers, and politicians controlled by developers who are bullied by immigrant and low-income lobbies continue to promote high-density housing in our urban centers without considering the consequences. For example, in 1991 an Argentine Airlines plane stopped in Lima Peru and picked up a dozen people with cholera and then went on to LA the same day. Think about how fast these diseases will be spread, as waves of poor immigrants are continually packed into our new high-density subsidized inner city housing.

Let the politicians fix San Jose's potholes, which number among the highest for a city its size, rather fixating on delusions of grandeur. With uncontrolled growth, overstaffed city workers with fat pensions, and liberal immigration policies, San Jose resembles LA more and more each day. The city gives millions to a group sponsoring a road race downtown, while the potholes grow. Corruption charges were recently filed against the mayor; the con man from "The Music Man," who smooth talks the government of "River City" into buying instruments for a grand parade, would get a red carpet welcome by the wasteful politicians that run San Jose.

The Nova Scotia Model

At one time in Nova Scotia, it was mandated that civil servants, security personnel, and public sector / government employees should not be allowed to unionize, and that their compensation should always be lower then comparable jobs in the private sector. This policy still makes sense, but public unions have become too powerful. Rather than defend the public interest, elected officials now simply bend to their pressure.

Puppets of Developers

Often, there is little interest in local politics, so anyone with a large group of friends, an exaggerated resume, and big bucks can run for office. Developers, who have big bucks, are able to overwhelm mom and pop candidates with those they hand pick. These candidates support unbridled housing and commercial development, as well as government payment, for infrastructure that makes their personal ventures even more profitable. In this way, major developers and campaign supporters often have access to local and state officials, while the public does not.

After a long and contentious series of public meetings about open space development and control, the largest developer in Santa Clara County, Stanford University, met individually and privately with County Commissioners to discuss the University land. Most commissioners changed their views after the closed-door meetings, voting for Stanford and against the open space coalition. Stanford packed the one public council chamber meeting by bringing in senior citizens and giving them dinner just before the vote. Only one council member, Joe Simitian, stood up to the developer's pressure.

Bureaucratic Power

We have all had our run-ins with bureaucrats who relish the power of their position. For example, a friend of mine received a notice that her car was involved in a crime and that city property, a stop sign, had been destroyed as the car sped away. The Finance Department of the City of San Jose submitted a bill for the stop sign replacement. My friend tried to explain to the clerk, unsuccessfully, that the license and the description of the car did not match hers. Plus, she knew nothing of the "crime" or the accident.

When I called to help correct the matter, the Finance Department employee showed no interest or empathy for facts, reason, or logic. This rude bureaucrat told me that the bill must be paid or she would initiate legal action against my friend. She followed up by saying, "people like [us] are always lying." I then asked for a copy of the police report, but was told that she would not release it. She told me that we would have to deal with Police Department records. After paying a fee and waiting four months, we were finally able to track down a busy homicide detective and asked him to call this woman in the

Finance Department to explain their mistake. The detective had agreed that a different car was involved in the accident and damage. The bureaucrat did not acknowledging the calls, but instead continued to send bills.

In the private sector, such an incompetent, obnoxious loser would have been fired for treating a client so rudely. This woman obviously felt very secure in her position, protected by civil service unions and her boss. Somehow these petty bureaucrats have forgotten that the public pays them their salaries for service, not abuse.

Bureaucratic Majorities

Public service unions are growing so large that they are influencing public policy to further their own interests, rather than serving the public. I think that the very concept of public service unions is patently unfair. In California, police and fire unions are large, well funded, and active in securing unreasonable pay and benefit packages. The very communities they serve are rarely in precarious condition or threatened by incidences of fire or crime. Perhaps an all-volunteer force should be considered, since most bureaucrats yield to union demands.

The San Jose bureaucrats have allowed the city to be liable for more than $1 billion in lifetime benefits to employees who work for the city a mere 15 years. And unbelievably, these elected representatives are planning to meet to talk about giving themselves the same lifetime benefits for even less service. The unions have dictated their terms to these spineless bureaucrats, and the obtained for their members enough compensation and time off to start second businesses, moonlight, or just play.

Irresponsible, large-state transportation unions likewise have enough clout to swing the vote for huge unnecessary state highway bond projects that require debt financing for years in the future. Teachers' unions, like all public service sector unions, should be outlawed. School administrators without backbone to stand up to the diversity and Left wing ideologues should take their fat severance packages and find real jobs. You know a system has become troubled when the

Left-leaning University of California becomes one of the largest campaign contributors in the state.

Term Limits Can't Get The Bums Out Of Office

Career politicians are bad for the country. Many states have passed laws automatically forcing longtime legislators out of office. Congressional efforts to limit the terms of members of the House and Senate died, but limits for members of state assemblies are flourishing. There have recently been a record number of newcomers with little or no political experience. Opponents of term limits argue that such inexperience will hurt voters because rookie legislators find it hard to navigate the bureaucracy. They say that limits force out well-regarded politicians, who have formed strong ties with their constituents. Further, they think limits will erode democracy by taking away voters' rights to choose their representative.

Proponents like me, however, see career politicians as the greater threat. The longer a careerist stays in office, the more likely they are to betray their constituents and give in to corruption. Newcomers need to be encouraged to take risks and enter elections free from entrenched, highly funded incumbents.

The Supreme Court let term limits stand for state lawmakers, permitting California, which has some of the country's strictest tenure restrictions, to continue enforcing them. Some states have even tried to limit the terms of their Congressional representatives. The Supreme Court ruled, however, that letting states establish such restrictions would violate the Constitution and weaken "Congress' national character." By not limiting Congressional terms, "Congress' national character" will eventually appear on the most wanted posters in our post offices, in my opinion.

Public College Bonds

State and community bonds put too much money into colleges and universities. Some community colleges have budgets large enough to allow representatives to travel and recruit internationally. Money is also wasted on numerous unnecessary programs and courses, including those that provide support for featherbedding diversity and Left-wing radicals. People in the system have told me how teachers' unions get almost anything they want because inflated bond measures go unquestioned and are accepted. Gutless administrators and trustees are also complicit in creating an overpaid and spoiled staff.

In the next chapter I will objectively look at how much of the decline of Western values and other problems in education, security, and healthcare can be traced to the lie that illegal immigrants help rather than harm our country.

Chapter 7
MASS, NOT MESS, IMMIGRATION

Emma Lazarus' quote, "Give me your tired, your poor, your huddled masses yearning to breathe free," still chokes me up. I'm proud of America's immigration record, and grateful that my Russian grandparents were allowed to pass under Lady Liberty's torch into this blessed land. Emotionally, I am pro-immigration, and value my many immigrant friends, but as an objective reviewer of immigration facts and impact on the future, I am deeply disturbed.

In this chapter, I will dispel the myths related to the premise that mass and illegal immigration is good for America. Illegal immigration is good for Agra-businesses and others looking for cheap labor, for politicians always ready to sell out the American public for votes, and for the Catholic Church, when they are looking for a source of new members. But the reality is that America's immigration policies have launched us into a risky experiment unlike any experienced by another country.

This country does not have the capacity to accommodate and assimilate an unending wave of mass migration. We are already seeing many signs of a Balkanized, fragmented, strife-torn, and dysfunctional America. The politicians just don't get it; they will destroy our culture with their open border / amnesty programs. Already, almost half of all children in our country under five years old are the children of immigrants. I don't remember voting to turn the US into a Third World country, to change our culture by allowing millions to cross our borders illegally, or to make a superhighway through the middle of our country for Mexican truckers. I would only support this asinine DOT plan if the truckers were going to fill those trucks with illegal aliens and take them back home.

It Pays to Wave the Flag in Washington if it's Mexican

After recent street demonstrations against immigration reform, we watched the embarrassing spectacle of political eunuchs in our government accelerating the rush to sell out our country's culture and language. These legislators gave illegals free passes to raid our treasury, destroy our healthcare and education systems, fill our jails, and maintain their special status for jobs and schooling, while declaring their loyalty by waving the Mexican flag. Immigration has become a ticking time bomb that is dramatically changing American society, and I don't think it's for the better. Sun Belt states like California, Florida, and Texas are becoming Third World states, with huge immigrant populations separated from White America by loyalty, poverty, violence, education, and racial tension.

Time for a Reality Check

The thousands of brainwashed students who walked out of classrooms to support illegal alien rights in the US should try this reverse logic exercise. Imagine walking across the border from the US into Mexico, skipping legal stuff like visas, passports, immigration quotas, and laws. Then, once you've slipped into Mexico illegally, demand the following:

- No severe jail term for entering Mexico illegally
- Free medical care for your entire family
- English-speaking government bureaucrats to serve you
- All government forms printed in English
- Your kids be taught by English-speaking teachers
- Schools that teach American culture
- Your kids be fed breakfast and lunch at school
- Public television for kids featuring cartoons of US kids with American names, speaking English
- Mexican drivers licenses so you can easily get to government services, though you do not have car insurance
- English-speaking police officers so you can understand when caught committing crimes

- Right to fly the US flag from your housetop
- A gigantic 4th of July celebration, paid for by Mexico City
- Wages paid in cash so you do not have to pay taxes
- Special admission status at the top universities, even though you are much less qualified then Mexican students
- Majors in American studies and professors who spew hatred against Mexico
- You must press one to speak Spanish

Before You Read the Myths, Know the Facts, as Reported by the *Los Angeles Times*

- **40%** of all workers in LA County (LA County has ten million people) are working for cash and not paying taxes, because they are predominantly illegal immigrants working without a green card.
- **95%** of warrants for murder in Los Angeles involve illegal aliens.
- **75%** of people on the most wanted list in Los Angeles are illegal aliens.
- **Over 2/3** of all births in LA County are taxpayer paid and to illegal alien Mexicans on MediCal.
- **Nearly 25%** of all inmates in California's detention centers are Mexican nationals here illegally.
- **Over 300,000** illegal aliens in LA County are living in garages.
- **50%** of all gang members in Los Angeles, according to FBI reports, are most likely illegal aliens from south of the border.
- **Nearly 60%** of all HUD property occupants are illegal.
- **21** radio stations in LA are broadcast in Spanish.
- **3.9 million** people speak Spanish, and 5.1 million people speak English, out of the 10.2 million people in LA County.
- **98% of the 275** California gangs' **17,000 members** are either Mexican or Asian, and reside in Orange County.

Did you know that Mexico regularly intercedes on the side of the defense in criminal cases involving Mexican nationals? Mexico has **NEVER** extradited a Mexican national accused of murder in the US, despite agreements to do so. I thank the Federation for American Immigration Reform (FAIR) for their help in debunking some of the following immigration myths.

Myth – Illegal immigrants are Abiding the Laws in the US

Fact: According to FAIR, criminal aliens – non-citizens who commit crimes – are a growing threat to public safety and national security, as well as a drain on our scarce justice resources. In 1980, our Federal and state prisons housed fewer then 9,000 criminal aliens. By the end of 1999, these same prisons housed over 68,000 criminal aliens. According to the Federal Bureau of Prisons, 29% of all inmates are not citizens (mostly Mexican illegals). These prisoners represent the fastest growing segment of the Federal prison population. Some 270,000 illegal immigrants spend time in local jails or state prisons. Over the past five years, an average of more then 72,000 illegal aliens have been arrested annually on drug charges alone.

Rather then complaining about overcrowded prisons and the need to build new prisons, government should deport these illegal prisoners and take border security seriously. (The Border Patrol estimates that they miss two or more illegal border-crossers for every apprehension.) If they did so, schools and cities would be able to use the funds earmarked for gang prevention to help serious students, who come to school to learn, instead of those who use the schools as centers for turf wars, drug dealings, and cultural genocide.

Myth – The US is Hostile to Immigration

Fact: The foreign-born population has exploded in the last decade, growing from 19.8 million in 1990 to 31.1 million in

2000. Projections indicate that the foreign-born population could reach 45 million by 2010, making this wave of immigration the largest in US history.

Each year, a national "lottery" selects approximately 50,000 aliens to become legal permanent residents of the United States. But in a report entitled "The Underground Labor Force is Rising to the Surface," the Wall Street investment firm Bear Stearns, conducting its own research on illegal immigrations' impact on the economy, concluded that the illegal alien population of the US is about 20 million people. That's roughly the equivalent of New York State's population ... more than double the official government estimate of about 9 million.

The US is the only nation that accepts hundreds of thousands of immigrants each year. **In the past decade, we've absorbed more immigrants than all other industrialized nations combined.**

The net annual cost of illegal immigration to California, home to 30% of the US illegal alien population, as estimated by the Bear Stearns report, is approximately $10.5 billion. The fair-minded people of California did finally stand up and say very clearly that immigration is more problematic than beneficial when they overwhelmingly passed an anti-immigration initiative called Proposition 187. Unfortunately, activist courts snubbed their noses at the voters of California and overturned the legislation.

The media and the amnesty for illegal aliens lobbyists have framed the immigration debate so that it appears between those supporting immigrant rights and those who do not. Most Americans support immigrant rights, but are against illegal aliens crossing our borders. Of interest is the fiction that Republicans still want illegal aliens charged with felonies, when it was the Democrats who refused to drop the felony language from the House bill after the Republicans reconsidered making illegals felons.

Myth – Immigration is Related to Labor Needs and Economic Conditions

231

Fact: Census Bureau data demonstrates that immigration to the US is unrelated to labor needs and economic conditions existing in this country. But despite a weak US economy and rising unemployment in the country since 2000, immigration has significantly outpaced the record levels seen in the 1990's, and shows no signs of abating. The two magnets attracting illegal aliens to the US are jobs and family connections. The typical Mexican worker earns one-tenth the salary of his American counterpart, and numerous American businesses are willing to hire cheap, compliant labor from abroad. Such businesses are seldom punished, because our country lacks a viable system to verify new hires' work eligibility. In addition, legal immigrant communities provide entrée for illegal-alien relatives and fellow countrymen through networks that serve as incubators, by supplying information on how to use the system to find jobs, housing, and services. Legal aliens continue to champion illegal immigration, even though it is destructive to their adopted homeland.

One of the most important findings of the INS report is the intimate link between legal and illegal immigration. The INS estimates that it gave out 1.5 million green cards to illegal aliens in the 1990's. This was not due to amnesty legislation, but rather reflects how the legal immigration process encourages illegal immigration by embracing legal exemptions. According to the INS, only 412,000 illegal aliens were removed during the decade.

Myth – Illegal Aliens Pay Taxes That Benefit the Economy

Fact: Most illegal aliens do not receive a typical paycheck with tax deductions. They are typically paid in cash, and therefore do not pay taxes. Even when they do pay taxes (it is possible, if they use fraudulent social security numbers or government-assigned tax ID numbers), their income does not allow enough in taxes to cover medical expenses for all the children.

In the last several months, how many times have you heard a media talking head or a liberal politician say that the illegal

232

immigrants are primarily "hard-working people who pay their taxes?" The truth of the matter is that illegal immigrants pay less than 0.1% of all Federal income taxes, even though they represent over 4.0% of the population. Just look at the statistics or visit the maternal ward at the LA County hospital. The illegal immigrant women have thousands of children per year, free of charge, and then can't afford to support them. Most learn quickly how to get cash assistance and food stamps, based on these children.

Modern America is a welfare state, and waves of low-skilled immigrants and their political lackeys are continually using that welfare to unravel our social safety net – one that is already torn. According to TREA Senior Citizens League, under the proposed "totalization" plan known as the US / Mexico Social Security Treaty, Mexican citizens who worked in the US could start collecting as much as $1 billion a year in Social Security benefits, even if they are here illegally.

Myth – It's About Cheap Labor

Fact: From the socialists who are so anxious to blame business, we hear that it is all about cheap labor. Isn't that what the whole immigration issue is about? Businesses don't want to pay a decent wage. Consumers don't want expensive produce. But the phrase "cheap labor" is a myth, a farce, and a lie. There is no such thing as "cheap labor."

Take, for example, an illegal Mexican who sneaks into the country with his wife and five children. He takes a job for $5 or $6 an hour. **At that wage, with six dependents, he pays no income tax, yet at the end of the year, if he files income tax, he gets "earned income credit" of up to $3,200, for free.** He qualifies for Section 8 housing and subsidized rent. He qualifies for food stamps. He qualifies for free (no deductible, no co-pay) health care. **His children get free breakfasts and lunches at school**, and bilingual teachers and books are provided. **He qualifies for relief from high energy bills. The aged, blind, or disabled qualify for SSI, and once qualified, they receive Medicare.** All of this is at that taxpayer's expense.

Myth – America Has Room for Immigrants

Fact: The open spaces one sees from an airplane are not where the multitude of new immigrants and their families will settle. They continue to settle in the already-overcrowded urban area of the country, just like immigrants always have. Much of America's open spaces are occupied by food production, national parks, wilderness, and uninhabitable land. All of our open space is threatened by population encroachment, as well as resource grabbing by business. Both of these threats are made worse by the sudden influx of illegal immigrants.

Myth – Illegals Come to the US for Jobs So That They Can Support Their Wives and Kids in Their Homeland

Fact: Many do. But record numbers of those wives and kids are sneaking over the border to join their breadwinner, rather than staying at home in Mexico. Even more common is that record numbers of dead-beat dads find an easy escape from responsibilities in their homeland, and actually abandon their families. Strong empirical evidence exists to suggest that even illegal aliens with good jobs in their homeland still want to be in the US. Indeed, most of the world's people come to the US because it is a very good place to be, rather than simply for a job.

Myth – The Cost of Not Educating Undocumented Children is Higher Than the Cost of Educating Them

Fact: This kind of statement is absurd. It assumes that disallowing illegal alien children from entering our schools and/or deporting them are not options. The idea that undocumented children are being punished for their parents' bad deeds is ludicrous. Undocumented children already have citizenship and the right to an education in another country. California's schools have a "don't ask don't tell" policy regarding who gets to go to school. This policy is a powerful magnet that attracts illegals to California. The costs are enormous. Undocumented children are being rewarded, often with special grants and privileged programs. We do not want to punish children for illegal status, but why should we reward them?

Breaking the Piggy Bank

With states straining under gaping budget shortfalls, public schools are facing some of the most significant decreases in state funding in decades. While these massive budget deficits cannot be attributed to any single source, the enormous impact of large-scale illegal immigration is dramatic. The total K-12 school expenditure for illegal immigrants costs states nearly $12 billion annually, and when the children born here to illegal aliens are added, the costs more than double, to $28.6 billion. Few disagree that if the current rate of illegal immigration continues, one school will have to be built each day to accommodate the undocumented children and citizen children of undocumented parents. Nearly all the increase in public school enrollment over the past 20 years is due, not to the Baby Boom generation having children, but rather to lax federal immigration policies and practices.

The taxpayers' hard-earned contributions towards school expenditures does not represent the total costs. The special programs for non-English speakers incur not only an additional fiscal burden, but also present a hindrance to the learning environment. A study found that dual language programs represent an additional $279 to $879 per pupil, depending on the class size.

Is Education Important to You?

Here are the words of a teacher who spent over 20 years in the Los Angeles school system:

Imagine teachers in classes containing 30 to 40 students of widely varying attention spans and motivation; many of whom aren't fluent in English. Educators seek learning materials likely to reach the

235

majority of students, and that means fewer words and math problems and more pictures and multicultural references.

We have heard often enough that we are a nation of immigrants. True enough, but the immigrants that came through Ellis Island wanted to learn English and to become Americans in every way. Now, too many immigrants come here demanding that lessons be taught in their own language, special privileges called affirmative action, and ethnic studies that glorify their cultures. The government uses taxpayer money to provide signs, bulletins, printed material, and automated recordings in immigrant languages. While illegal immigrants receive $20 to $30 an hour in benefits, working Americans are lucky to have $5 or $6 left after paying the bills, not to mention paying for increased crime, graffiti, and trash cleanup. **Cheap labor? Yeah right!**

Myth – Issuing California Drivers Licenses to Illegal Aliens will Make Our Roads Safer

Fact: Many Illegal aliens currently drive without licenses. Society must assume that anyone who would break the law and drive without a license would continue to break driving and other laws even if they were licensed. It is absurd to think that illegal aliens are going to run out and buy car insurance, just because they are given a license. Indeed, one of the most profitable documents now being sold to illegals is fraudulent proof of insurance documents.

Myth – Lack of Academic Achievement and High Drop-Out Rates are Caused by the Poor Economic Conditions of Immigrants.

Fact: This is a good example of the "just accept it as truth" clichés that motivated me to write this book. Poverty in itself does not cause school failures, as we know from the well-documented successes of other poor groups that have come to our shore. *Scientific American* magazine pointed out that many refugees from Southeast Asia with large families arrived

236

in the US with little more then the clothes on their backs, and with no exposure to Western culture or knowledge of the English language. Yet their children display stunning scholastic achievement in American schools.

In the US, the effect of poverty on education has been focused mainly on two ethnic groups: Black and Hispanics. Ironically these groups, as we have shown in Chapter 1, are represented by leaders whose livelihoods depends on excusing poor academic performance for any reasons except the obvious one – not doing the hard work it takes to succeed in academics.

Myth – Illegals are Enjoying the Fruit of the Recent Robust American Economy

Fact: While many Americans are benefiting from the good economy, a record number of Americans are falling into poverty, despite 35 years of record government spending on social programs. This downward slide can be directly linked to illegals flooding the low scale job market. We are very simply importing poverty faster than we can eradicate it. Had there not been massive illegal immigration in the past 20 years, poverty in America may well have been reduced significantly.

Back during the Great Depression, President Herbert Hoover ordered the deportation of all illegal aliens in order to make the jobs available to American citizens who desperately needed work. Again in 1954, President Dwight Eisenhower deported 1.3 million Mexican nationals (called "Operation Wetback") so that returning American WWII and Korean veterans had a better chance at getting jobs. It took two years to deport these people. So why aren't we deporting illegals today, for the same reasons? If you doubt the veracity of this information, just type Operation Wetback into your favorite search engine and confirm it for yourself. Remember … don't forget to pay your taxes. There are 12 million illegal aliens depending on you!

Myth – If You Could Get Americans to Pick Vegetables, You Would End Up Paying $10 a Head for Lettuce

Fact: It would be cheaper to hire Americans. Hiring illegals doesn't save the country money, it shifts costs from their employers to the government. Since illegal wages don't include health care benefits or enough money for food and housing, the American taxpayer subsidizes their wages in the form of food stamps, Welfare, hospital treatment, free clinics, bilingual services, etc. Add that to the retail price, and the cost of overwhelmed public services and infrastructure, and you will correctly estimate what that head of lettuce really costs. Why not allow the free market to set a wage at which Americans will take jobs that are now filled by illegal aliens?

Myth – Illegal Aliens Don't Affect Politics Because They Can't Vote

Fact: The main reason politicians support amnesty for illegal aliens is to include these voting blocks in their political parties. When illegal aliens ultimately become voting citizens, most vote in blocks – not for the good of America, but for economic gain and benefits for their crowd. Their gains usually come at the expense of another group. One such example is promoting policies of amnesty for their illegal countrymen in the US.

As these minorities become a majority in many congressional districts, the legislators with Hispanic and Asian surnames set agendas that continually take more from the system than they give back. They exert political pressure on business and government to supply money and jobs to help solve the problems of their needy districts. This demographic shift continues to exert what Robert Dahl called "minority rule," in which public policy is arrived at by neither a majority nor a minority, but rather through the compromises of various organized and vocal minorities. The old squeaky wheel syndrome is the oil that moves our politicians to cater to the needs of a vocal and growing minority.

Myth – The Immigrants / Illegals Will Assimilate Into Society

Fact: Many do. But most Third World illegals come to the US for personal economic reasons, not to cherish our democratic system. Many so-called immigration rights groups are Left-wing radicals that fan the fire with their rhetoric, encouraging immigrants to preserve their culture and language at taxpayers' expense. Among these groups, the word assimilation is considered xenophobic. Most Americans did not give politicians permission to exchange our country's high moral values into an "I hate America" gang culture. I don't remember voting to allow massive illegal immigration into the country, or to allow our way of life to be turned upside down in order to make lawbreakers feel more at home.

The United States is the only nation that accepts hundreds of thousands of immigrants each year. We continually absorb more immigrants than all other industrialized nations combined. California will soon be the first state to have a "minority majority." Los Angeles already has that minority majority.

Despite recent restrictions, liberal US immigration policies are a time bomb that will change American society even more dramatically in the future. There will be problems galore. Sun Belt states like California, Florida, and Texas will become Third World countries themselves, with huge immigrant populations isolated from White America by poverty, violence, education, and racial tension. Finding the right level of Welfare support to provide a safety net without undermining immigrants' incentives to succeed will be particularly difficult. Education and job creation will also pose major problems for government at all levels. These new Americans are assimilating into one society, but the pace will continue to be painstakingly slow. And the society into which they are assimilating isn't American.

We will not have the predicted labor shortages that have justified our lax US immigration policies. Severe underemployment in newly developing nations will fuel the

239

migration of millions of workers to industrialized nations, particularly to the US Sun Belt. In the United States, it would be possible for zero population growth to be reached in the next decade, with immigration alone accounting for population increases. Without volatile birth, but based on death and immigration rates, the US population will peak at about 300 million in about 2038, and then begin to decline for the first time ever. This decline would be a blessing to the overpopulated world, since natural resources are becoming scarcer. However, unless increased immigration from Asia, Latin America, and Eastern Europe is checked, a decline in US population is highly unlikely.

US immigration is now approaching the record levels of the early 1900's. Asian-Americans have a growth rate eight times that of Whites. If Hispanic immigration and birth rates increase, theirs will be four times that of Whites, and will double in the next decade.

Growth in immigration will also have a profound effect on household markets. Immigrants from Asia and Latin America are likely to be young adults, so in the next decade a large share of new householders, especially in cities, will be Hispanic or Asian.

Our culture is also changing due to growing Hispanic and Asian influence on food, fashion, and customs. We will become more aware that the food we eat, the music we hear, and the clothes we wear will have a Latin flavor. For example, tacos have surpassed pizza for the first time as the most popular ethnic food. Rather than assimilating into the US melting pot, we will see instead a cultural mosaic of highly concentrated Asian and Hispanic-speaking markets. If marketers are to succeed, they will need to deal in Spanish, Chinese, Arabic, and other languages. Like most people, I enjoy exploring ethnic foods and cultures. But when immigrant groups apply pressure on companies and governments that force me, an American who speaks the native language, to endure the "Press one for English" messages, something is terribly wrong. Does any sane person believe you would have to press a person in Mexico to speak in Spanish?

Public education will continue to be radically changed to help immigrants. There will be continuing disruptive and misguided pressure to require school districts to provide teachers who speak the numerous immigrant languages. We see this hybrid culture played out on the Public Broadcasting System (PBS) children's programs, where cartoon kids with Hispanic names continually present Spanish words, concepts, and idealized immigrant lifestyles into their stories. This is understandable, since nearly half of all kids less than five years old in the US are Hispanic or from another racial minority. When the minorities become majorities, perhaps some shows will allow English to be tossed into the Spanish programming to satisfy the White minority activists.

The US vs. Mexico

On February 15, 1998, the US and Mexican soccer teams met at the Los Angeles Coliseum. The crowd was overwhelmingly pro-Mexican, even though most lived in this country. **They booed during the National Anthem, and US flags were held upside down.** As the match progressed, supporters of the US team were insulted, pelted with projectiles, punched, and spat upon. Beer and trash were thrown at the US players before and after the match. **The coach of the US team, Steve Sampson said, "This was the most painful experience I have ever had in this profession."**

This wide cultural diversity reaching our shore will generate a distinct culture of its own that will be neither traditional American nor identical to the country of origin. Hopefully, the US will escape the assimilation problems experienced in Europe. They have learned in France, as Paris burned, that millions of Muslim immigrants allowed into France to do low-end jobs, while the economy was healthy, never assimilated into the French society. Instead, throughout Europe, clerics who minister to the growing Muslim population continue to indoctrinate poorly educated workers against Western values.

Myth – Americans Support Illegal Immigration

With hundreds of thousands of demonstrators shouting in the streets, demanding rights for illegal aliens, and the US Congress and President supporting their efforts, one might believe the myth that Americans support illegal immigrants.

Fact: Americans think that illegals have a lot of gall coming here and demanding rights that aren't theirs to have. A *USA Today* / Gallup poll revealed that 61% of Americans say that the US should make illegal immigration a crime, while 81% say illegal immigration to the United States is out of control. Almost 80% believe that controlling our borders to halt illegal immigration is extremely important.

Hopefully, Congress will understand that they are once again failing to march in step with the American public. Instead they are marching with illegals, carrying the Mexican flag. Speaking of the Mexican flag, it does not help the immigrants' cause for Americans to see the heart-stopping photo of the Mexican flag being put up over an upside down American flag. Students at Pioneer High School in Whittier, California perpetuated this maltreatment of our flag. (The pioneers for whom the town is named must be turning in their graves.) The same students also walked out of classes to protest proposed Federal immigration legislation. We would all be better off if they stayed in class, to learn English and the history of why the US is the greatest democracy on Earth.

Once again, the US Senate is out of step with the American people. Since immigration is getting press, these senatorial media addicts will unleash their inflated egos and float an immigration reform package rather than protecting our borders, a top priority for keeping lawbreakers out. More likely, our congressional eunuchs will come up with a plan to give the lawbreakers a free pass to become citizens, and an option to become a majority, making the USA "Mexico Norte."

More Rewards for Being an Illegal Alien
Uncle Sam Wants Us to Help Illegal Aliens Buy Homes

The Federal Depository Insurance Corporation (FDIC) and the Mortgage Guarantee Insurance Corporation (MDIC) now facilitate lending money to illegal aliens so that they can buy homes in this country. Both of these agencies encourage their insured banks to tap into the large and growing illegal alien market for loans.

With the approval of the Federal government, banks are authorized to accept an Individual Tax Identification Number (ITIN) in lieu of a social security number when considering applications for home mortgages or other types of loans. According to the FDIC, "Banks aren't legally required to verify legal status" of the people applying for loans. Banks have been at the forefront in allowing potential customers to use foreign consular ID's to open accounts, and fought a provision barring their use in last year's homeland security bill.

The state governments are also getting into the act of helping illegal aliens buy homes. Wisconsin State Housing Authority, for example, underwrites bank loans made to illegal aliens purchasing homes and encourages banks to lend to this population. These loans, for which the taxpayers are ultimately responsible, are being made to people who could be deported at any time.

Unlike legal residents with Social Security numbers and ten-year credit histories usually considered when applying for a mortgage, illegal aliens with ITIN's need only demonstrate a two-year credit history. Encouraging illegal aliens to enter the housing market will likely exacerbate already-skyrocketing housing costs at the expense of homebuyers.

In-State Tuition Rates for Illegal Aliens

Efforts are underway in several states and in Congress to allow illegal aliens to pay steeply discounted in-state tuition for public colleges and universities – rates not available to American citizens from other states. As state universities limit enrollment, the increased number of illegal aliens at these schools will reduce opportunities and aid to legal immigrants and US citizens. State taxpayers will pay higher costs; out-of-state tuition is typically 2 to 3.5 times higher than in-state tuition. FAIR estimated that illegal aliens in 2004 cost the taxpayers between $581 and $756 million for in-state tuition.

Some university admissions policies actually favor new immigrants over White Americans.

This advantage for freeloading illegal aliens is not a problem for the brainwashed students at Columbia University, who embarrassed their school by rushing the stage and trying to attack an invited speaker. The speaker was a representative of the Minute Man Project, an effective grassroots citizens group helping to bring attention to the problem of illegal aliens and to prevent these lawbreakers from entering our country. The University proved again that our education and value systems have become corrupted when they released a report about the incident on Christmas day, a damage controlling, quiet news day. Columbia did not even demand that the speaker be given an apology. First Amendment rights seem to apply only to Left-wing topics and to people ignorantly parroted by the "new Red Guard" students who have been brainwashed within our university fortresses.

Myth – Illegal Immigration is not a Security Threat or Crime

Fact: Each year the Border Patrol makes more then a million apprehensions of people who flagrantly violate our nation's laws by unlawfully crossing US borders to work and receive publicly funded services, often with the aid of fraudulent documents. Such entry is a misdemeanor and, if repeated, becomes a punishable felony.

In addition to sneaking into the country without legal documentation, these people might enter with legal documentation, and then violate the terms on which they have been admitted by taking unauthorized jobs or by overstaying authorized periods in the country. Immigration and Naturalization Service (INS) estimates that in January 2000 there were 7 million illegal aliens living in the US; a number that was growing by half a million a year. The half million annual increase is the net growth in the illegal-alien population. Note that immigration minus deaths, and minus legalizations, and minus exodus stands, is at about 8 million, conservatively. Included in that estimate are approximately 78,000 illegal aliens from countries who are of special concern in the war on terror.

The government recently asserted the right to indefinitely detain in jail whole classes of immigrants deemed security risks. The ruling was originally passed after Haitian immigrations, when Ashcroft observed that mass immigration was putting a strain on national and homeland security resources. He particularly noted the heavily taxed Coast Guard's limited capacity and capabilities.

Ashcroft stated that the State Department had detected an increase in aliens from countries such as Pakistan, who used Haiti as a staging point for their entry into the United States. According to *Infiltration* author Paul Sperry, there are now 1,209 officially recognized mosques in this country, with an estimated 80% of them controlled by Saudi Arabia. Saudi money and the Saudi brand of Wahhabi Islam gave rise to al-Qaeda. This ideology, fueled by immigration, is now finding a well-financed home on these shores.

Terrorist Ties to Hiring Center for Illegal Alien Workers?

Why is an individual with close ties to radical Islamic groups interested in having the town of Herndon, Virginia build a hiring center for illegal alien workers who hail from Mexico and Central America? FAIR uncovered information that Mukit Hossain, director of Project Hope and Harmony (the group behind the day laborer hiring center), also serves on the board of organizations investigated for links to Middle East terrorist organizations.

This particular group has offices that serve as headquarters for about 100 interlocking Islamic organizations, many of which are presently under investigation for ties to Islamic terrorist groups. Nearly all of these organizations are the creation of Dr. Jamal Barzinji. In Paul Sperry's book, *Infiltration*, Barzinji is described by Federal investigator David Kane as "not only closely associated with the Palestinian Islamic Jihad, but with Hamas."

Another entity is interested in seeking $170,000 from the town of Herndon, Virginia to run a hiring center known as the All Dulles Area Muslim Society, or ADAMS, Center. The Adams Center, according to Sperry "is another Saudi-controlled Wahhabi mosque," where violence against America and the West is regularly preached.

As I watched members of the illegal alien movement and the flag-waving Palestinians march side by side in San Francisco to protest our war on terrorism, I only speculate as to why Islamic groups with suspected ties to terrorism are at the forefront of promoting a hiring center for illegal aliens. Whatever the reasons, it is clear that exploiting America's chaotic immigration system is a tactic that terrorist organizations aim to employ.

Former 9/11 Commissioners Warn That Security Recommendations are Ignored

Among the 9/11 commission's recommendations were calls for tightening many of the loopholes in our immigration laws and lax enforcement policies. The 9/11 terrorists exploited these immigration law shortcomings to carry out their attacks, and others will follow their example in the future. The recommendations of the commission include tighter border security, more rigorous interior enforcement, and improving the security of vital government-issued identity documents. Adding to the urgency of the former commissioner's warnings was the recent arrest of an Iraqi national with ties to al-Qaeda along the US / Mexico border. "God help us if we have another attack," said one of the commissioners, former Governor Thomas Kean, "and if we have not done all that we can reasonably do to prevent it, what will our excuse be?"

Security Loses in Our Immigration "Lottery"

Another security concern is the way aliens become legal permanent residents of the United States. Each year, approximately 50,000 successful applicants are chosen at random and given permanent resident status based on pure luck. Usually, immigrant visas are issued to foreign nationals that have an existing connection with a family member who lawfully resides in the US or with a US employer. However, under the visa "lottery" program, visas are awarded to immigrants at random, without regard to such minimal criteria. Recently, Congress held an eye-opening hearing on the problems with the visa lottery program, revealing that many specific terrorism-related offenses in the US have occurred at the hands of those who have benefited from the visa lottery.

One such case was that of Hesham Mohamed Ali Hedayet, the Egyptian national who killed two and wounded three during a shooting spree at L.A. International Airport in July of 2002. He was allowed to apply for lawful permanent resident status because his wife was a visa lottery winner, and despite his own admission to the INS that he had been accused of being a member of a known terrorist organization.

If that wasn't bad enough, the visa lottery program is also wrought with fraud. The State Department confirms that the lottery is "subject to widespread abuse," and more specifically that 364,000 duplicate applications were detected in one year alone. Furthermore, the lottery is unfair to immigrants who comply with our laws, because it does not prohibiting illegal aliens from applying for visas through the program. Thereby, foreign nationals that comply with our laws are treated the same as those blatantly violating them.

As Congressman Bob Goodlatte noted,

> The visa lottery is a flawed policy and is foolish in the age we live. Those in the world who wish us harm can easily engage in this statistical gamble with nothing to lose. Our immigration policy should be based primarily on our national security and economic needs, not on arbitrary systems lacking basic safeguards.

Myth – The US Economy Benefits from Immigration

Fact: Realistic estimates suggest that since 1980, immigration raised the total income of native-born Americans by no more then a fraction of 1%. Many of the worst-off native-born Americans are hurt by immigration, especially from Mexico. Because Mexican immigrants with much less education then the average US worker increase the supply of low-skilled labor and work for less, they drive down the wages of the worst-paid Americans. The most recent authoritative

Harvard study of this effect estimates that US high-school dropouts would earn as much as 8% more if it weren't for Mexican immigration.

Myth – Americans will not do the Work Illegals do

Fact: Prior to 1965, when the disastrous Immigration Bill was passed, very little immigration occurred. In fact, there was even a period of net emigration from the US between 1925 and 1965. During this time, our grass was cut, our meat packed, our children cared for, our houses cleaned, and our restaurants cooked and served food. The idea that somehow we suddenly cannot run a country without an unlimited supply of foreigners is absurd. The willingness of Americans to do a job depends on how much the job pays, and the main reason some jobs pay too little to attract native-born Americans is competition from poorly paid immigrants.

A Magnet for Immigrants

The destructive force of Hurricane Katrina also destroyed one of the favorite arguments posed by immigration advocates: namely that immigrants, especially illegal aliens, do the jobs Americans don't want. As Katrina evacuees spread out across the country, many found themselves in direct competition with millions of illegal aliens for scarce jobs. The government estimates that some 400,000 jobs were lost in the Gulf region as the result of the hurricane. The workers who lost their jobs report that they are finding jobs in their new or temporary homes filled by illegal aliens. The hurricane area already had wages lower then average, and Federal rules waivers created a surge of low-cost immigrant labor.

Before Katrina, foreign-born Latinos made up 17% of the US construction workforce and accounted for 40% of the 2004 employment growth in that sector. Twenty percent or more of US construction laborers were unauthorized migrants; the percentage was even higher among cement masons, roofers, and dry wall workers.

After being victimized by Mother Nature, these displaced Americans are now victimized by government policies that continue to place the interests of illegal aliens above those of law-abiding American citizens. Shortly after the storm, Homeland Security Secretary Michael Chertoff announced that his department (DHS) was suspending deportations of illegals and that the DHS would not enforce employer sanction laws for at least 45 days.

It should be noted that the government was not enforcing sanction laws even before Hurricane Katrina struck. Indeed, the number of Federal fine notices issued to employers for knowingly hiring illegal workers dropped from 417 in 1999 to only three in 2004. Arrests of unauthorized workers dropped from 2,849 in 1999 to 445 in 2003.

Even more dismaying are reports that large numbers of foreign workers, mostly Mexican, are already working for labor contactors and have begun rebuilding New Orleans and the surrounding communities. Desperate American workers, including Blacks looking to get their piece of set asides allocated as a preferential race, may not find work rebuilding their own communities.

Myth – The Mexican Government Wants to Stop Illegal Immigration

Fact: The government of Mexico views its citizens' illegal immigration into the United States as a way to unburden Mexico of excess labor and as a source of revenue in the form of remittances sent home. For a long time, Mexico has tacitly encouraged such migration, but the encouragement is tacit no longer. The Mexican government began distributing a guidebook instructing would-be illegal migrants how to enter the US as safely as possible, how to avoid detection once across the border, and what to do if apprehended by US authorities. Since Mexico's former President was considering legislation that would allow the personal use of cocaine, LSD, heroin, and other drugs, doped up illegals and drug traffickers, when caught, were told that they would be able to say that they were only bringing in drugs for their personal use.

Mexico is not the only country that encourages their citizens to immigrant to the US. Many countries go out of their way to support their nationals who have come to the US illegally. For example, I watched in awe as a meeting of foreign affairs ministers from Central America discussed a major tenet of their foreign policy. They stated that they intend to acquire and keep "rights" for their citizens who have come to the US illegally. This Latin American chutzpah is another example of reality being turned upside down.

Illegal Immigration is not only from Latin America
Lost in the immigration debate are Asians – they are not a large majority of the illegal aliens in the US, but have joined Hispanic-led protests in ever greater numbers. This public display of support must be in light of the 200-year history of discrimination against Asians immigrants in the United States.

The Pew Hispanic Center estimates that of more than 11 million illegal aliens in the United States, 78% are from Mexico or other Latin America countries. Some one million of the 14 million Asian illegal immigrants in the United States are Chinese. One in every five of the million Koreans in the US is here illegally. More are on the way: there are 1.5 million Asians in the backlog of applications for permanent residency status or citizenship.

Immigration from China to the US is proving as contentious as China's policies regarding human rights, protection of terrorist states (Iran and Hamas-led Palestine), and the trade imbalance. China has proven time and again to be reluctant to take back its illegal immigrants, including the 19,000 being held by American authorities.

Canada has become the gateway for Chinese criminal activity in the US. Chinese and biker gangs smuggle booty and illegals through the Indian reserves that straddle the Canada / US border in Ontario and Quebec. Police can't do much, since these reserves have their own police force that is often corrupt.

Myth – English is the Official Language of the United States

Fact: The Arizona Supreme Court overturned as unconstitutional a 1988 law requiring that state and local government conduct business in English. Arizona was one of 23 states that previously passed laws making English the official language of the state. Who would think that expecting immigrants to speak English would become a violation of the law? This is just one more example of how brainwashed and screwed up our country has become. And things will become more ridiculous as liberal politicians pander to immigrant groups, knocking those who stand up to protect our culture, borders, and treasury from a tidal wave of uncontrolled, illogical immigration.

As immigrants flock to the US, the nation's work force is becoming more and more multilingual. Today, 322 languages are spoken in America. Indeed, according to the most recent census, 21.3 million Americans barely speak English – a disturbing increase of 52% in only ten years. Some companies, who responded by creating ad hoc language policies, have landed in court. This happened to Sephora USA, when five employees filed a complaint with that dangerous army of legal storm troopers, aka the US Equal (Unequal) Employment Opportunity Commission. The commission filed a lawsuit on behalf of the five and a class of Hispanic employees. The suit alleged a double standard that required that Hispanic employees speak Spanish with customers, but refrain from speaking Spanish in their free time.

Sephora claimed that the EEOC allegations were groundless, denying that it ever had "an English only rule" that expected workers speak English to customers unless the customer wishes otherwise. A judge ruled that the company's written policy on English usage was "permissible," but the issue of discrimination against employees told not to speak Spanish is still pending.

The EEOC and their diversity business partners are always looking for new markets to exploit. English seems to be the issue that makes up the soft underbelly of business and government, ready for destructive parasite attack. Indeed, cases involving English-only policies are growing for the EEOC, as well as for their "dawgs," aka "friends," in private law firms across the country. Complaints filed with the agency jumped to 155 in 2004 from 32 in 1996. Most grievances usually involve Spanish, and are likely to be handled by private attorneys looking for an easy mark to pay for the addition of a new wing on their house.

In the 2000 census, 47 million people – an astounding 18% of all US residents – reported speaking a language other than English at home, up from 14% in 1990. To accommodate immigrants, many states offer drivers license tests, hospital questionnaires, and election ballots in as many as eight foreign languages. Due to the increase in Spanish speakers, even the US Census Bureau is testing a bilingual questionnaire in preparation for the 2010 census.

These tower of Babel forms add considerable confusion and cost to the American public.

Some municipalities are even considering Spanish-language-only courts. They may be needed at this year's Cinco de Mayo festivities in San Jose. The *San Jose Mercury* reported that there were 54 arrests and 27 citations given out on Friday night, with 44 more arrests and 142 more citations on Saturday. Of course, the pro-immigrant paper printed in the front-page article "It was a mostly peaceful, family friendly affair..."

Highland Hospital in Rochester, NY, according to hospital CEO, asked its housekeeping staff to speak English after receiving several complaints from non-Spanish speaking employees who felt ostracized by a group of Hispanic workers and a supervisor. You can be sure the EEOC did not file a lawsuit on behalf of the English-speaking employees, but instead filed suit against the hospital and its owners on behalf of Hispanic employees who said they were subjected to an English-only rule and disciplined for violating it. The suit seeks financial compensation for past humiliation and emotional distress. Uncle Tony, can you believe this shit? The hospital denies ever enforcing an English-only policy, according to CEO Becker. The Hispanic plaintiffs all speak English and were asked to communicate in a "common language," but the EEOC maintains that most of the claimants have only limited English proficiency. The workers are still employed by the hospital, even while the case is in litigation.

English only matters when it impacts you. As I wrote this book, my Dell computer with Microsoft Office software developed a bug that suddenly decided my spell check should be in 'Mexican Spanish.' I wasted a day trying to get the problem fixed, as I unsuccessfully dealt with what is laughingly referred to as support services in "Indian English."

"Press number one if you would like to continue in English." It makes me boil as more and more companies force me, born an American, to choose to speak in English. Do you believe that shit Uncle Tony? How about pressing one if you speak English or press two to get disconnected until you CAN speak English!

Hispanic Leaders Speak Out!

Like other minorities, Hispanics need to quickly change their leaders' "su casa es mi casa" attitude. They continue to hurt the impoverished immigrants – the ones we care about – with their rhetoric. What did the illegal immigrant leaders and some losers have to say at the various demonstrations a couple of months ago?

Augustin Cebada, Brown Berets: "Go back to Boston! Go back to Plymouth Rock, Pilgrims! Get out! We are the future. You are old and tired. Go on. We have beaten you. Leave like beaten rats. You old, white people. It is your duty to die. Through love of having children, we are going to take over." (This comment proves again that Hispanic "leaders" belong in school rather than spending their time ranting on the streets. The Pilgrims this guy berated were also illegal immigrants.)

Richard Alatorre, Los Angeles City Council: "They're afraid we're going to take over the governmental institutions and other institutions. They're right. We will take them over. We are here to stay."

***Excelsior*, the national newspaper of Mexico:** "The American Southwest seems to be slowly returning to the jurisdiction of Mexico without firing a single shot."

Professor Jose Angel Gutierrez, University of Texas: "We have an aging white America. They are not making babies. They are dying. The explosion is in our population … I love it. They are shitting in their pants with fear. I love it."

Art Torres, Chairman of the California Democratic Party: "Remember 187 – proposition to deny taxpayer funds for services to non-citizens – was the last gasp of white America in California."

Gloria Molina, Los Angeles County Supervisor: "We are politicizing every single one of these new citizens that are becoming citizens of this country. I gotta tell you that a lot of people are saying, 'I'm going to go out there and vote because I want to pay them back.'"

Mario Obledo, California Coalition of Hispanic Organizations and California State Secretary of Health, Education and Welfare under Governor Jerry Brown, also awarded the Presidential Medal of Freedom by President Bill Clinton: "California is going to be a Hispanic state. Anyone who doesn't like it should leave."

Jose Pescador Osuna, Mexican Consul General: "We are practicing 'La Reconquista' in California."

Professor Fernando Guerra, Loyola Marymount University: "We need to avoid a white backlash by using codes understood by Latinos."

Are these just the words of a few extremists? Consider the fact that I could fill up many more pages with such quotes. Also, realize that these are mainstream Mexican leaders. I guess our politicians don't understand the meaning of these Spanglish threats to our culture and country. The threats to our society often evolve into cases brought before our judicial system.

We will see in the next chapter, however, that the judicial system, like government, is often the source of our problems, rather than the solution.

Chapter 8
JUSTICE IS JUST

A blindfolded woman holding a pair of scales is symbolic of America's justice system. The system is indeed blind, but not necessarily to guilt or innocence, but rather to the damage the legal system itself is causing our country. Indeed, judges and lawyers are most often the problem rather than the solution. In this chapter, lawyers and their politician cousins become easy targets. I'd like to acknowledge the important insights of Don Wolfe to this chapter.

Lawsuit Abuse

The number of lawsuits in the US has tripled in the last 30 years. The business community must pick its battles carefully, to survive the risks of fighting this abuse. Staggering legal costs, extensive delays, and huge judgments can severely affect a company's bottom line.

The US has gone overboard in protecting individual liberties at the cost of endangering the economy. Indeed, polling corporate executives revealed that 83% say that their decisions are increasingly affected by the fear of lawsuits. Small wonder, with law firms grossing well over $100 billion, according to Department of Commerce estimates.

The legal system is rigged in favor of big business – lawsuits are a devastating competitive weapon for those like Microsoft, who can afford them. Indeed, tort reform, including ending class action suits and preventing people from suing a company if they misuse a product, would spark an explosion of productivity in America.

Not just business, but all society as well, suffers as Left-wing professors and diversity exploiters use lawsuits and tenure to protect their dangerous, irrational ideas and lies. They put a chill on those who want to expose their lies, by silencing the critics trying to tell the truth. Lawyers and judges act like the secret police of totalitarian regimes around the globe. By killing dissent and controlling the thinking of the masses, they keep evil dictators in power.

Here Comes the Judge, There Goes the Constitution

In the last few years, Federal courts have ignored the separation of power and begun to interfere with laws enacted by the Legislative branch of government. The courts now impose their own rulings as laws on communities that never voted for them. In 1994, voters in California passed by a substantial margin the ballot measure known as Proposition 187, denying most public benefits such as Welfare to illegal aliens. Within a year, a Federal judge ruled the law unconstitutional. Similarly, in 1996 the voters of California passed Proposition 209, a ballot measure that effectively abolished Affirmative Action programs and prohibited racial discrimination by state government. Again, a Federal judge ruled the new law unconstitutional – this time in just three weeks.

Furthermore, the US Ninth Circuit Court struck down as unconstitutional the official English language amendment to the Arizona state constitution. Likewise, a US district judge ordered the Kansas City School District to spend $740 million to meet education standards set by his dictate.

A California judge contributed to the "civil wrongs" that continue to allow the race victim card to be used. This time, it was to trump the minimal standards required to graduate high school. Judge Freedman, just weeks before graduation, said he intends to block the state's exit exam. This would allow students to receive diplomas even if they couldn't pass basic English and math tests. The judge said that he found merit in the argument that the exam was unfair, since all California students do not have access to the same quality of education. So by dropping the bar, this activist judge presented our businesses and colleges with more dead-enders and devalued the diplomas of students from the same schools, who had worked hard to master basic survival skills. The only bar these "students" will raise will be the corner bar. Yes Uncle Tony, some judges still believe that victim shit, but thankfully, this decision was overturned.

This Judicial Revolution

The Federal courts have appointed themselves as virtual dictators to determine which laws are valid or not, without regard for the wishes of voters, legislators, or even the text of the Constitution. Judges since the 1920's have used a variety of pseudo-constitutional doctrines and devices to override laws they have disliked.

One such device is the misinterpretation of the Constitution's Commerce Clause empowering Congress to regulate commerce among the several states, with foreign nations, and with Indian tribes. They purposely misinterpret this clause to justify Federal regulation of virtually any activity that remotely affects interstate commerce. This includes upholding the 1964 Civil Rights Act and its prohibition against racial discrimination by private enterprises in hotels restaurants and theaters. The courts used this Clause in ways having nothing to do with the intent of the language or of the principles of those who originally drafted and adopted it. **This alteration of the Commerce Clause's original intent is an example of one subtle change negatively impacting our future.**

Original intent is an important concept worth understanding when selecting judges at every level. Simply stated, original intent is the only legitimate means of interpreting any law. We should look to the intentions of those who drafted and enacted law as essential reliable guides to the law's application. In recent history, there has been a Judicial revolution in the United States, intent on overthrowing the doctrine of original intent.

Even some Supreme Court justices think it is their job to "evolve" our laws to meet their own subjective view of reality. Retired Supreme Court Justice William Brennan was one of the architects of this judicial revolution. In a *New York Times* editorial, he acknowledged his own abandonment of the original intent principle. "I approached my responsibility of interpreting it [the constitution] as a 20th-century American," Brennan recalled, "for the genius of the Constitution rests not in

257

any static meaning it may have had in a world dead and gone, but in its evolving character."

Wrong – the whole point of a written Constitution lies precisely in its "static meaning!" By fixing its meaning in writing, the framers tried to make it impossible for people to change the meaning of the laws to suit their own purposes. If we employ Brennan's evolving document, courts could simply impose on the written laws whatever meaning they wish, without regard to the original meaning in the language.

Our Judicial system can no longer be considered just, when its Judicial revolution seriously compromises the American values won in our own revolution. Since most of us are not directly impacted, we have not begun to consider seriously the ways to halt the judicial revolution and restore the Constitution. Who will be our next Paul Revere and sound the alarm? If not reversed, expect to feel more anger as you continually learn of more arrogant judges using the Constitution as notepaper to compose agendas for their buddies and themselves.

International Criminal Court (ICC)

Whatever the motives behind the creation of the International Criminal Court, let's not be blind to the fact that the preservation of a decent world order depends chiefly on the exercise of American leadership. For both geo-political and constitutional reasons, we should not be in the business of delegating leadership or compounding difficult exercises by creating unaccountable, supra-national bodies.

Like most attempts at building international convention, the ICC created a Frankenstein similar to the UN, which is now its partner in crime. The ICC is based on an emotional attachment to the abstract ideal of an international justice system, and runs contrary to American standards of constitutional order as well as the principles of international crisis resolution. The concerns expressed by John R. Bolton (our great former US Ambassador to the United Nations), before the Senate Foreign Relations Committee about the 1988 creation of the International Criminal Court (ICC) in

Rome, are as valid today as they were then, since no major, substantive change has been made to the treaty.

Bolton stated that the conference created "not only a court with sweeping and poorly defined jurisdiction, but also a powerful and unaccountable prosecutor." Bolton saw through the obvious but concealed agenda of those states looking to create more international organizations to bind nations in general and the United States in particular.

Unfortunately, President Clinton signed the ICC treaty – one that he himself admitted was flawed – having no intention of submitting it to the Senate for ratification. His purpose was to put the US in a position to help correct the flaws. But as others have noted, the treaty was not only flawed, but actually dead on arrival. Without the US, the ICC would have hopefully rested in peace, but the naïve support for the ICC left the US in a weaker position than if we had simply declared the treaty a non-starter in the first place. The ICC was created as an organization outside the UN system; a decision I would normally say was wise. Unfortunately, by excluding the UN, the Security Council and the veto power of the US, as one of the Council's five permanent members, was also eliminated.

The American concept of separation of power reflects our belief that the various authorities legitimately exercised in government are placed in separate branches, as a necessary system of checks and balances. Europeans, however, may feel comfortable with a system that vests the ICC Prosecutor with enormous law enforcement powers accountable to no one. Bolton concluded that the ICC is in fact a "stealth approach to eroding constitutionalism. Americans should find this unacceptable."

Be aware of liberal Democrats under pressure from Left-wing Europeans to pump life back into the ICC Frankenstein. The Left would love to have such a weapon to use against US troops and their leaders; a type of Nuremberg trial to denigrate our courageous war heroes. Uninformed, biased, Left-wing Euro-trash prefer to support terrorist regimes in Palestine, and the cowardly toads that run Iran would love to target our troops in their kangaroo courts. These are the kinds of things we can expect from an overly powerful ICC.

Judicial Speed Traps

The American Tort Reform Association (ATRA) identified 13 jurisdictions where the law is constantly applied unfairly. The result is lawsuit abuse that costs consumers, compromises access to affordable healthcare, and acts as a drag on the economy. Personal injury lawyers bring cases to these Judicial hellholes because they know that these courts will produce a large verdict or settlement, a favorable precedent, and usually both. This kind of injustice has a tremendously negative impact on our system of government. Even some personal injury lawyers agree that there is a problem. A trial lawyer who won $1.4 billion in legal fees admitted that it's almost impossible to get a fair trail if you're a defendant in some of these places.

In Madison County, Illinois, county judges receive three-quarters of their contributions from personal injury lawyers. Not surprisingly, Madison County saw a 2,050% increase in class action lawsuits from 1998 to 2001. Mississippi's 22nd Judicial District is infamous, and subject to FBI investigations for some jurors receiving payments for their verdicts. In Orleans Parish, Louisiana, one judge celebrated with his jurors after a large verdict, inviting them to have their pictures taken with him and the plaintiff's council, the late Johnnie Cochran, who we all remember for helping O.J. escape a first-degree murder charge.

Prejudging Judges

Experienced law professors and litigates, as well as the general public, are reporting that too often judges are simply unwilling to listen to facts and reason. They start instead with predilections heavily favoring one view. If asked, of course, they deny ever having made such predictions. They then prove impervious to facts and viewpoints contrary to their bias, and are steadfast in their opinion even when there is evidence supporting different facts, or when those facts are not denied by opposing council. In many cases, judges literally make up counter facts. An analogy to the typical judges' resistance to facts is the O.J. Simpson jury, who were not going to let facts get in the way of prejudices. Another is Justice O'Connor's support of Affirmative Action for the simple reason that she had negative experiences as one of a few female law students.

When judges act on the basis of their prior predilections, ignore facts, and even make up supposed counter facts, they destroy a central tenet of the Judicial system: decisions of cases are to be based on facts rather then prejudice. They injure persons by such decisions, and in the case of the Simpson jury, destroy faith in the Judicial system, leading to bitterness toward a system that reneges on its promise to be fair.

This bad situation is made worse when the disregard for facts is combined with other acts that compound the bias. For example, a judge may insure that facts contrary to the side he favors are kept to a minimum by denying discovery of those facts. Discovery is the legal process occurring before trial, where each party receives documents from the opposing side and questions the persons involved. Judges sometimes, almost unbelievably, hold secret hearings barring one party from examining witnesses and learning facts.

There are also examples of judges disqualifying knowledgeable and experienced counsel who would be best qualified to uncover and present those facts.   Judges have refused to be excused from hearing a case, even when they have ignored or buried facts and have then been accused of bias. I was involved in a vote recount that involved an entrenched New York Democratic Congressional incumbent, a former judge himself, who was running against an idealistic reformer who I worked for. The vote was very close, with the incumbent winning by about 300 votes, so a recount was ordered. The recount, after taking out scores of invalid votes from dead people and double counting, showed the reformer as the winner by a few votes, say 15. The incumbent challenged the recount in court. The sitting judge, a known associate of the incumbent, refused to disqualify himself saying, "though he was a friend of the Congressman for 30 years he could be impartial." He then reviewed the recount and gave the reformer all but 18 of the challenged votes – just enough to assure another victory for the incumbent.

Who Is Judging Judges?

Political conservatives continually charge that judges are overriding the will of the people, as expressed in statutes relating to abortions, gay rights, Affirmative Action, religion, and so forth. The Left, on the other hand, makes charges of bias by businesses against women, minorities, handicapped, Spanish speakers, and so on. In the meantime, the lawyers charge trial judges with tyrannical and arbitrary misuse of their position, and even bribery.

However, conservatives, liberals, and lawyers all agree that the commissions and boards dealing with Judicial misconduct are not effective. Due to this lack of power, few judges are taken to task by commissions, which are largely comprised of judges themselves, and staffed by defenders who are predisposed to protect wayward judges rather than punish them for misusing their position.

Legal Vultures

Looking for a growing business opportunity? Go on TV and find anybody who claims to have an asbestos-related injury. A RAND report states that over 600,000 people in the US filed claims for asbestos-related injuries, costing businesses more then $54 billion by the end of 2000. The study reports that 500,000 to 2.4 million more claims could be filed in the years ahead, costing businesses another $210 billion more.

The study found that 65% of compensation over the past decade was paid to people with non-cancerous conditions. Increasing claims by those with no cancer and little functional impairment explain the recent growth in the asbestos caseload. There are too many lawyers in America already, and 500,000 more are graduating from Law School this year. Too many lawyers mean too many frivolous lawsuits.

Here are just a few of the thousands of suits that clog up our courts:

Top that off – A college student was unknowingly caught on camera cavorting topless in New Orleans during Mardi Gras. Lawyers are suing the makers of "Girls Gone

Wild" video for exploiting her. Who would have expected there to be cameras snapping a bare-breasted woman during Mardi Gras?
Source: *Tallahassee Democrat*

One for you millions for me – A class-action lawsuit filed in Texas accused two of the largest auto insurers of over billing by $100 billion. The lawsuit was filed, even though state insurance regulators declared the practice of rounding off twice annual premiums to the next dollar to be legal. In the end, both companies settled. The policyholder plaintiffs received $5.50 each. The lawyer got $8 million.
Source: *San Antonio Express*

Caught in a pickle – A West Virginia store worker was awarded $2,699,000 after she injured her back opening a pickle jar. The worker also received $130,066 in compensation and $170,000 for emotional distress. This "outrageous sum" was reduced to $2.2 million by the state Supreme Court.
Source: *Charleston Daily Mail*

Fax this – A Hooters restaurant in Georgia was bankrupted after a $12 million judgment in a class action lawsuit. It seems a third party sent an unsolicited fax, advertising to hundreds of folks. Hooters' defense was that it was a third party. The judge, however, ruled that Hooters had knowingly violated the law, and, having the discretion to triple the amount, did so. Plaintiffs will receive about $6,000, and the lawyers will rake in over $4 million in fees. Now you know who owns those fancy houses we drive by, and how they got them.
Source: *The Augusta Chronicle*

Lap this up – A quadriplegic sued a Florida strip club because he allegedly could not get his wheelchair into the club's lap dancing room. His lawyer sued over 100 companies for alleged Americans with Disabilities Act (ADA) violations. I predicted in my last book that the ADA law would "open a Pandora's box of lawsuits," but this one is special.
Source: *Inclusion Daily Express*

How sweet it is – A German judge who is diabetic sued Coca-Cola and Master Food for not putting health risk labels on their products. The judge is convinced that Coke and chocolate bars are responsible for his diabetes rather than his

263

decision to consume them. The judge, who is vice president of his court, is suing for 3,500 Euros plus costs.
Source: *The Independent*

A bout of shopping – A couple sued JC Penny, seeking $600,000 in damages for injuries she claimed happened during the store's after Christmas sale. She claimed that she had been attacked and verbally assaulted by another customer who wanted to buy the same figurines. The retailer prevailed against the shopper when a state appeals court judge noted "the dangers of the cut-throat arena of after-Christmas bargain shopping."
Source: *Gomemphis.com*

Booty of a story – A woman sought $50 million from a snack food named Pirate's Booty because it made her fat. When tested, the product contained 147 calories rather then the 120 written on the label. The problem was blamed on a change in the food maker's manufacturing process, and it immediately recalled the product from the shelves. The plaintiff claims to represent all consumers who ruined their diets and had to spend more time at the gym.
Source: *The Guardian*

You are a bad Barbie – A British doll maker who turned Barbie into a partly nude, "Dungeon Doll," complete with rubber bondage dress and helmet, did not violate the Mattel Inc. copyrights, a judge concluded.
Source: *Court TV*

Hold that thought – A man unsuccessfully attempted to sue the city of San Diego and Jack Murphy Stadium for $5.4 million, claming that the unisex bathroom policy at a concert caused him embarrassment and distress. He tried six or seven different bathrooms, only to find women in them all. Because of his embarrassment, he asserted that he "had to hold it in for four hours."
Source: *The Fresno Bee*

It is called a killer whale – The parents of a man found naked and dead on the back of a whale are suing the marine park for several million dollars, alleging that the dangerous Orca was portrayed as a huggable stuffed toy. Park officials determined that the man had drowned after slipping past security and trying to swim with the whale. The suit claims that the park should warn visitors that the animal could kill people who enter the water.

Source: *San Antonio Express News*

Good vibrations – A woman who was pulled off a plane in Dallas and asked to take a vibrating sex toy out of her checked bag sued Delta, citing public humiliation. The woman told a newspaper that she didn't want to be embarrassed any more than she had been, and then promptly filed a lawsuit that made her the target of talk show hosts around the country.

Source: *The Dallas Morning News*

An ass of mine story – A Montana man sued media giant Viacom, saying that the MTV show "Jackass" plagiarized his name and defamed his good character. The guy's name is Jack Ass. This fellow legally changed his name to raise awareness about drunken driving. He claims the show, Jackass, committed trademark and copyright infringement and is seeking $10 million in damages.

Source: CNN

Go team – A doctor who is a University of Kentucky fan was sued for using a cauterizing tool to inscribe the letters "UK" on a woman's uterus to mark it prior to performing a hysterectomy. He did it to remain oriented, for the patient's safety. The woman and her husband sued the doctor for emotional distress.

Source: *CNN.com*

Fear of Lawsuits is Changing the Way We Live

Don Wolfe, President of Silicon Valley Citizens Against Lawsuit Abuse (CALA), is a contributor to this book, and shares his views about another trend that needs to be reversed. Don's thoughts follow.

The fear of lawsuits is changing the way we live. Our society is being unnecessarily punished by the escalating cost of our civil justice system. I'll illustrate what I mean, but first let me relate this story. A couple of months ago, I got a call in my office from French National Television. "Happy to chat with you," said I, "but why would you call us?" They said that,

"There are many people in our country who would gladly make investments in America, but hesitate to do so because you are such a litigious society, and we hear that you (CALA) are doing something about it." So we chatted on and I gave them a statement – some of which you will hear today. But by all means, next time you're in Paris, check it out.

Perhaps that call was related to this the fact that in the United States last year, there were 70,000 product liability lawsuits. In England there were only 200. Why? We'll get into that, but first let's get a little closer to home. The Girl Scouts in Santa Clara County, for example, have had to sell an additional 20,430 boxes of Girl Scout cookies this year in order to cover their cost of lawsuit protection.

And do you remember those friendly Neighborhood Watch signs you used to see around town? They indicated that some neighbor was willing to look after youngsters and homes in the area and kindly see that things were safe. Well, have you noticed that those signs are hardly seen any more? Some lawyers have found a way to sue those kindly volunteer neighbors for "neglect" of some sort, and so **Neighborhood Watch signs are going away**. **Lawsuits are changing the way we live.**

In another example, a source of less expensive housing for young families or retirees is seriously affected by what is known as **construction defects litigation**. We desperately need housing for you, entry-level families – the first time homebuyers. These used to be smaller homes, often in the form of condominiums. Well, new condos have all but disappeared. In this valley, you'll hardly see a condo going up that is not backed by public agency financing. That's because private builders can no longer risk or afford to build them. It seems that Home Owner Associations (HOA) have been enticed to sue builders in enough instances that these builders are pulling out of the market. I have heard of situations where law firms or their agents will video tape condo projects while they are under construction, and when completed, go to the new board of the HOA. Then they tell them that they have observed defects in the construction of the complex and that the board is obliged to bring suit against the builder. "...And by

266

the way, we have the only evidence," say the lawyers. Some consider this a new form of whiplash lawyering.

A builder friend of mine did have a legitimate problem in a complex that he built. It turned out that there was some sidewalk damage in the condo project that he completed. There was loose soil that caused a few yards of walkway to sink. He was perfectly willing to correct the matter. It would have been about $60,000 to fix the problem. The Home Owner Association lawyer, however, filed suit for $1,600,000. The builder wasn't willing to pay that. So there is now a cloud over the title of all the units in this complex. There will continue to be great disruption and distraction on the part of scores of families in the complex until the matter is resolved, and the lawyer awaits his fee. The builder now vows never to build another condo unit. And he's not alone. Almost everyone in the construction industry – those that supply shelter for families – has walked away from condominium building.

That's the case with the builder of my own home, Jerry Lohr, who is a marvelous builder and engineer, and who will no longer go near the condo market. Now you might say, "How does this affect me? I've got a big $600,000 home on the hill. Who cares?" But unless you have someone coming up the economic food chain that is able to sell the less expensive home in order to have the equity to buy your home, then you have merely puffery on a financial statement. Forms of unmerited construction defects litigation places artificial deformities on the supply of housing for all of us. Again, ladies and gentlemen, frivolous lawsuits are changing the way we live.

Many of you volunteer to help at local charities. One with which I'm involved, The San Jose Shelter Foundation, is a kind of "beggar" for the homeless. For some 20 years, we've gathered bedding and materials for shelters in the area. A few department stores have been cooperative and generous. But we were informed recently by the legal department of the JC Penney stores that they can no longer fulfill our requests for pillow cases, sheets, and the like because shelter inhabitants have found a way to have lawyers sue if they trip over or are otherwise "injured" by the donated goods.

267

Let's take the football helmet that you gave to your youngster or grandchild last season or for the holidays. It cost about $200 didn't it? Well, about 50% of that was the manufacturer's cost of lawsuit protection. Twenty-five percent of the cost of the last stepladder that you purchased to use around your house went to the cost of the maker's protection against claims, whether they had merit or not.

Can frivolous lawsuits endanger your health? Well, in a recent article in the *San Francisco Chronicle*, Congresswoman Anna Eshoo sites a study by the National Institute of Health saying that litigation is crippling biomedical research and having "an immediate and significant impact on health care."

You readers can probably come up with other examples. And that is the very reason that Silicon Valley Citizens Against Lawsuit Abuse, or CALA, was formed. We are a nonprofit, public education organization dedicated to serving as a watchdog over the civil justice system and those who would seek to abuse it for undeserved gain. Our mission is to educate the public on the cost of lawsuit abuse, expose the flaws in our legal system, and hold our legislators accountable for restoring some sanity to our civil justice system. We have grown from a handful of people to now over 6500 supporters from 75 cities in eight Bay Area Counties.

Do we as taxpayers get hit with lawsuit madness? Let me tell you another brief story. In my town of Saratoga, a man that we let go from city employment was suing us for $100,000. He claimed sexual discrimination. It seems that after he was fired, only female employees remained in the department. Therefore, he "must have been" discriminated against. Well, we don't discriminate in Saratoga; we rejected the suit and so instructed our attorney, whom we pay by the hour – we don't have a full time attorney – to bring that message to the former employee's attorney. Our attorney came back to us and said that the fellow would drop the $100,000 discrimination charge if we would give him two weeks severance pay. That would only amount to about $1500, and if we had to go all the way to court it might cost as much as $10,000.

Our attorney advised that it would be prudent to settle for the two weeks pay. But I told him that I wanted to take the jackpot out of the justice system. Our severance policy is to give two weeks notice. We had done that, so we didn't owe the ex employee a dime. Besides, I thought it might have been worth the $10,000 to send a message to the rest of the employees that you can't shake down Saratoga! The rest of the City Council hesitated for a moment but then agreed with me. So we instructed our attorney, and went to deliver our decision. And guess what? The fellow dropped the suit. I guess he was impressed by our resolve not to buckle under pressure.

So did we win? Of course not – it took several thousands of dollars of Saratogans' tax money for our attorney to talk to the other attorney, just because one young man decided to use the civil justice system for unearned personal gain. But the most shocking part of this story is that our attorney, who has represented scores of cities for over three decades, told us that this was unprecedented. It was the first time in his experience that a city had held firm. The moral is that it isn't enough to have tough-minded, clear-thinking, justice-seeking good citizens on your city council, county board, or school board – it takes a change in public attitudes.

Lawsuits Have Changed Our Lives

We at CALA will be able to measure success when the time comes that it is a public embarrassment to file a lawsuit that is frivolous.

Did you know that our society's enchantment with lawsuits is strangling business expansion and destroying innovation? The California Business Roundtable just did a survey, on which the State Chamber of Commerce reported. They found this: 84% of business leaders, and 65% of voters, identified reform of liability laws and civil suits as being "extremely important" policy issues for the state's future economic well being. A frivolous lawsuit, ladies and gentlemen, is a job-killing machine – and it kills the Christmas bonus for those who may still have a job.

Having said all of that, let me share this with you. It's from a letter-to-the editor, recently published in the *San Jose Mercury News*. It says in part, "Most attorneys are honorable and practice their profession with dignity, compassion and sensitivity." I wrote that. I meant it, and I still mean it today. It describes the attorney that most of us know – the fellow that married our daughter, our sister-in-law, or our friend, and the good guy that represents our business or us. The point is that CALA is not about lawyer bashing. We are about the conduct of civil justice.

Who else is affected by this frivolous, out-of-control lawsuit system? Consider – every taxpayer, any business owner – big, or a small business that wants to get bigger, retirees, working families, anyone who pays health insurance, and anyone who's trying to create jobs … they are all affected by this trend that is destroying the business world.

Let me ask you this. Is there anyone you know who has had to pay out recently on a frivolous lawsuit? I know it's an intrusive question – kind of embarrassing. So let me rephrase the question. Have any of you shopped recently? That is, have you gone through the checkout counter of any store of any description recently? If you have, and I think that might include all of us, then you have paid for frivolous lawsuits. It's in the cost of our products and produce. Studies indicate that it costs every person in America approximately $800 to pay for this avalanche of unwarranted lawsuits. That's about $3,200 for every family of four. Even if you've never been sued, you pay. We all lose, and we all pay. Yes, ladies and gentlemen, lawsuits are changing our lives.

You might ask at this point, "Why is it this way?" When, how, and why did we become such a litigious society? In another recent article in the *Mercury News*, Joseph Calafano, a former Secretary of Health, Education, and Welfare, and an attorney, identified and faulted a certain self-indulgent element of the legal profession.

I was mentioning this to a Rotary Club not long ago, and someone shouted out from the audience – you know how Rotarians are – "Why is that allowed? Who lets it continue to happen?" My first inclination was to say that we do – we as a people. But I responded by saying that judges are very reluctant to close the courthouse doors in any way because our

270

very wise Constitution holds those doors open so that we all might enter to find redress for grievances.

The problem is that we have redefined what a grievance is in this country. And why is that? For the answer to that I'll have to refer to my resource manual. I hold up a copy of the telephone book yellow pages. In my resource manual, I find that there are 17 pages of florists, 22 pages of restaurants, 45 pages of physicians of every type, four pages of accountants, and 126 pages of attorneys, many of their ads screaming at you to transfer responsibility for your own actions onto someone else for financial gain at the expense of justice.

In the center of the scales of justice is balance. But our system is gravely out of balance. Is not swift justice surely denied when someone has to wait years for a decision because our courts are clogged with frivolous matters? Sometimes they lose their entire life savings, although they are innocent and not at fault. What justice occurs when one neighbor receives a huge award, but 17 other neighbors lose their jobs because the firm where they all worked went out of business due to the settlement?

Recently I learned that a jury in a Texan town addressed just this. A woman was suing for one million dollars. She had been injured on the job, and had suffered real pain. The jury foreman on the case asked of his fellow jurors during deliberations what their average incomes were. After deliberation, they went back to the courtroom and awarded the woman $40,000. She was absolutely delighted. She had never seen $40,000 at one time before in her life. It took care of medical costs and some of the punitive claim as well. Justice was done; everyone was pleased, except whom? Her attorney, of course. He wanted 40% of that million dollars rather than of $40,000. But justice and not greed prevailed in this case.

The most illuminating part of this story is that there had been a CALA group in that area for about five years. Attitudes were beginning to change. The scales of justice are returning to balance.

Are Class Action Suits Running Amuck?

These are, all too often, the type of lawsuit that use consumers as victims only to benefit plaintiff lawyers. Here's proof. This is a case that landed in my own mailbox. It's a judgment form the Superior Court in San Francisco. I bought a computer monitor within the last five years, the 15-inch kind. Maybe some of you have done the same. It seems that the viewable screen of my monitor was not a full 15 inches. I was not offended by that; in fact I didn't even notice it. Though it was kind of like my TV screen, it didn't annoy me. I wasn't blinded by it or inconvenienced in any way. But a law firm in San Diego was so "outraged" on my behalf that they, unbeknownst to me, and lots of others, brought suit against every manufacturer, parts supplier, packager, distributor, retailer, or anyone who could spell monitor. So for my aggrieved condition, this document was offering me $6. What will the lawyer get? $5,800,000. In other words, the only meaningful recovery for this so-called injustice went to the lawyers. Doesn't it sound like the whole suit was cooked up just for their benefit? And who's going to pay for it? Why you are, of course – the next time you buy a PC monitor.

A couple of years ago, at the invitation of the President of the United States, George W. Bush, I had the privilege of meeting in the Oval Office to discuss the misuse of our courts through merit-less class action lawsuits. The result was the passage of the Class Action Fairness Act of 2005.

It's my understanding that there are what is called "pet-plaintiffs" hiding out in Silicon Valley who are on the payrolls of some law firms, and own one or two shares of hundreds of high-tech firms, just so they can look for opportunities to cash in at the expense of the consumer.

So what do we do about all of this? What are some of the remedies?

Jury Service

The American public seems to enjoy serving as jurors as long as the case is wrapped up in an hour, give or take a few minutes for commercials. Criminal trials, real and imagined, dominate the airwaves. There are entire television channels and programs that fill every hour in the TV Guide with programs about trials, including such favorites as "America's Most Wanted," "Law & Order," "CSI," and "Court TV." These programs' ratings are evidence of our desire to witness stories about criminals and their victims, and we rarely turn the channel until we're sure justice has been served.

On TV, the burden of proof is on the director, actors, and writers. In the real world, the burden is on the shoulders of the attorneys prosecuting and defending cases. In both instances, however, the jury is the same – the American public. But there's a glaring disconnection: how can we be so consumed with the application of fairness in our justice system and ignore the call to serve on a real jury?

To illustrate the nationwide problem, I will use California as an example. More than eight million lawsuits were filed in California courts last year. And each lawsuit often represents multiple plaintiffs or defendants who went to the courts seeking fairness over a family dispute, a civil matter, or a criminal case. Not all of these cases made it to the courtroom, but conservative estimates suggest that nearly one in every four Californians relied on the Judicial system to resolve their dispute last year.

The data we have on the number of Californians who participate in the court system as jurors is not as easily quantified. Each courthouse keeps its own records, decides what information is important, and then shares the data on a limited basis. That said, in 2002, there were nearly 21.5 million eligible voters in California. Being eligible to vote follows similar criteria as being eligible to serve on a jury. For instance, individuals need be residents of the state, over the age of 18, and not convicted felons.

Out of these 21.5 million potentially eligible jurors, less than half were summoned to serve on a jury, and only 2% of those actually served. That means that while one in every four Californians wanted to use the court system, the current system's inefficiencies failed to reach a majority of eligible Californians for jury duty, and those who actually received summons either never bothered to show up or found some reason to be excused.

Jury service does not necessarily reflect all the dramatizations we see on television. Usually, juries are applying simple intellect and principles of fairness to property or civil rights disputes between two people or for crimes that don't make the nightly news. Nonetheless, whether a trial takes a day or a week, the outcome to those seeking justice is equally important.

Often jurors seated for lower profile civil or criminal matters may only need a mere day or two to resolve the case and dispense a fair verdict. Still, far too many Americans continue to ignore the fact that the very court system they may some day rely upon requires their participation to work.

The consequences of disregarding a jury summons – not to mention one of our most important rights – are significant. Fewer people available to be seated on a jury means the chance are less likely for a person to be judged by a fair and representative jury from the community. Here in California, the evidence shows that citizens, and even their local governments, may not understand the importance and value of jury service. A recent study by Daniel Klerman of the University Of Southern California School Of Law sought out the reasons that so many Californians were avoiding jury service.

Findings show that more than eight million Californians were called to serve on a jury in 2000 – the most recent year for which court data is available. Yet only an astonishing 27% completed their service. The other 73% consisted of no-shows, disqualifications, excused participants, and undeliverable summonses. These results suggest serious shortcomings on the part of citizens, as well as by the court system.

That means that a good majority of California residents are sidestepping this principal obligation and right – one that our Founding Fathers fought so hard for over 200 years ago, and that our soldiers continue to fight for today. Thomas Jefferson thought it was so important that he wrote, "The jury is the ultimate safeguard of our civil rights." Jury service is the best contribution we can make to improving our court system and ensuring the continuation of our democratic principles. Think of the alternatives. In some countries, the closest things to a jury of peers are dictators, who order firing squads, or fundamentalists who advocate public stoning and amputation.

It's clear that the drama is not over. Americans will continue to rely on the court system to resolve their legal differences and to seek justice for victims of crime. It remains to be seen if they will continue to judge from their couch while expressing outrage at the ludicrous verdicts rendered by some courts, or whether they will accept their role as lead players in the quest for fairness and serve on a jury when called.

With our troops still serving valiantly in Iraq and elsewhere around the world, many people have asked what they can do on the home front to help protect democracy. One answer is for each of us to embrace our civic duty and serve on a jury when called. After all, if we can't preserve our Judicial system here at home, how can we hope to serve as a model for other countries? If we can't lead, how can we ask the Iraqis and others to follow?

Junk Science – Take out the Trash

Just in time for spring-cleaning, Citizens Against Lawsuit Abuse (CALA), headquartered in San Jose, CA, is launching the "Take out the Trash" campaign to encourage judges, legislators, and the public to dump the junk science and dubious "experts" from our courtrooms. This is the only way we are going to protect our legal system and public health.

The goal of the program is to shine a spotlight on the use of junk science and how it trashes our civil justice system. Junk lawsuits based on junk science undermine the integrity of our courts, drive up the price of medicine and doctors' fees for consumers' healthcare, and divert funds and attention away from researching and developing medical cures.

"Junk science can be found in the so-called 'expert witnesses' who will say anything for the right price, greedy personal injury lawyers bringing questionable claims, and plaintiffs filing lawsuits without experiencing any injury."

Whatever form junk science takes, the problem has reached national proportions, and something needs to be done about it.

CALA is launching this program as more and more personal injury lawyers are using "expert witness" – usually doctors who have never even met the plaintiffs they diagnose. Asbestos and silicosis litigation are just the latest examples of how questionable facts are being used to exploit our legal system. Personal injury lawyers should not be able to alter the facts; when they do so they tamper with our courts. Bogus lawsuits based on junk science clog our courtrooms and take money away from legitimate victims.

To kick-off the "Take out the Trash" program, CALA is providing local judges, legislators, and the media with trash bags filled with some of the most egregious examples of junk science in the court. Examples include: In recent fen-phen litigation, an independent physician hired by plaintiffs' attorneys to review 120 echocardiograms diagnosed with heart damage by two cardiologists found that only 6% of them actually showed heart problems. One of the doctors received an extra $1,500 for every positive reading. An employee of the plaintiff's attorney trained the other doctor's sonographer.

US District Court Judge Jack of the Southern District of Texas tossed out many silicosis claims as manufactured diagnoses. Of the 10,000 alleged silicosis victims in the multi-district litigation, the same nine doctors had diagnosed 99% of them. One doctor had his secretary fill out patient diagnoses on blank forms, while another analyzed 1,239 patients in 72 hours. Many of the alleged victims in the lawsuit had at one time been diagnosed with and filed claims for asbestosis.

In California, Dr. Gary Ordog, dubbed "Dr. Mold" by Forbes, has appeared as an expert witness in hundreds of California mold lawsuits, claiming that mold can cause a terrifying array of diseases, from lung cancer to cirrhosis of the liver. This is despite the American College of Occupational & Environmental Medicine, the Federal Institute of Medicine, and even the vice president of Ordog's own professional association, the American College of Medical Toxicology, saying that there's no evidence for such claims.

276

We want to be sure this information gets in front of judges. Just as judges in Texas and Florida have begun throwing out testimony from questionable "experts," judges everywhere must take an active role in throwing junk science out of the legal system.

What Is Junk Science?

Junk science is questionable, unfounded, or misleading information that is put forth as medical or scientific fact, and is driven by speculative theories outside mainstream, peer-reviewed science. Junk science is medical or scientific claims that are not supported by fact and not validated by others within the scientific and medical community. Junk science is used to advance a specific, hidden agenda – often political or litigation-driven. The purpose of real science is to discover the truth; the purpose of junk science is to support a preordained conclusion. Those looking to fuel public alarm for their own gain often perpetrate junk science.

Potential Indicators of Junk Science

Doctors and scientists, who provide expert opinions or interpret data outside of their areas of expertise, and individuals offering "expert" opinions without having the necessary educational background and training, indicate junk science. Examples are doctors or scientists who are paid on the basis of their findings. Health or science institutes created by personal injury lawyers or organizations with a political agenda, who use sensational "findings" and "studies" that are released through the media without the endorsement of other scientific or medical experts, are the creators of junk science. Others are the firms who use paid advertising about new "health threats" but do not document the basis of the threats, or those who refer the public to personal injury lawyer firms or organizations.

Why Is Junk Science A Problem?

Junk science is often used as the basis for highly speculative litigation, especially health-related lawsuits such as so-called toxic mold, or cell phone lawsuits. Sensational junk science claims needlessly confuse and scare consumers. Junk science props up baseless cases that clog our courtrooms and delay and dilute justice for the truly injured. For instance, the thousands of silica lawsuits that are based on bogus x-ray readings mean that the claims of the legitimately injured are held up and that all claims, including those of people who are truly ill, are brought into doubt. Junk science is often used to try to make a case when the facts won't otherwise support it.

So-called "expert" witnesses who peddle junk science undermine the integrity of the medical profession and qualified expert witnesses. Junk science in our courtrooms undermines the integrity of our courts, and misleads jurors who are predisposed to believe that information presented by a doctor, or other person billed as an "expert," is credible. After junk science is printed in the media and posted on Internet sites, untrue myths may be circulated among the public for years, potentially harming public health, innocent individuals, and organizations.　　　　–Don Wolfe

Criminals Rights Injustice for Victims

This year, almost six million Americans will be the victims of violent crime. When it happens, the victims will be in for a number of surprises. Somewhere along the way, the criminal justice system began to serve lawyers, judges, and defendants. Victims are now treated with institutionalized disinterest. The neglect of crime victims is a national disgrace. They may suffer untold emotional grief, financial hardship, and public humiliation, only to watch the offender become the center of attention in a legal system that tips the scales ever more heavily in favor of the criminal. Criminals are the bottom feeders of society, and do not deserve the attention and rights they are currently receiving.

Plea Bargains

About 95% of all felony convictions in the United States are results of plea-bargaining. Albert Alschler, professor at the

University of Chicago, thinks, like many others, that there is nothing good about plea-bargaining. Alschler starts with what the sentences lead to. "You have two people who've committed the same crime. They have the same background, and one is going to get twice as severe a sentence as the other because he's exercised the right to trial."

The argument in favor of plea-bargaining asserts that by pleading guilty instead of going to trial, the uncertainty of trial outcome is reduced. For the state, it also saves time and money. The bottom line is that almost all felons serve less time and are out on the street earlier to become repeat offenders as a result of this revolving door justice. I do, however, agree that the system would collapse if every case went to trial; we squander too much money on the judicial system as is.

Sentencing Guidelines

To check plea-bargaining abuses, we must have sentencing guidelines like the Three Strikes Rules that take away discretion from liberal judges, who allow repeat felons to prey on society by continuing the plea bargain game. In response to rising crime rates, California instituted these strikeout laws. Under these laws, the second or third felony offense is met with more severe punishment then the first. Opponents and those who care more about these losers than protecting society claim that the laws are expensive and do not deter crime, but as usual, convict coddlers are wrong.

Data from the FBI Uniform Crime Reports and the Bureau of Justice estimates that during the first two years after the legislation's enactment, approximately eight murders, 3,982 aggravated assaults, 10,672 robberies, and 384,488 burglaries were deterred in California using the three strikes legislation. The law resulted in an increase of 17,700 further larcenies, as criminals substituted strike able offenses with non-strike able offenses. The deterrence of these crimes saved victims approximately $889 million.

Since some criminals substitute other crimes not on the list of strike able offenses, the study suggested that the list be expanded to include the most common substitutes for strike able offenses as well.

Getting Away With Murder

What do Lefty, "never-met-a-killer I didn't like" journalists and political activists, naïve, "all criminals are innocent" student lawyers, and their media-savvy, "watch me again twist DNA evidence to free the guilty" experts have in common? They all use shoddy statistics!

Jaime Sneider in the *Columbia Daily Spector* reviews a Columbia University study that claimed there was an amazing 68% "error rate" in capital punishment. The study concluded that capital punishment is "collapsing under the weight of its own mistakes." The widely circulated study immediately set off my right brain bullshit meter when I first heard it. Instinctively, I know that more O.J.'s were getting away with murder, and every con claims to be innocent, but 99.9 % are as guilty as hell.

Sneider points out, and **the media failed to mention, that Columbia Law Professor James Lieberman's meaning of "error rate" was not that 68% of people on death row were found to be innocent. On the contrary, Lieberman and his co-authors were unable to find a single case in the 23 years they reviewed cases in which an innocent man was executed.** *This was another case of a big lie told long enough to become truth.* In the *Wall Street Journal*, professor of law Paul Cassell revealed that the 68% error rate "turns out to include any reversal of a capital sentence at any stage by appellate courts – even if those courts ultimately upheld the capital sentence."

Likewise, the one in seven ratios, commonly purported to expose the egregious level of errors made in death penalty cases, are misleading. Disseminators of the statistic say that for every seven people executed, one has his sentence overturned. MIT professor Arnold Barnett called the ratio "meaningless," because it does not constitute an error rate as many people ignorantly assumed.

An error rate is computed by dividing the number of innocent persons executed by the total number executed.

(Remember not a single innocent person was executed in the 23-year Columbia study.) Reporting how many people were not executed "yields no insight," according to Barnett, simply because it does not necessarily represent a flaw in the system. It instead shows that the system corrected itself, not that any execution was or has been incorrectly performed.

Ah, the Criminal Version of the Racism Song Again

Another lie perpetrated to help murderers and rapists supports the misconception that those sitting on death row are victims of racism. Unfortunately, the ranting, anti-death penalty, diversity crowd and their professors at Left-wing law schools have just one more lie to use in their propaganda mill.

The Bureau of Justice Statistics shows that convicted White murderers are more likely to be sentenced to death than their Black counterparts.

In looking for another means to push their agenda, capital punishment opponents argued that Black murderers with White victims are more likely to get the death penalty than White murderers with Black victims. The numbers are easily distorted because 80% of the United States is White, and only 13% is Black. If murderers selected their victims at random, for every ten murders committed by Whites, only one victim would be Black, whereas for every ten murders committed by Blacks, eight victims would be White.

Justice Delayed Is Justice Denied

Many activists also argue that the death penalty is too expensive, saying it costs more than simply giving convicts life sentences. But of course, the reason for the added expense of executing people is not the result of added due process, but the unnecessary delays in Federal courts. Writing for the *National Review*, a former assistant attorney general, Andrew Thomas, observed that between 1977 and 1996 the average time a condemned prisoner sat on death row almost tripled from just over four years to over eleven years.

The positive consequences that the death penalty has in reducing crime should not be overlooked, although the media does so continually in death penalty stories. During a ten-year increase in the number of executions, the number of murders simultaneously dropped.

William Tucker, in the *National Review On-Line*, remarked about another fact that supporters of murderers and the media ignore: Over the last decade, the most dramatic decline in murders was precisely in regions utilizing executions. Since 1990, Texas, Oklahoma, Louisiana, and Arkansas performed half the nation's executions, resulting in murder rates in these four states falling faster than anywhere else in the country.

This strong correlation between high rates of executions and reduced murder rates suggests that we need to protect society, and not vicious killers, by supporting advocates who are not afraid to use the death penalty as a deterrent and will lobby to reduce length of the appeal process from over eleven years to just over four years, as it was in the 1970's.

Society overcompensates for the risk of sentencing an innocent person to jail by going to the other extreme and freeing many guilty people, who are then allowed to elude punishment in this life. As the O.J. trial clarified, society must lower the ridiculously high burden of proof, the DNA game, and the "if it doesn't fit we must acquit" circus games. We are innocent victims suffering as "innocent" criminals slip though the growing flaws in our justice system.

A major contributor to the brainwashing of America and the reversal of society's moral compass is the manipulation by the dangerously biased, unprofessional media, as I will expose in the next chapter.

Chapter 9
MEDIA SMEAR AND MALICE

There is no such thing as objective reporting ... I've become craftier about finding the voices to say the things I think are true.

— *Boston Globe* reporter Dianne Dumanoski

The major responsibly for disseminating and reinforcing the misguided beliefs and lies that have brainwashed a generation and will terribly damage Western civilization can be directly attributed to today's media. Through the power of selecting what topics to cover, which commentators to interview regarding certain stories, what polling data to use, what part of a story to highlight, and whom to favor and whom to attack, the media continually uses smear and malicious propaganda techniques to promote their agenda.

Thirty million Americans rely on broadcast television for their news. They form their opinions based on what they hear and see, and to a lesser extent, read. Citizens cannot cast informed votes or make knowledgeable decisions on matters of public policy if their information is distorted. Western Democracy depends on fair and unbiased television and other news media. Instead, the press promulgates the Ten Great Lies, spreading a deadly cancer throughout America and other countries. To prevent the continued spread of lies, the media must be sanitized and studied using the clean and well-lit microscope of truth to detect and eradicate this pathology.

PART 1 – IS THERE A LIBERAL BIAS IN THE MEDIA?

Left-leaning media watchdogs like FAIR (not to be confused with the immigration policy group) claim that they are being objective when they are really wolves hidden in academic sheepskins, bent on attacking the few conservative news programs found in the mainstream media. Organizations like this claim that there is not a liberal bias in the media. In all fairness to FAIR, much public confusion exists regarding what is liberal and what is conservative.

A UCLA political scientist, for example, found that the *Wall Street Journal* has a conservative editorial page but liberal news pages. They are, in fact, even more liberal than those of the *New York Times*. While public television and radio were found to be conservative compared to the mainstream media, public and media professionals themselves strongly disagree, saying that almost all "major media outlets tilt to the Left."

The public understands this bias at a gut level. In 2003, the Gallup Organization polled 1,002 people about the media's accuracy and objectivity. Americans, by three to one, say the media is too liberal (45%) rather than too conservative (15%). In addition, 63% of conservatives think that the media are too liberal, as do 43% of moderates.

Even self-described liberals agree that there is a liberal bias: 41% see the media as liberal, compared to only 22% that find the news conservative. Seventy percent of self-described liberals surveyed in a 1997 Harris survey reported a "fair amount" or "great deal" of bias in the news.

There is an interesting perception that the higher your level of education and the more you participate in politics, the more biased you are. This might help explain why Left-wing faculty members and students tend to be such biased liberals.

Public opinion of media bias was looked at in 1997 by the Pew Center for the People and the Press. Some key findings included: Seven percent of those interviewed said, "In dealing with political and social issues, news organizations tend to favor one side." This is up from the 53% who answered in 1985. Those who believed the media deals fairly with all sides fell from 34% to 27%; the percentage that felt "news organizations get the facts straight" fell from 55% to 37%.

Newspaper Editors Concede Liberal Bias

Highlights of a Newspaper Association of America (ANA) survey of editors, publishers, and executives reported by

"Media Watch" in 1993 admitted bias. **Key findings disclose that over half of the respondents believed there was a bias in the general media's political coverage. When they were asked "toward which agenda," conservative or liberal, 70.8% said liberal.**

Another survey conducted by *Editor and Publisher* in 1998 found many editors willing to concede a liberal slant, with more than three times as many describing American dailies as liberal over conservative. Asked how they think the American public perceives newspapers, 89% of newspaper editors said "liberal" as compared to a measly 1.2% that responded "conservative." Yet if you listen to liberal blowhards, you would think that a cabal of Right-wing extremists controls the media.

The Public Is More Conservative Than the Media

There is also a clearly conservative bias on certain networks like Fox. Bill O'Reilly tries to portray himself as fair and balanced, usually when his conservative rants no longer shoot his ratings to new heights. Why do more people watch Fox? The media tends to forget that members of the public were more likely than journalists to consider themselves conservative.

In 2001, a Princeton Survey Research Associates report for the Kaiser Family Foundation compared views of media professionals and the public. Here are some key findings: Members of the public were six times more likely then journalists to consider themselves "conservative," and seven times more likely to identify themselves as "Republican" than were members of the media.

In truth, of course, there is a liberal bias. Indeed, 89% of Washington-based reporters said in a study that they voted for Bill Clinton in 1992. Only 7% voted for George Bush. A Lichter and Rothman survey of journalists discovered that 54% placed themselves to the Left of center, compared to only 19% who chose the Right side of the spectrum. Fifty-six percent said that the people that they worked for were mostly to the Left, and only 8% to the Right: a margin of seven to one. Fifty-four percent did not regard adultery as wrong, compared to only 15% who said it was. Only 1% strongly agreed that environmental problems were overstated, 90% favored abortion, and 80% supported strong Affirmative Action for Blacks. No wonder the diversity gang continues to loot the country and not be unmasked by the press.

In 1992, the Freedom Forum commissioned two Indiana University professors to survey journalists about their political affiliations. They interviewed more than 1,400 journalists, and found that the percentage identifying themselves as liberals had grown since the first poll in 1971. The results, published in *Media Watch*, clearly show a Left-wing bias.

With about 41% of journalists identifying themselves as Democrats, compared to only 16% who tagged themselves as Republican, journalists are 5% to 10% more likely to be Democrats than the general population and 10% to 15% less likely to be Republicans.

The study found that minority journalists are much more likely to call themselves Democrats than are White journalists: Blacks – 70%, Asians – 63%, and Hispanics – 59%. The liberal trend is clear and continues to be fueled by government-mandated programs to hire minorities. The American Association of Newspaper Editors (ASNE), in a 1997 survey, found that 61% of newspaper reporters identified themselves as leaning liberal Democratic, as compared to only 15% who identified themselves as leaning conservative Republican.

More Recent Data

The trend is continuing and clear. The Kaiser Family Foundation survey, released in late June 2001, found that members of the media were four times as likely to identify themselves as liberal than conservative. Similarly, the survey found that members of the media were more than seven times more likely to identify themselves as Democrat than as Republican.

Need more proof? If the media leans more to the Left, it will fall on its face. Read the decennial survey, "*The American Journalist* in the 21st Century," by Weaver et al, in collaboration with Indiana University School of Journalism. They surveyed 1,149 journalists in 2004. Some key findings were: In

American newsrooms, Democrats outnumber Republicans by two to one (37.1% to 18.6%), one-third claim to be independents, and a poll by *Journalist and Financial Reporting* that surveyed 151 business reporters revealed that these newspaper and magazine reporters are as liberal as their colleagues covering politics.

Liberal bias in the news media is not the result of a vast Left-wing conspiracy, but rather an unconscious groupthink mentality that allows only one side of a debate to get a fair hearing. When that happens, the truth suffers. This makes it so important that news media reports be politically balanced, and not biased. When was the last time you heard a positive report about post-war Iraq?

A Harris poll confirms what the public already knows; the media is biased and uses their bias to try to move the public toward their distorted view of reality. The results of the poll are as follows.

- Most Americans think the media is biased, and almost 49% think the media usually doesn't "get the facts straight."
- Some two-thirds believe the media doesn't "deal fairly with all sides" in social and political reporting.
- Almost three-fourths of Americans see a "fair amount" or "great deal" of political bias in the news. And by a more then 2-to-1 ratio, poll respondents said the bias is liberal rather then conservative.
- More then 60% surveyed prefer media to "simply report the facts," not "weigh the facts" or offer suggestions about how to solve problems.
- Nearly 60% believe the news media has "too much influence." Some 47% believe journalists have values different from their own.

PART 2 – 25 WEAPONS OF MASS MEDIA SMEAR AND BIAS (WMB'S)

In Part 1, I objectively proved that the media has a strong Left-wing bias. In Part 2, I will explore the unethical methods used daily by the media to successfully brainwash the public into accepting their dangerous agenda. Don't take it anymore! Be aware at all times that you cannot trust most of the media. Find people and several media sources you can trust, to objectively learn the truth. Only after learning to distinguish truth from propaganda can we right our moral compasses and identify good from evil.

1. Find a Critic to Parrot Your Agenda

The Left-wing media is interesting to watch as it coordinates efforts. Find a critic of the administration or America, and for sure, Wolf Blitzer will be giving the person "ear" time on CNN. The media repeats their lies daily until they collapse, based on their own weight. Joe Wilson's take on Sodamn Insane's attempt to acquire uranium in Niger, and the Valerie Plame nonsense, are good examples already presented in Chapter 2.

Here are Some More

Oak Leaf posted an excellent expose of some politically timed publications aimed at the military, asking for Rumford's resignation. These publications are news because they seem to be military endorsements. This is false.

First, it appears as though four different "military magazines" called for Rumsfeld to resign. They are basically all from the same publication, except that they are titled separately as the *Army Times*, *Air Force Times*, *Marine Corps Times*, and *Navy Times*. They are not even "professional military publications" such as *Proceedings of the Naval Institute* and *The Officer*, by the Reserve Officers Association. The *Army Times* formerly had a wide circulation, but then became part of the Gannett Group (*USA Today*). The writers for all four "military papers" also work at *USA Today*!

The front page of the *San Jose Mercury* ran a headliner declaring that five retired generals wanted Rumsfeld ousted. Why are five disgruntled retired generals being featured, rather than hundreds of other active and retired generals who understand and support Rumsfeld and his brilliant policies? By relentlessly presenting only the views of the Rumsfeld critics, the Left-wing media successfully forced the Secretary of

Defense's retirement, causing America to lose one of the brightest and most knowledgeable Secretaries of Defense in our history.

On the other hand, the *San Jose Mercury* missed the opportunity to highlight the failures of a truly lousy Secretary of Defense, Casper Weinberger, whose recent death was covered by the *Mercury*. For example, the paper didn't mention Weinberger's unilateral decision to call off a low-risk attack that would have decimated the terrorist group Hezbollah after they blew up the Marine barracks in Lebanon, killing hundreds of our finest.

The *San Jose Mercury* has long suffered from the "Peter Principle," stating that people rise to the level of their incompetence, as well as a terminal case of political correctness. When Knight Ridder, the former parent of the *San Jose Mercury*, tried to use its own reporters to cover the Middle East, minority events, or other Left-wing causes, they proved to be so biased and naïve that I suggested they be reassigned to writing garage sale announcements.

For example, a Knight Ridder's story euphemistically entitled "Palestinians Besiege Buildings Hours After Israeli's Leave Gaza" included an "explanatory" quote at the top of the article: "I want to destroy everything here as they did the Al Aqsa mosque," said Mahmoud Malahi. "It is a symbol of occupation. Destroying it is a symbol of Islam." Israel is actually well known for protecting the Muslim places of worship under its control. The very site mentioned, the Al Aqsa mosque, is an outstanding example of Israel's policy. The way the Knight Ridder article quoted these lying hotheads is typical of the press, however. Another article published Palestinian rappers' hateful rants about Israel without challenge or criticism. The article served to give voice to these crazy dummies, validating their words through correspondent ventriloquists. Even when a correspondent is invited to write in the paper's "Prospective," a section written to "enlighten" the public, you can be assured that only voices known to parrot pro-immigrant, anti-Israel, anti-Bush party lines are selected.

2. Handle with Care: Minorities, Muslims, and the Left are Sacred and Revered, so Don't Criticize

Mainstream policies at Gannett require editors and reporters to quote enough Blacks and Latinos from a minority source list to reflect "the face of the country." Some newspapers also have numerical formulas for evaluating managers on their success in running positive stories and pictures of minorities. A reporter in Gannett's *Vermont Free Press* was fired after a Black activist named in the paper threatened to sue and march unless the reporter was fired and an apology printed. The reporter wrote about a Black mayoral aide who had ejected a White woman who was defending Vermonters charged with racism from a community meeting, saying the meeting was for people of color only.

Another example is Nancy Grace's libelous television incrimination of the Duke lacrosse players accused of rape by a drunken Black stripper. As it turned out, the DNA did not match, and the only physical evidence was a report by a nurse documenting signs of sexual trauma. DNA evidence from the stripper's boyfriend was found to be present from before the time of party. CNN presented this woman as another Towanda Brawley, the Black woman defended by good old Al Sharpton in a false accusation of police rape. The paper was too afraid of Black backlash to present what seemed obvious to most people; the District Attorney jumped to conclusions and then proceeded with the case, to save his political ass.

As expected, Jessie Jackson didn't miss his chance to steal the spotlight. This time he offered to pay for the Black stripper's education, no matter how the trial turned out. Hopefully, she'll attend school after serving her jail time for false accusations. Will Jessie offer to pay tuition for the 44 lacrosse players vilified by false accusations now that they were all found innocent? As I had predicted, the case was thrown out and the DA censured.

Mainstream media continues to almost deify Jackson, rather than condemning his sordid past, as they should be. CNN and other networks always give this showboat an opportunity to transform news into his personal publicity platform, from whence he can throw mud at others.

Then there is the story of a Stanford professor's claim that he was being silenced for his Middle Eastern political views by being pictured on the cover of a new book by David Horowitz. But it seems that Horowitz is really the victim of an attempt to silence him. For the professor has chosen to sue Horowitz for not getting a release for the picture, rather than debating with Horowitz on the merits of the case published against him.

Somehow in this case, the *San Jose Mercury* sees the professor as the victim of an attack on academic freedom. Again the media tries to brainwash the public by trying to paint a true hero in the fight to save Western Civilization as a villain. Why would the media spotlight Horowitz, who is a true hero fighting for academic freedom and exposing those that promote agendas of hatred against America and Israel? Horowitz is famous for shining a spotlight on the media and university phonies that perpetuate chilling black lists and thwart genuine academic freedom on campuses by systematically brainwashing students with their warped views of our country and the real world. Their weapons of mass destruction are the lawsuits funded by deep Left-wing pockets, an association that is ignored by most media, with its Left-wing-biased agenda.

Horowitz is a target because he highlights media, academic, and government hypocrisy and lies. For example, the politically correct believe that it is offensive to associate Muslims with terrorism. Horowitz noted that Canadian officials bent over backward to avoid describing the 17 Islamic Canadians suspects arrested for plotting to behead the Prime Minister as Muslims. And so did the US media. The first *New York Times* story identified them as "Canadian residents" and "mainly of South Asian decent."

Listeners to the BBC World Service Radio are made aware of efforts not to "offend" Arab extremists even in reports of ethnic cleansing and genocide in Sudan. They avoid saying who the perpetrators are (Arab militias) and who the victims are (hundreds of thousands of Black Sudanese Africans-Muslims, Christians, and Animists). And there is no mention of the long history of mass slavery in Sudan carried out by Arabs against non-Arabs.

Yet, in the same news bulletins, the BBC mentioned that the settlers in Gaza were "Jewish," and the lands on which they were settling were "Palestinian." (See Chapter 4 for a dispute of the legal and historical accuracy of even referring to the territory as Palestinian.) Indeed, I believe the BBC always mentions ethnicity or religion when referring to Israel, but not when it comes to those Islamic terrorists who continue a program of ethnic cleansing.

Why is it that Hillary and Bill Clinton always get a pass from the Left-wing press when they invoke God in their public discourse, but if President Bush mentions God, it is time to warn of an impending theocracy? Higher oil prices generate media attacks on the oil companies, but the anti-American behavior and alleged human rights violations of well-oiled Venezuelan dictator Hugo Chavez receive less critical coverage.

3. Spinning Lies from the Truth

The Associated Press often makes dubious claims. In response to claims like this, the website *Honest Reporting.com* questions reporter Sara El Deeb's article blaming Israel for ruining a supposed "cease fire" by responding to Hamas' rocket firings. "The new (Israeli) offensive dubbed 'Operation First Rain' dashed hopes that Israel's recently completed Gaza withdrawal would help restart peace talks and left a **seven month old cease fire teetering on the brink of collapse.**" Say what? Whose offensive "dashed hopes"' of positive change? And how exactly were 40 rockets fired during a cease-fire?

4. Omit Crucial Points

When a reporter presents only one perspective or passes along only the "facts" espoused by the Palestinians without acknowledging that the Israelis disagree, it is bias by omission. For example, "hostilities between Israel and Palestinian militants have escalated since an explosion at a Hamas rally on Friday in Gaza killed at least 19 people. Militants blamed the blast on Israel which denied the claim." **CNN failed to mention that the Palestinian Authority**

concurred with Israel's assessment that Hamas itself was to blame for the explosion. Omissions create more misunderstanding and doubt about an issue. When the misreported action is justified, as in this case, with Hamas using the explosion as a pretext for its rocket attacks, the harm is double.

Remember the Falun Gong protester whose shrill outcries disrupted President Bush's reception for Communist China's leader Hu Jintao? She said on May 4, 2006, that CNN told her not to discuss Beijing's gruesome practice of organ harvesting during a recent TV interview because it would disturb viewers.

5. Pander to Your Target Demographic Bias by Making Israel a Target for Dangerous Media Bias and Propaganda

Media bias is very dangerous and, like the Nazi propaganda of Goebbles, indirectly led to the death of thousands of people in the Middle East. By glamorizing terrorists, understating and misrepresenting US and Israeli policies, intentions, and actions, and ignoring historical facts, the press emboldens terrorists, reinforces hatred, damages the reputation of two of the world's greatest democracies, and makes the world a more dangerous place.

The amazing big lie about the existence and victimization of the Palestinian people, as explored in an earlier chapter, can be directly tied to global media bias. In this section, I will explore examples of media bias against Israel from around the world. In my analysis, I refuse to recognize and thus legitimize the Arab propaganda machine, jokingly called the Arab media, which fuels the hate mongers responsible for the deaths of so many people.

Britain and the BBC

Britain's media is among the least objective in the world when it comes to covering Israel and the US, and shows little sign of improvement. They make a mockery of their charter, which states, "due impartiality **lies** at the heart of the BBC." Perhaps "lies **are** at the heart of the BBC" would have been a more accurate statement. Indeed, criticisms of the BBC in a report by an official commission set up by the UK government, the "Hutton Commission," were so scathing that both the BBC Chairman of the Board of Governors and the Director General had little choice but to resign.

Any fair-minded person will concur: the BBC coverage of the Middle Eastern and Arab world seeks to undermine, even de-legitimize, Israel, the region's sole democracy, while at the same time bending over backwards to excuse extremist Islamic clerics and the worst of the Arab dictators.

The BBC's biased Middle East coverage has become an international problem, and CNN International copies their "pander to the Arabs" style. The emergence of a global news media presented institutions like CNN with a dilemma: pro-US versions of the news, broadcast outside the US, are dismissed as so much blatant propaganda. Critical US journalism broadcast in the US is discarded as biased and unprofessional. CNN seems to have decided to stay in the Left lane in the US, but makes hard Left turns following BBC bias in the rest of the world.

Throughout the world, the BBC enjoys exceptional influence. The BBC pours forth in almost any language of the Middle East: Pashto, Persian, Arabic, and Turkish. Needless to say, it declines to broadcast in Hebrew. An article in *Haaretz* quotes a leading campaigner against anti-Semitism in Lithuania, who believes that inflammatory and biased BBC news coverage against Israel helped to revive anti-Semitism against the few remaining Jews who survived the Holocaust.

Some might argue that this anti-Jewish sentiment is not limited to BBC news programming. Each summer, for example, BBC Radio 3, a station largely devoted to classical music, carries a broadcast of "The Proms." "The Proms" are a British institution, a jovial annual event at the end of the British summer during which classical favorites and lighthearted flag waving tunes such as "Rule Britannia" and "Land of Hope and Glory" are sung at the Royal Albert Hall in London. Yet in 2002, the BBC Radio 3 producers shamelessly decided to fill the intermission time of the live broadcast with a recitation of poems that compared Israeli actions to those of the Nazis, and asked Holocaust survivors why they had "not learnt their lesson."

6. Bias by Commission – Synagogue Desecrations

Mere hours after Israel completed its historic withdrawal from Gaza, Palestinian mobs descended on former Jewish settlements, desecrating their synagogues by burning them to the ground and looting anything left. While observers the world over were saddened and outraged, some media outlets tried to justify the sacrilege, and even blame it on Israel.

The BBC TV report by Orla Guerin was guilty of *bias by commission*, by passing along assumptions that tended to support a pro-Palestinian view. She justified the arson mobs by stating that Palestinians came streaming into the settlements that caused them so much pain, to sightsee and to loot. **"Israel stole 38 years from them, so they were ready to take back anything they could."**

7. Bias by Labeling

Another common BBC prejudice is *bias by labeling*. In a BBC report, the correspondent casually referred to a "fanatical rebel group" in Uganda. This contrasts with the term "Palestinian resistance group" that BBC reporters often use to describe Hamas, a group the BBC clearly doesn't find fanatical at all.

But then Hamas, one of the most vicious murderers of Jews since Hitler, appears to enjoy a certain degree of sympathy at the BBC, which obscures the true nature of the group by using misleading language. There are innumerable examples of this since they occur almost daily.

8. Bias by Recommendation and Condemnation

Some BBC staff are quite open about their sympathies for Hamas, and are guilty of *bias by recommendation and condemnation.* On May 26, 2001, the senior BBC Arabic Service correspondent in the Gaza Strip, Fayad Abu Shamala, told a Hamas rally attended by the late Hamas leader, Sheikh Ahmed Yassin, that journalists and media organizations in Gaza, including the BBC, were waging a campaign of resistance, shoulder-to-shoulder with the Palestinian people, against Israel. Sheikh Yassin, spiritual leader to Hamas homicide bombers, was described by the BBC as "polite, charming and witty, a deeply religious man."

Again printed by the BBC: Sheikh Abdur-Rahman al-Sudais, from Saudi Arabia, who opened London's biggest mosque, is a respected leader who works for "community cohesion" and building communities. Not mentioned were some of these racist's own words: "In the name of Allah, the Jews must be annihilated. They are the scum of the human race, the rats of the world ... the murderers of the prophets, and the off spring of apes and pigs." But none of this seems to have penetrated the BBC bubble. On the BBC website, a video clip of the rally was flagged with the caption: "The BBC's Mark Easton: Events like today offer grounds for optimism."

The real story, of course missed by the BBC, is that the wacko they were praising was not just another Islamic racist imam; his hate-filled sermons are not just delivered in some peripheral setting. He is the preacher at the most important mosque in Mecca, the very heart of Islam, and could easily influence the Islamic extremists who are killing British troops in Iraq and civilians in their subways. Even in 2006, the top cleric at the hajj called for an Islamic victory over those who are fighting the war on terrorism.

9. Bias Trying to Make a Silk Purse out of a Sow's Ear – Yasser Arafat

Instead of doing a documentary about human rights abuses in the Arab world, Palestinian anti-Semitic textbooks, bomb belts for nursery school kids, and Palestinian authorities using EU aid to funds terrorism, the BBC tries to paint a pretty picture of Islam. Using the non-existent history of the Palestinian people before 1948, the BBC rarely misses an opportunity to denigrate Israel or its prime minister. One program even staged a mock "war crimes" trial for Ariel Sharon. The BBC verdict: Sharon's cause to answer for war crimes was never in doubt.

On the other hand, Yasser Arafat, the late corrupt terrorist leader of the PLO, received very different treatment at the hands of the media. One 30-minute profile of Arafat described him as "hero and an icon," speaking of him as "being the stuff of legends." Adjectives applied to him included "clever," "respectable," and "triumphant." These words were broadcast just two weeks after President Bush called for a change in Palestinian leadership following revelations about Arafat links with suicide attacks.

10. Bias of the Double Standard Muslim and Arab Media

Cartoons that were published in the European press depicting caricatures of the Prophet Mohammed have been met with extreme outrage, death threats, rioting, and targeting of Danish and other European embassies and institutions. But let's make no mistake. The real cartoon issue is the fact that every day, state controlled Muslim and Arab media publish cartoons with virulently anti-Semitic and anti-Israel themes. These cartoons have one goal: stirring up hatred against Jews.

The hypocrisy of world media is evident by the daily coverage of the cartoon caper, which always expressed sensitivity to Muslims and usually had a spokesman representing them as victims and the wonderful Danes as perpetrators of a terrible act. The fact that anti-Semitic and anti-Israel cartoons appear daily in Arab media was rarely mentioned anywhere in the world media. This is typical of the perverted double standard that says Arabs are victims of aggression by Israel and the West.

11. Bias of Blatant Anti-Semitism

France – Always a bastion for anti-Semitic opinion, the French media was finally officially chastised for their racist bias by the French Court, in a landmark ruling that a leading paper was guilty of slandering Israel and Jewish people. The court found three writers for *Le Monde*, as well as the newspaper's publisher, guilty of "racist defamation" against Israel and the Jewish people. In the groundbreaking decision, the Versailles Court of Appeals commented that the 2002 piece, "Israel-Palestine: The Cancer" in *Le Monde* had whipped up anti-Semitic opinion.

Australia – The Australian media focuses disproportionately on Israel. Beyond the obvious bias of public broadcasters and some newspapers, certain themes in the media are examples of a "new anti-Semitism." These include the alleged financial and media power of the Jewish lobby, an extreme demonization of Israel, extravagant assertions about the supposed worldwide effects of Israel toward Palestinians, conspiracy theories about American Jewish neo-conservatives, and a tendency to claim that anti-Semitism is a response to Jewish behavior and attitudes.

The Australian media gets much of its news about the Middle East, both in print and electronic form, from international services such as AP, CNN, and the BBC, and so absorbs many of the biases and problems documented in this chapter.

12. BBC's USA Bias – Reagan Obituary

Most newspapers around the world began their obituaries of Ronald Reagan by saying that many, including Mikhail Gorbachev, credit Reagan with helping to bring an end to the Cold War. But the BBC online obituary (*World Edition*, June 6, 2004, titled "Reagan's Mixed White House Legacy") ran almost a thousand words, a full four pages, without mentioning the Cold War, let alone Reagan's call to tear down the Berlin Wall. Instead, the BBC reminded us that Reagan was "a B movie actor" and stated that as President his "foreign policy was criticized for being in disarray." Accompanying photos were not of Reagan meeting Gorbachev, but of Ollie North and the invasion of Grenada: "a clumsy sham," according to the text.

13. Bias of Public Broadcasting: Who's Public?

American taxpayers have long subsidized the indoctrination efforts of the Public Broadcasting Service (PBS). PBS has now become a major component of Leftist broadcasting, "The News Hour" being the exception to the rule.

For example, on the PBS website, a student who clicks on "Environmental Defense" will discover how to oppose drilling in the Artic. Is it useful to include every point of view simply to cover every base? Even PBS Senior Producer Linda Harrar said that PBS' programming is virtually impossible for their audience to sort out. We agree, but PBS' listeners are more conservative and do not appreciate the historical revisionism and moral relativism found in PBS programming.

14. Piling on Hot Air and Bias

The accidental shooting of Harry Whittington while he was on hunting trip with Dick Cheney has nothing to do with government policy or the Vice President's official duties. Nevertheless, the mainstream media harped on the incident involving Cheney. The "Big Three" networks aired 34 stores about the Cheney hunting incident in the following 48 hours of newscasts. They treated the accident not as a mishap, but as a national scandal.

15. Making Mountains out of Molehills Bias

How quickly enemies in the Left-wing press, the UN, Arab countries, Congress, and the military tried to exploit the unfortunate "hazing" of some Iraqi prisoners at Abu Grarib, turning the circumstances into major war crimes. Hell night at my fraternity was as bad as any night most prisoners spent under American restraint. Indeed, "60 Minutes" reran its piece on the Mai Lai massacre the same week the mistreatment became news, thereby using the inference to slander one of the well intentioned, trained, and professional fighting forces in the world, as well as their leader Don Rumsfeld.

16. Guilt by Association Bias

Chris Matthews introduced his talk about Karl Rove and Valerie Plame by declaring, "What did the President know and when did he know it?" The words are an obvious attempt to link President Bush to President Nixon.

17. The Fog of News Bias

After the attack on September 11th, the President spoke about an NSA surveillance program and promised the American people that our government would do everything within the law to protect them against another terrorist attack.

299

I authorized the National Security Agency to intercept the international communications of people with known links to al-Qaeda and related terrorist organizations. In other words, if al-Qaeda or their associates are making calls into the United States or out of the United States, we want to know what they're saying.

The President made some important points about what our government was doing, and what the government was not doing. Our international activities strictly target al-Qaeda and their known affiliates. Al-Qaeda is our enemy, and we want to know their plans. The government does not listen to domestic phone calls without court approval. The authorized intelligence activities are lawful, and appropriate members of Congress were briefed, both Republican and Democrat. The privacy of ordinary Americans is fiercely protected in all activities.

He continued in defense of government activities, saying that they are not mining or trolling through the personal lives of millions of innocent Americans as the media implies. Efforts are focused on links to al-Qaeda and their known affiliates. Another attack on our soil has been prevented. The President asserted,

As a general matter, every time sensitive intelligence is leaked, it hurts our ability to defeat this enemy. Our most important job is to protect the American people from another foreign attack, and we will do so within the laws of our country.

The following is a perfect example of how the media clouds the simple facts and confuses the public by blowing smoke and then shamelessly yelling fire where there is none. Look how the media obscured the President's clear, fair statement above. *USA Today's* front page, and the network morning and evening newscasts, rehashed a six-month old *New York Times* non-story to hype their Left-wing agenda, alleging that the President's plan to listen in on phone calls infringed on personal privacy. By their objections, the media

300

clouded the issue and confused the public by diverting attention from the task and making it more difficult to fight terrorism.

Remember the simple facts: our international activities strictly target al-Qaeda and their known affiliates. Al-Qaeda is our enemy, and we want to know their plans. The government does not listen to domestic phone calls without court approval. The intelligence-authorized activities are lawful and members of Congress, both Republican and Democrat, were briefed. Finally, the privacy of ordinary Americans is protected in all activities.

18. US Media Bias

After the fog comes the spin. Listen to the spin: Seismic! Shocking! Startling! Bombshell! That's how the ABC, CBS, and NBC morning shows described a *USA Today* headline touting that "NSA has a massive database of Americans' phone calls." The TV coverage and the newspapers insinuated that the existence of the database was a major violation of Americans' privacy rights and evidence that the President was lying when he described the NSA's eavesdropping on suspected terrorists communications as targeted and limited.

Diane Sawyer declared, "New this morning: NSA bombshell. A new report that the government is secretly tracking your phone calls, seeking information on every call made in the US. The war on terrorism versus your privacy." With Big Brother on screen, NBC's Matt Lauer warned, "This morning a shocking new report that the NSA has been secretly collecting phone records of tens of millions of Americans."

Jack McCafferty played the outraged role to straight man Wolf Blitzer, an expert on how to use "weapons of media bias" as a means to push Left-wing agenda. McCafferty angrily stated that Specter "might be all that is standing between us and a full-blown dictatorship in this country." He was referring to Judicial Committee Chairman Arlen Spector, who wants his committee involved in anything controversial. After this completely asinine remark, the "sheep in Wolf's clothing" amazingly heralded the McCafferty stupidity as "words of

301

wisdom." Do you people get it? Instead of announcing the four simple facts about the NSA program, we were entertained with "fire in the theatre," hot headlines, and misrepresentation of the facts.

Additional facts were completely ignored and unheard, as the usual congressional clowns joined the media circus. According to ABC's George Stephanopoulos, the "core members of both the House and Senate Intelligence committees were fully briefed, including the details of the program described in *USA Today*. One source in the Senate said that no senator raised any legal objection to the program." Lisa Meyers reported on NBC's Nightly News, "House Democratic leader Nancy Pelosi pounced on the headlines even though she had been briefed long ago." An intelligence source told NBC News that two-dozen members of Congress had known about the program for years and had been completely uninterested until today.

Media polls have repeatedly shown a public dissatisfaction with the economy under President Bush. A January 2006 Pew Research Center survey found that 64% of those questioned thought economic conditions were fair or poor, and this wasn't Bush's low point. In May 2006, a joint *New York Times* / CBS poll gave Bush only a 28% approval rating on the economy.

Network news stories painted a bleak picture of an economy in decline. Reporters treated gas prices as a metaphor for the economy – only when the prices were high. A slowing housing market after two record years was just another club used against Republican incumbents by a pessimistic press.

But the truth about the economy is far different. The United States continued to enjoy solid job growth. New jobs increased by 1.7 million, with nearly six million created after August 2003, a three-year streak of positive growth. Unemployment was at a low 4.7%. Gas prices decreased once again, by more than 75 cents, from their recent highs. And though the economy actually grew just 2.6% in the second quarter of 2006 following a rapid expansion in the first quarter, the rate was revised upward to 5.6%.

That is not how things looked on the evening news shows of all three broadcast networks – ABC, CBS, and NBC. The Media Research Center's Business & Media Institute (BMI) looked at all stories referencing the economy or economic news between August 1, 2005 and July 31, 2006.

Here are some key findings:

Reports Negatively Charged – More than twice as many stories and briefs focused on negative aspects of the economy (62%) as compared to good news (31%). News broadcasts dwelled on one prospective cataclysm after another, yet each time the economy continued unfazed. Negative stories were given more airtime; bad news was emphasized on all three networks. Negative news appeared in full-length stories twice as often as it appeared in shorter, brief items. Good news was relegated to briefs; more good news appeared in brief form than as full-length stories.

Man-On-The-Street Interview Spin Stories – Reporters used ordinary people to underscore negative stories by roughly a 3-to-1 ratio over positive. Since these are interviews chosen entirely by the reporter, this shows particular bias. NBC was especially bad at this, featuring negative accounts six times as often as positive ones.

Worst Network – More than 80% of the full-length stories on CBS Evening News delivered a negative view of the economy, easily the worst of the three broadcast news programs. The networks hid the news of job or economic growth in short items. More than 56% of CBS's brief stories were positive.

Best Network – ABC was hardly the "best" at anything for its economic coverage. It simply wasn't as negative as either NBC or CBS. More than 56% of ABC reports were negative, compared to slightly more than 36% that were positive. To improve coverage, BMI recommended that the networks carefully select a range of economists and analysts to balance negative reports, cover stories that reflect the actual economic data rather than the reporter's opinion, educate the public about what the economic data really means, and do more than report changing numbers like sport scores.

From the misrepresentation of these stories and others it seems that only the White House is stating the facts in a coherent honest way. The media coverage simply stinks of bias and spin.

19. Putting Some English on Media Spin

The BBC correspondents can teach the master course in perfecting the *bias of spin*. "Over the years, Hamas has been blamed for scores of suicide attacks on Israel," says the BBC, thereby trying to suggest to listeners and viewers that Hamas has perhaps been wrongly accused of such attacks. Hamas, however, has proudly and repeatedly claimed responsibility at mass celebratory rallies in Gaza, Jenin, and elsewhere for these very actions.

Two Palestinian gunmen opened fire indiscriminately in the heart of the Northern Israeli town of Afula, killing two young Israeli civilians and wounding 50 others. The gunmen were then shot dead by Israeli policemen. The headline on the BBC website read: "Four Die in Israel Shooting Rampage," suggesting that four innocent people had died at the hands of the Israelis.

Again, when suicide bombers killed 26 Israeli civilians in attacks on Jerusalem and Haifa, the BBC used the word "terror" only when describing Israel's retaliatory (and largely non-lethal) attack on Palestinian military targets. The word terrorism of course appeared when one of their own correspondents, Frank Gardiner, was shot and badly wounded by an al-Qaeda gunman in Saudi Arabia.

20. Heating Global Anti-American Sentiment

We hear every day about the bombing story of the day, but we don't hear about the issue that most people believe is an oxymoron: "Arab constitutional democracy." There has been a lot of undeniably bad news in the Iraq war, but are network reporters giving the public an inordinately gloomy portrait of the situation? Are the positive accomplishments of US solders in Iraq being lost in news agendas dominated by assassinations, car bombings, and causality reports? The answer to both questions is "Yes."

The conclusion is based on a Media Research Center (MRC) study of broadcast network news coverage in 2005. MRC reviewed 1,388 stories broadcast on ABC, CBS, and NBC nightly news. The conclusions were that network coverage has been overwhelmingly pessimistic. News about the war has grown increasingly negative. Terrorist attacks are the centerpiece of TV's war news. Even coverage of the Iraqi political process has been negative. Few stories focused on the heroism or generous actions of American soldiers.

It is not as if there were no "good news" stories to report.

By accentuating the negative, the networks reinforce the negative global anti-American propaganda being pumped out by Arab, European, and Third World media outlets, giving aid and comfort to our enemies in our war on terrorism. Indeed, the insurgents are very media savvy. They know that if they blow something up every day, the bombing will be in the news. Also, reporters know no one wins a Pulitzer Prize for a headline reading "The US is Making Amazing Progress in Iraq."

21. Let the Lie Stand – Don't Question – Jenin Massacre

In the annals of Israel's wars, the battle in the Jenin refugee camp stands out. This clash between IDF (The Israel Defense Force) soldiers, who entered the camp as part of a wide, anti-terrorist campaign, and the hundreds of armed Palestinians, who had taken up positions there, was one of the biggest engagements to rage between Israel and the Palestinian Authority in years. For eight days, Israeli fighters fought an intensive house-to house battle in a densely populated urban area filled with hidden explosives. According to the United Nations, 23 Israeli soldiers and 52 Palestinians were killed.

It came as no surprise that Jenin became the focus of media coverage within hours after fighting began, and any eyewitness accounts took on enormous significance before the actual facts came to light. Throughout the next few months, journalists widely and maliciously quoted the rarely reliable Palestinian Authority propaganda spokesperson, Hanan

Ashrawi, who claimed that the IDF massacred many hundreds of Palestinians. The international press, particularly in Europe and the Arab world, reported continuously on war crimes Israel was said to be committing in the camp. The British press in particular reached a new low in journalism and a new high in malicious intent.

The Independent, in a lying smear article, wrote that nearly half of the Palestinian dead were identified as civilians, including women, children, and the elderly. According to the report, they died amid a ruthless and brutal Israeli operation in which mass atrocities occurred, and which Israel sought to hide by launching a massive propaganda drive.

On a similar vein, a lead article in London's once prestigious *Guardian* embarrassed civilized people when it called Israel's actions in Jenin every bit as repellant as Osama bin Laden's 9/11 terror attacks on the US. One of the *Evening Standard*'s most influential columnists, A.N. Wilson, sullied his reputation forever and was guilty of libel when he emphatically announced a massacre and a cover up of genocide.

Such charges cannot be dismissed lightly. If proven well founded, serious questions should be raised about the standards of the Israeli army, not to mention the officers responsible. But is there really anything to the allegations?

In the year since the event, a great deal of reliable information has become available, revealing what really happened in the battle of Jenin. The picture that emerged is strikingly different from the images that filled the media in the weeks after the clash. Not only was there no massacre of innocent civilians in the Jenin refugee camp, but in the vast majority of cases, IDF soldiers took unusual measures – even at the risk of their own lives – to prevent harm to the civilian population. These efforts were not simply isolated acts of restraint, but the result of decisions made by both the military command and the civilian leadership as part of a deliberate policy aimed at keeping casualities to a minimum.

The IDF followed these orders to the letter, though they significantly complicated fighting in a residential area. Other armies, even the most enlightened among them, have not shown such a level of concern for civilian populations in times of war.

A military history scholar, Y. Henkin, who studied urban warfare and the lessons of Jenin wrote, "Indeed, in the history of modern warfare it is difficult to find another example of an invading army that took upon itself such restraint in order to minimize civilian casualties." **The relatively low number of civilian causalities in Jenin reveals the lies made by accusers in the months that followed, but also testifies to the high moral standard employed by the IDF; a rare demonstration of humanity in the midst of battle, for which they paid a heavy price.**

Another unquestioned media lie originated with ABC's White House correspondent, who charged that GOP leader Dick Armey echoed former war criminal Slobodan Milosevic in calling for ethnic cleaning of Palestinians – something Armey never said.

22. Whose Headline is it Anyway?

The *San Francisco Chronicle* used six columns on the front page to print a headline story, saying that a Vice Presidential aide **may** have lied. Though there was no proof that he did lie, the aide and the administration suffered damage, given that this type of headline is usually reserved for world war or significant global or national events.

The *San Jose Mercury* also used six columns on the front page in a two-day headline exploiting the plight of our brave soldiers, who suffered traumatic injuries, in an effort to push their anti-war, anti-administration agenda.

On April 18th, a Palestinian homicide bomber killed at least nine people and injured scores more in Israel. This, the most violent terrorist act in nearly two years, was wildly celebrated on the trash-strewn streets of Gaza. These Palestinian actions were not mentioned in the *San Jose Mercury* article. The paper's front-page headline read instead, **"Hamas says suicide blast is defensible."** Using the same twisted logic that continually tries to make silk purses out of these pig-headed, sow-eared murderers, one would expect the

307

headline after 9/11 to read, **"Al-Qaeda says attacks on World Trade Center are defensible."**

American reporters are the ones who are **indefensible**, when they promote the agenda of Hamas and their brother hate groups who are considered by the civilized world to be mass murderers and a threat to world peace. **Are you beginning to see how immoral it is for the mass media to assist the terrorist agenda by giving voice to their propaganda machine, and how the media acts to reverse our moral compass?**

Today, April 17, 2006, the damn *Mercury* newspaper has once again pressed my hot button, this time with a picture accompanying an article that clearly provides a very obvious example of malicious anti-Israel agenda. The caption next to the picture of that small, despicable loser Ahmadinjad, who belongs in a mental institution for the criminally insane rather than at the head of the government of Iran, reads "**Ahmadinjad comments on Israel, a slight retreat from earlier remarks."**

The article by this irresponsible paper is in itself nothing more then an opportunity to repeat all the racist, anti-Semitic remarks, images, and propaganda that this anti-Zionist, Islamic vermin could spew out. What was missing from the *Mercury* story is the one line from Ahmadinjad that today's *Wall Street Journal* and responsible media thought was worth reporting, "**Israel is heading toward annihilation."** Some "slight retreat from earlier remarks." Whose payroll are these Knight Ridder reporters on? Why did they repeat Iranian garbage without a line that provides even more justification for the West and Israel to go to war with this rouge, terrorist, nuclear state? Perhaps they, like so many in the Left-wing press, see their role as spreading propaganda for the Islamic terrorists in Iran, Gaza, and elsewhere.

Reportedly, after the West stopped sending funds to those countries that refused to renounce terrorism and to recognize Israel, Iran's homicide bombing, Hamas government spent millions on public relations, while the Palestinian people suffered and waited for them to help. I 'm already reading positive stories in the *Mercury* and other media outlets about

Hamas, nonsense and lies about Israel, and how the so-called Palestinian people are poor victims.

23. Blatantly Biased Correspondent

Meredith Viera came on the air in 2004, as the Republican Convention was beginning, and boasted that she had marched in an anti-Bush, anti-war protest in New York. NBC News hired her to replace Katie Couric as co-host of "Today," paying her an eight-figure salary for her Leftist biases. Perhaps they should pair her with MSNBC's Keith Olbermann, another liberal, and put them both on Air (head) America, the Left-wing radio station.

The number of Mid-East correspondents with a blatant pro-Arab bias is staggering. See the excellent media watch group CAMERA website for numerous examples of Mid-East reporting bias.

24. Omit Story

During the past decade, a great many newsrooms have been driven by publishers, militant organizations of minority journalists, and mandates of diversity training to suffer from a terminal case of political correctness disease. The disease regards any dissenting views about race preferences as racist, and to be avoided like the Bubonic plague, or conveniently forgotten.

For example, the media failed to report how Affirmative Action in university admissions grew into a blatant system of race preferences. The impact of these failed programs on their "beneficiaries" also goes unreported. Take the case of Patrick Chavis, a Black physician and one of the beneficiaries of a quota system at UC Davis medical school. Nicholas Lemann lionized Chavis in a major piece in The New York Times Magazine, and Senator Edward Kennedy and others lauded him for his service in the Black community. A "perfect example," Kennedy said, of the benefits of Affirmative Action. I could not agree more about this being a "perfect example." Afterwards, when Chavis was investigated for gross negligence in connection with a set of botched operations and stripped of his license by the state medical board, the Times ignored it.

Then there was the attempt to fully integrate women into

the armed forces. The *San Diego Union-Tribune* printed a report based on the Navy's investigation of Lt. Kara Hultgreen's fatal crash. She was the first female Navy pilot to be assigned to combat duty on a carrier. Her errors were attributed to "lowered training requirement," and hence to politically driven "preferential treatment" for women, not to engine failure, as announced by the Navy's official pronouncement. Most media outlets did not pick up the *Union Tribune* story. The *New York Times* called the crash a "gender-neutral tragedy."

If you listened only to CBS, you would not know that former CIA Director George Tenet specifically denied in a speech at Georgetown University that the Bush administration improperly influenced intelligence on Iraq, or that pacifist Mark Hatfield, the 82-year-old former governor and senator from Oregon, announced his strong support for the war.

Another big story that has been ignored by the media told how the president of the firefighters union engineered an endorsement of John Kerry for president without asking for his members' vote. Most of the union members are Republicans who supported Bush.

Finally, though patriotic citizens in the tens of thousands have attended rallies to support our fighting troops, the liberal media prefers to ignore them, instead portraying sparsely attended anti-war rallies as the sentiment of most Americans.

Sometimes omitting a story can be dangerous. Although conditions in Zimbabwe continue to deteriorate, with ongoing seizures of White-owned farms, state-sanctioned murder, harassment, and a dangerous famine, the misery failed to gain the attention of the establishment Western media, leaving many in Zimbabwe hopeless.

25. Just Make Up the Story

Gary Webb is one of the many *San Jose Mercury* and other Left-wing reporters who belong in the Journalism Hall of Shame. This loser, who tried to link the CIA to the crack cocaine epidemic in Los Angeles, killed himself after several major newspapers followed up reports questioning his conclusions. Even his own newspaper was forced to turn on him. Black reporter Jayson Blair joins Webb in the Hall of Shame. Blair gave the *New York Times* a black eye when he was caught fabricating many of his stories. *Times* Executive Editor Howell Raines said Blair "had gotten the breaks he enjoyed because of his race."

CNN TV puts fairytale stories on the ticker running across the TV screen during regular programming. For example, today, December 19, 2006, a deceitful, Palestinian story was naively repeated by CNN. The story was an obvious smoke screen to hide the current civil violence occurring between the Hamas and Fatah terror organizations. In another story, we learn, "according to CNN sources," always unidentified, that Israeli solders killed two Palestinians, including a teenager. No other news network seems to know anything about the story, and as I predicted, the story evaporated.

The media failed us when they didn't cover major issues such as our pending environmental disaster. The threats discussed in our next chapter should be seen regularly in six column headlines.

Chapter 10
MAN IS LISTENING TO MOTHER NATURE

I've saved the lie that man can control nature until last. It will literally be our last problem, if we fail to understand the destructive changes that man is making to the planet and act to reverse the trend. All the threats to western civilization presented in this book won't matter, since man's basic needs such as air, water, food, and shelter will always trump other societal concerns.

The human population of the world, and the pace and scale of its demands upon the earth, is reaching its "carrying capacity." This refers to the largest number of any given species that a habitat can support indefinitely before the habitat declines, along with the population. The decline of our environment is happening much faster then the scientist and politicians are predicting. To reverse this trend, we should have taken action years ago. Unfortunately, governments will not act unless pushed by their constituents, and people will not act until they are personally feeling the impact. By the time either of these things happens, it will be too late.

We must pulverize this last false idol – the mistaken belief that man can with impunity continue to exploit, destroy, and mismanage the resources of our blue planet while ignoring all the warning signs of impending disaster. Indeed, much of the World Community has shown a fundamental disregard for the ecosystems that provide life on this planet. Even where there is rare scientific agreement that a problem exists, there is a widespread failure to summon the political will needed to solve the problem.

In this chapter, we will discuss the Army Corps of Engineers (protectors of estates built by rich homeowners on flood-prone barrier islands), the Environmental Protection Agency (EPA) (favorers of power plants and economic growth over the environment), industrialists (neglecters of the environmental impacts of their products), scientists (non-believers who must see their microscopes melt from global warming), Right wingers (pillagers supporting their "right" and an inherent destiny to control the Earth), cattle ranchers (breeders of CO2), bigger-the-motor-the-better SUV owners (gas-guzzling polluters), developers and their political cronies (pavers of Nature's beautiful and bountiful gifts for more green in their pockets), and right-to-life groups (promoters of the major cause of environmental degradation – population growth).

Population Growth

A growing population is sowing the seeds of an environmental disaster, and population control is the most crucial program we can undertake to assure that our future on this planet is sustainable. A global struggle exists between production and reproduction. While production has long been predominant in industrialized countries, three-quarters of the world's people live and reproduce in developing nations, and **reproduction is winning over production.**

Indeed, world population is likely to exceed 7.8 billion by 2020. Nearly 95% of this growth will occur in less developed nations. To understand the enormous implications of this "so what" statistic, let's give it some perspective. A staggering increase of 2 billion people is twice the population of China and eight times that of the United States. Every 24 hours, enough people are added to the earth to fill a city the size of Newark, New Jersey or Akron, Ohio. Most are Chinese.

This extraordinary population rise is not precipitated by higher birthrates, as occurred during America's post-World War II baby boom era, but rather a drastic decline in Third World death rates, due to foreign aid programs that provide public heath programs and assistance. Another reason is obviously the large numbers of young women having children in the developing world.

As the prediction of permanent population excess over available resources is actualized during our lifetime, we will be continually bombarded with press reports of famine and deprivation in Africa, Latin America, and Asia. Population growth will overwhelm the capacities of underdeveloped and newly developing nations, forever dooming millions to subsistence living. There will be no business as usual when starvation and war continually threaten millions of lives in Africa and parts of Asia.

Though experts have cried wolf before, these figures actually mean that the earth's resources cannot feed, clothe, house, and educate a population that in the next couple of decades will become almost 30% larger then the earth's present 5.6 billion people. **In 1927, after 4 million years, humanity reached the 2 billion mark. In just 70 years, the span of one lifetime, that number will triple.**

China's economic growth is quickly pushing the earth to its environmental tipping point. China is not only the world's most populous country, containing one-fifth of humanity, but also the fastest growing economy. With its large size and extraordinary growth rates, I tell my clients that China will predictably impact the future and also provide a window into how other developing counties might influence the environment as they reach new levels. It is not a pretty picture. China is teaching us that the industrial model will not work, simply because there are not enough resources in the world.

China is already the world's leading consumer of resources: consumption of grain and meat in the food sector, coal in the energy sector, and steel in the industrial sector. China is now the world's largest producer of the greenhouse gases that case global warming. The Earth Policy Institute predicts that with the current economic growth of 8% per year, China's per capita income will reach the current US level in 2031. If the consumption level in 2031 is the same as in the United States (currently China's grain use per person, both direct and indirect, is roughly half the US use.), then China's projected population of 1.45 billion will consume an amount equal to two-thirds of the current world grain harvest. For example, if China, with its new wealth, was to just increase meat demand by one-kilogram per person, then those additional Chinese burgers would require a 4% world grain increase to produce enough cattle feed. Indeed, having recently returned from a trip to Brazil, I became very aware of how that country was developing into a huge grain bin simply to feed China.

While it is not particularly surprising that China's total consumption of some basic resources has now overtaken that of the US, the rest of the world is startled and potentially devastated. China surpassed the US in consumption per person of some basic goods such as pork and eggs. By 2031, China paper consumption is expected to be double the current world production. There go the world's forests. The US alone was originally blanketed with a billion acres of forest. Now only 40 million acres remain uncut.

China is already paying a high environmental price for its booming economy. A heavy reliance on coal, for example, has led to that country experiencing some of the world's worst air pollution problems. **China is turning into one of the greatest environmental threats the earth has ever faced.** Soon it will be the world's leading source of deforestation, extinction of wildlife, consumption of resources, and emitter of greenhouse gases.

Even with pollution controls, China faces a formidable challenge because of the density of its population. Although it has a landmass that is almost exactly the same as the US, most of China's billions of people live in a 1,500 kilometer strip on the eastern and southern coast. To understand the density of China, squeeze the entire US population into an area east of the Mississippi River and then multiply it by five.

Economic Logic Will Destroy the Earth

Population growth alone will end civilization, but when conspicuous consumption is added to population, the destruction increases exponentially. As countries like China copy our consumer-driven capitalist model, they, like us, will collect, waste, overuse, and abuse the earth's limited resources. They will eat more fish and meat protein, and buy and consume things that they were able to live without for generations.

My late SRI colleague, Willis Harmon, shared my concern about our political leaders, who do not take pending environmental problems seriously enough. He noted how fast parts of the world are turning into desert and how the predominance of economic logic over other forms of logic is tearing the earth apart.

Harmon observed how we squandered resources to build products, and then got rid of them so that we could create more. We've pushed other cultures aside and developed a Western "economic mono-culture" around the world, because we have all been taught that this would be a good thing. With no strong diverse counter-culture to balance the system, native cultures are being destroyed. People who once lived on the land become impoverished and flock to the cities, where there is nothing for them.

Environmental degradation correlates with poverty just as it does with consumption. Indigent people are more worried about their economic survival than the health of the planet. While economists may be oblivious to the relationship between the global economy and the earth's ecology, the public must not be. As you will see in this chapter, evidence of mounting environmental stresses can be seen everywhere, as more and more long-range sustainability thresholds are crossed, and waste absorptive capacities are overwhelmed.

Environmental Interdependency

As countries of the world become economically linked, they must also deal with another form of interdependence: environmental interdependence. Problems such as global warming, resource depletion, and overpopulation cross borders without passports. If a German factory pollutes the Rhine, someone in the Netherlands may suffer the consequences.

Technology creates as many problems as it solves. These problems are increasing, while our skills to deal with them are decreasing. Today, more people question technology's value in our lives, and wonder what to do about the problems it has created. For example, NIMBY (Not In My Back Yard) grass roots groups are very effective at stopping things from happening. Even things we once considered normal, such as living near high-tension power lines, are starting to be questioned. "Living close to strong electromagnetic fields may or may not be good, so don't run it by my backyard." On the other hand, environmental laws have been challenged for unnecessarily forcing out entrepreneurial competition. Big business more than the government is able to afford costly environmental impact studies.

Global Warming

One of the major consequences of ignoring the subtle impacts of overpopulation and consumer logic is global warming. Global warming occurs when carbon dioxide, mostly from the burning of coal, gasoline, and other fossil fuels, traps heat within the atmosphere that would otherwise radiate into space. Global temperatures have increased about one degree Fahrenheit during the 20th Century, and international panels of scientists sponsored by world governments have concluded that most of the warming is probably due to greenhouse gases.

These heat-trapping gases, such as carbon dioxide, act like a blanket over the earth, warming the planet at an increasingly alarming rate. According to NOAA (National Oceanic and Atmospheric Administration), the gas that is largely blamed for global warming has reached record-level highs after growing at an accelerated pace in the past year. The Energy Information Administration said that during the past 20 years, about three-quarters of human-made carbon dioxide emissions came from burning fossil fuels. What most people don't understand is that the remaining 25% of carbon dioxide emissions today are coming from deforestation. Trees, absorbers of CO2, are cut down, or burned and left to decompose, thereby releasing more carbon dioxide into the air. As climatologists forecast a continued rise in global temperature, credible threats to our long-term survival on this planet are being ignored and denied by special interest groups. Their "can't see the forest for the trees" scientists and politicians are beholden to the industrial and resource sectors of the economy, rather than the planet.

Rising temperatures can cause the seas to rise and lead to other unpredictable consequences – unpredictable in part because of the uncertainties in computer modeling of future weather. **Need proof?** No, not if you watched the curtains of dust turn Australia's skies orange as drought-fueled fires swept the nation. Not if you experienced shock and awe as Hurricane

Katrina devastated the Gulf Coast. Not if you watched sections of ice the size of small states collapse in the disintegrating ice caps of the Arctic and Antarctica. Changing weather patterns affect every area throughout the world.

The 2005 Atlantic hurricane season was the busiest on record, according to the National Oceanic and Atmospheric Administration (NOAA). The season included 26 named storms, including 13 hurricanes, of which seven were listed as major (Category 3 or higher).

Yes, scientists have been warning us for years that this is what would happen if we continued putting greenhouse gases into the atmosphere, trapping the sun's heat, and raising global temperatures. **It is abundantly clear to people who can think strategically that global warming is another example of a slowly brewing but critical threat to our future existence. Climate is one of the most important factors in determining the quality of life we will have in the future.**

Paralysis by Analysis

Government and industry-sponsored scientists remind me of those people standing in several feet of water on the Titanic, refusing to believe that the ship could actually sink. US government experts continue to say that the reason for the faster buildup of greenhouse gases "will require further analysis." As MIT professor Dr. Richard Lindzen notes,

> In the public arena, global warming is commonly used as a source of authority with which to bludgeon political opponents and propagandize uninformed citizens... A fairer view of the science will show there is still a vast amount of uncertainty – far more then advocates of Kyoto would like to acknowledge.

Science, thereby, continues to stall the necessary measures to prevent a coming disaster. At least with increased monitoring, they cannot deny that these dangerous gases continue to reach record levels. After growing at an accelerated pace in the past year, carbon dioxide, the gas largely blamed for global warming, reached record high levels in the atmosphere,

319

say scientists monitoring the sky at the Mauna Loa Observatory in Hawaii.

Cyclical Thinking

Economic logic, or more acutely *illogic*, promotes the mistaken cyclical thinking dogma we discussed in the economics chapter. When scientists believe that conditions such as global warming are normal parts of the Earth's heating and cooling cycles, they fall into the same trap economists do. Like economists, climatologists make their forecasts about our long-term weather conditions by looking into the rearview mirror of the past. Therefore, they cannot see that the very thin ice they are standing on is melting away under their outdated cyclical beliefs. Yes, there is a record of cyclical climate swings in the past, but something critical has changed, and the old beliefs about the climate must change based upon new facts.

Getting in the way of progress is our government's own climatologists, who, like their brethren the academic economist, can't get out of the logic trap that weather and the economy move in cycles. They believe that an exceptional period of hot weather will be followed by a long period of cold weather. As proof, they show convincing evidence of these historical climate cycles in geologic and biological record.

Like economists, climatologists base their theories on past history. No wonder the scientific community is always surprised that so much is happening faster then anyone predicted. Still, conservative think tank groups like the Heritage Foundation want to eliminate Earth Day. They go against the tide of public thought. Even the conservative Evangelical Christian base now demands that Congress regulate greenhouse gases.

Questionable Experts

In September of 2005, a rather curious event happened, even considering our government's three-ring circus. Possibly for the first time ever, a chair of a Senate Committee, former Senator James Inhofe (R-OK), invited a science fiction writer, Michael Crichton, to advise the Environmental and Public Works committee on scientific facts. In this case, the subject was based on the facts behind climate change. The panel joining Crichton, of course, was also proficient in the fiction writer's art of half-truths and red herrings.

Over the course of the hearing, there was much talk about cooling in the Northern Hemisphere from the 1940's to the 1970's. Some scientists predicted an imminent ice age at that time, and proclaimed global warming disproved. The argument, however, is fallacious to most serious scientists. Others invalidate global warming, saying important scientific pieces have not independently been reproduced. That global climate models can't reproduce past climate change is not proof for non-existence. Climate cannot be predicted, because weather is chaotic.

Uniformed Public

The world is in deep trouble! According to a *Time* / ABC / Stanford University poll, most people are not aware of the broad scientific consensus on global warming. The majority of people see it as a problem for future generations. We are not aware of the problem's depth. Actions to reverse a devastating fate should have begun two decades ago. The good news is that 85% of us believe that the world temperature has been going up slowly for the past 100 years. We have at least that much understanding of the problem.

Resources are Finite

One of my heroes is Lester R. Brown and his former colleagues from the World Watch Institute. His **State of The World** books provide important information for those interested in the health of the planet. Lester, currently with the Earth Policy Institute, has been sounding the alarm for years. Hopefully more people are finally listening.

Endangered Species

"In effect, we are currently responsible for the sixth major extinction event in the history of the earth, and the greatest since the dinosaurs disappeared, 65 million years ago." – **Secretariat of the UN Convention on Biological Diversity**

Habitats raging from coral reefs to tropical rainforests face mounting threats. Years ago, rainforests circled the earth in abundance from South America to Africa, Malaysia, and

Indonesia, but by the time you read this sentence, another eight acres of rain forest will have been bulldozed and burned off the face of the earth.

Without firing a shot, we may kill one-fifth of all species of life on this planet in the next 30 years. The World Wildlife Fund gets it. They tell us that "pleading ignorance of these vital and fragile ecosystems can only spell global disaster."

Hunger will be the Wake Up Call

Fisheries – Oceans cover roughly 70% of the earth's surface and support an incalculable amount of bio-diversity. They provide us with ecological services valued at $21 trillion annually, yielding 8.5 million metric tons of fish and other raw materials. Beyond the narrow strip of near-shore waters, the oceans are the last unclaimed domains on Earth. Since the oceans belong to no one, and to everyone, they are perhaps the most unprotected ecosystem on Earth.

The US recently released the Federal government's first assessment of ocean policy in 35 years. Marine biologists who monitor oceanic fisheries reported that not only have we neglected our ocean resources, but we are also currently ill equipped to turn back the tide.

Chronic over fishing is a global problem. Marine biologists say that nearly all fisheries are now being fished at or beyond capacity. The total world fish catch has dropped since its high absolute tonnage in 1989. Right now it's at about 17.8 kilograms per capita, and that's down 8% since 1989. The world's oceans are being fished out. The current ban on fishing within a 200-mile limit of New England and the Newfoundland reefs is hoped to reverse the loss. By 1992, the cod of Eastern Canada had nearly disappeared, fished, almost to extinction. The Canadian government responded with severe restrictions, but was too late. After a ten-year moratorium in 1994, the ban on cod fishing was extended; there is no recovery in sight. The fishermen of New England face a similar fate. The cod, so abundant in 1497 that John Cabot bragged that he could catch them in a basket lowered to the sea, may be disappearing.

A new analysis of government data reveals that commercial fishing has harmed the rich Northwestern Hawaiian

Islands ecosystem as well. Report data revealed that the area closest to the main Hawaiian Islands was over fished – or dangerously close – in the years from 1998 to 2003. One culprit is long-line fishing, which involves setting out fishing lines up to 60 miles long, baited with many hooks. The line unintentionally kills roughly 40,000 sea turtles, 300,000 seabirds, and millions of sharks every year. The Federal government must be forced to better regulate long lining to protect marine species.

The growth in fish protein use will require fish farming and some type of feed protein. So seafood has declined in absolute terms, and has certainly declined on a per capita basis.

Other Food Sources – Global cropland per capita is down 35% since 1965. Simply put, most of the arable land has already been put under the plow. As population grows, the amount of arable land per person will continue to decrease. Grain harvests have dropped 1% per year since 1984 – another indicator that croplands are almost full utilized. In Africa, for example, output has declined yearly for 20 years, leading to chronic malnutrition.

At the same time, rising affluence is expanding the demand for grain in Asia. Billions of people move up the food chain, consuming more pork, beef, poultry, eggs, milk, beer, and other grain intensive crops. Meat production uses about 37% of the world's grain output. Cattle, sheep, and goats are rumens, meaning that they can convert grass to protein. But the world's rangeland is already in full use. In fact, productivity is falling due to overgrazing. Beef production per capita is down 4% since 1990, and mutton down 2%, impacting the amount of milk and cheese available. Raising pigs and chickens is a growing trend because they are not rumens, but they require a concentrated feed like grain or soybean meal. Normally as GDP increases, meat consumption grows. How can the world supply the amount of protein that will be demanded in the future? Today's protein shortages in seafood, meat, and soybeans will only get worse.

An increase in demand for meat with reduced grain, and at best flat soybean production, creates an imbalanced equation. Fertilizer can no longer replace new cropland in the effort to increase production. The world's existing crop varieties are quickly reaching capacity in fertilizer use. Fertilizer use per capita is down 11.5% since 1985, with a plateau or decline in the developed world. Use continues to climb in the developing countries, which are surpassing the industrialized world. **Rising grain prices may be the first indicator that the world is moving down an unsustainable economic and environmental path.**

Water Shortage

Since the 1950's, water use has tripled and is continuing to expand. Water scarcity now threatens economic progress and global security. Where there is over pumping for irrigation water today, there will be irrigation cutbacks tomorrow. Cuts in irrigation mean cuts in food production. Irrigation, and water shortages in countries such as Algeria, China, Egypt, India, Iran, Mexico, Pakistan, and Saudi Arabia, all continue to increase the need for imported water. And as populations outrun their water supplies, talk about conflicts over water will multiply. In areas such as the Middle East, future wars will more likely be over water then oil.

Playing Politics with Mother Nature Is a Deadly Game

If governments were both intelligent and capable (they are neither), they would not be giving amnesty to illegal aliens and set asides to minorities, or worrying whether telephone calls are being tapped legally. Instead, responsible leadership would immediately be planning for our country's biggest threats – those to the environment.

We must document when we approached sustainable yield thresholds, so demands can be adjusted before we set in motion the decline or collapse of the natural systems on which we depend. Government could calculate the sustainable yield of aquifers, fisheries, forests, and rangelands, restrict use to those yield levels, and fulfill our commitment to future generations. We could make certain not to plow lands that are prone to erosion or becoming wasteland. Instead, we could leave the land in grass or forest – productive uses that are sustainable. Furthermore, we could reduce fossil fuel use before carbon emissions permanently destabilize the earth's climate.

But instead, government just makes things worse. In 2002, more then 70,000 adult salmon died in the Klamath River as a result of low water flows – one of the largest fish kills in US history. Much of the river's water, flowing from Oregon into California, had been diverted for agriculture, leaving the salmon in warm, crowed conditions that breed disease. According to a 2003 article in the *Wall Street Journal*, Karl Rove and President Bush visited Senator Gordon Smith to hear the farmers' demands to divert water from the river for their farms. Rove reportedly leaned on the US Department of the Interior and the US Bureau of Reclamation to do just that, despite environmental repercussions.

The US Bureau of Land Management controls our public grasslands for the short-term benefit of the livestock industry. Cows and sheep have permanently destroyed 50% of the nation's grasslands, and are currently munching away on another 40%. This leaves only 10% of the nation's original grasslands available for wildlife, and most of this land is unprotected.

Pristine wild lands that are federally designated as wilderness enjoy the highest level of government protection. Road building, logging, vehicle use, and many mining activities are prohibited in wilderness areas to preserve their natural condition. Despite widespread public support for these wilderness areas, the Bush administration entered into a backroom deal with the State of Utah, resulting in the withdrawal of Federal protection for 300,000 acres of untouched wild lands, as well as an agreement not to consider wilderness designation for millions of acres of public lands across the nation.

Water Pollution

Public opinion polls consistently document that Americans value water quality. Although US waterways have become cleaner with pollution controls on industrial discharges and sewage treatment plants, extensive water quality problems remain. The Clean Water Act requires surface water quality to be high enough to support fish and wildlife populations, protect drinking water sources, and allow for human recreation. Nationwide, 36% of rivers and streams, 39% of lakes and reservoirs, and 38% of estuaries are not supporting at least one of these uses. Many more waterways are either threatened by degradation or lack the data required for accessing their condition.

Coeur D'Alene Mines Corporation, the world's largest silver mining company, plans to construct the Kensington mine near Juneau, Alaska. Although the company initially proposed a more reasonable method to dispose of millions of tons of its industrial waste, it has changed its plans to cut costs. Coeur is now planning to dump more then 4.5 million tons of waste directly into a freshwater lake in the heart of the Tsongas National Forest. Federal agencies concluded that the chemically treated waste will kill all fish in the lake, but those out of control, mission-less, over funded friends of special interests, the Army Corps of Engineers, nonetheless issued a permit for the mine. Discharges from the waste-filled lake will eventually flow into Berners Bay, which supports a diverse array of wildlife including bald eagles, grizzly bears, humpback whales, and Steller sea lions. The Kensington mine will set a bad precedent for other mining companies, allowing them to dispose of their waste in Alaska's waterways.

In the opposite part of the country, South Florida, sewage sludge is treated and spread on land as fertilizer. Unfortunately, the sludge often washes off the land and into nearby creeks, making the water unsuitable for swimming and fishing. The EPA said that one-third of the nation's lakes and one-quarter of its rivers are contaminated with mercury and other pollutants, which could cause health problems for children and pregnant woman who eat too much fish. States issued mercury and other pollutant warnings for nearly 850,000 miles of US rivers and 14 million acres of lakes.

We Can't See the Forest...

Our forests provide clean water and clean air. They regulate climate, and provide soil stability and wild life habitat, including habitat for fish and the pollinators of food crops. Many modern medicines are derived from the forest. Our survival as a species depends upon intact forests; yet, we have destroyed 96% of our forest. Each year another 16 million hectares of forest disappear as land is cleared by timber operations or converted to other uses, such as cattle ranches, plantations, and small farms.

Deforestation is not the only threat. Serious declines in forest quality are affecting much of the world's forests. Many of us that view tropical forests with concern are unaware that the temperate forests in our own backyards are the most fragmented and disturbed of all forest types. For example, we have logged 95% to– 98% of forests in the continental United States at least once. In Europe, two-thirds of the forest cover is gone, with less then 1% of old growth remaining.

The rising appetite for forest products and their trade is a major force behind the logging and conversion of many of the world's forests to other uses. Policies and subsidies that encourage logging for timber harvest, agriculture, and development drive the process. **A precursor to forest decline is government subsidizing the building of roads, whether in the Amazon jungle or in our national forests.** Road-less areas in our national forests are some of the most pristine wild lands in the country, providing valuable wildlife habitat, clean water for thousands of people, psychological sanctuary, and recreational opportunities for the public. Before leaving office, President Clinton designated road-less areas in our national forests.

When the Bush administration took office, it immediately suspended the Road-less Rule for review and refused to defend it in court when the rule was challenged by the timber industry. Instead, the administration bowed to this special interest group, as discussed in the chapter on government. The rule was formally repealed in 2005 and replaced with a new rule that does not guarantee any protection of road-less areas. All too often, governments look at their forests as a standing asset that can be liquidated to solve financial problems.

The Kyoto protocol came into force in November 2004, with the aim of curbing air pollution. When Russia ratified the treaty, the accord had to be ratified by nations accounting for at least 55% of greenhouse emissions to become valid. The US had not joined, saying that the changes would be too costly to introduce and that the agreement was flawed because large developing countries, including India, China, and Brazil, were not required to meet specific targets for now. If this agreement is the best the world governments can do, there is no hope for preventing a coming environmental disaster.

Signs and Predictions of the Global Environmental Threat

As we noted in the beginning of this book, subtle changes that shape our future are often not noticed in the early stages by those who are going to be most impacted. In the case of the environmental disaster that has begun, recent polls show that **most people believe global warming will be a problem for future generations but not the current one. They are very, very wrong!** Already our environmental decline is impacting us. Here are some of the many signs that futurists and others tracking a potential global disaster have found today.

Pollutants Cause Huge Rise in Disease

The number of sufferers of brain diseases, including Alzheimer's and Parkinson's, has soared in the West in the last 20 years. This alarming rise, including figures showing that the dementia rates in men have trebled, is linked to increases in the levels of pesticides, industrial effluents, domestic waste, car exhausts, and other pollutants, says a report in the *Journal of Public Health*.

Arctic Warming at Twice the Global Rate

Global warming in the Arctic is happening now. The most comprehensive scientific report to date warns that the northern ice cap is warming at twice the global rate, and that this will lead to serious problems for the planet. According to the average climate models run by the scientists, the Arctic will lose 50% to 60% of its ice distribution by 2100. One of the five models predicts that by 2070, the Arctic will no longer have any ice in the summer.

Duller Foliage, Less Syrup

Make that planned trip to New England next fall. Climate experts predict a warming trend over the next century that could make New England's fall foliage less vibrant and the maple syrup industry practically nonexistent. New England temperatures are experiencing a warming trend that affects the region's sugar maples – trees that are vulnerable to climate change.

Soaring Global Warming Can't be Ruled Out

The earth may be more sensitive to global warming than previously thought. A research project tested thousands of climate models and found that some produced a world that warmed by a huge 11.5 degrees Celsius when atmospheric carbon dioxide concentration reached levels expected to be seen later this century. The extreme result was surprising because increase was far outside the 1.4 to 4.5 C. range predicted by the Intergovernmental Panel on Climate Change.

Keep in mind that climate change is more likely to follow an exponential rather than a linear path. Prepare to often hear statements like, "Wow; did that happen fast. Nobody predicted it would happen that fast."

2005 – the Warmest Year on Record

A weak El Nino and human-made, greenhouse gases caused 2005 to be the warmest year since records were being kept in the late 1800's. The prior warmest years were 1998, with 2002 and 2003 coming second and third, respectively. The year 2007 is predicted to be the hottest year ever.

Greenhouse Gas Is Turning Oceans Acidic

Increases in the greenhouse gases causing global warming are also threatening the world's oceans and leading to the complete disappearance of marine life from cod to coral reefs. British scientists warn that huge volumes of carbon dioxide, already known to be threatening the future of our planet by changing climate, are also rapidly turning the world's oceans acidic. As carbon dioxide dissolves in seawater, it puts an enormous array of marine life at risk. Ocean acidification may destroy much of the microscopic plankton at the base of the marine food pyramid, and have a domino effect right up the food chain from shellfish to major human food species such as cod.

Ocean Changes May Cool Europe

Changes to ocean currents in the Atlantic may cool

European weather within a few decades, scientists say. Researchers from the UK's National Oceanography Center report that currents derived from the Gulf Stream are weakening, bringing less heat north. They say that European political leaders need to plan for a future, which may be cooler than warmer

Climate Food Crisis to Deepen

Climate change threatens to put more people at risk for hunger over the next 50 years than previously thought, according to new research. Scientists say that expected shifts in rain patterns and temperatures over time could lead to an extra 50 million people struggling to get enough food.

Critical Danger Warning on Fish

Deep-sea fish species in the northern Atlantic are on the brink of extinction, new research suggests. Scientists studied five deep-water species, including hake and eel. Writing in the journal *Nature*, they say some populations have plummeted by 98% in a generation, meeting the definition of "critically endangered." Scientists and conservation bodies are pressing for a global moratorium on deep-sea fishing, which they regard as particularly destructive.

Amazon Rainforest Vanishing at Twice the Rate

Loggers are cutting down trees in the Amazon rainforest at twice the rate of previous estimates, according to a new analysis of satellite images in the region. Earlier attempts to gauge the scale of deforestation were not sensitive enough to spot the occurrence of selective logging – the cutting down of individual trees without clearing the surrounding forest.

Old Ways of Life Fade As Arctic Thaws

In Russia, 20% of which lies above the Arctic Circle, melting of the permafrost threatens the foundations of homes, factories, and pipelines. The problem is also happening in Alaska, and the effect is an engineering nightmare no one anticipated.

Antarctica Losing Ice to Oceans

A new space-based study of Antarctica shows that its ice sheet is shrinking. Researchers used satellites to plot changes in the earth's gravity in the Antarctic during the period of 2002 to 2005. Writing in the journal *Science*, they concluded that the continent is losing 152 cubic km of ice each year, with most loss in the west.

Deadly Effects of Future US Heat Waves

In 2003, a summer heat wave killed between 22,000 and 35,000 people in five European countries. Temperatures soared to 104 degrees Fahrenheit in Paris. London recorded its first triple digit Fahrenheit temperature in history. If a similar heat wave struck the United States, a new study suggests that the results would be disastrous. Researchers looked at what would happen if a comparable extreme heat event settled on five major US cities, learning that not only would the country experience massive blackouts, but also that thousands of people could die.

The Coming Resource Wars

In a major London address, British Defense Secretary John Reid warned that global climate change and dwindling natural resources are combining to increase the likelihood of violent conflict over land, water, and energy. Climate change, he indicated, "will make scarce resources, clean water, viable agricultural land even scarcer," and this will "make the emergence of violent conflict more rather than less likely."

World's Largest Rivers Drying Up

A United Nations investigation revealed that half of the planet's 500 biggest rivers are seriously depleted or polluted. The world's great rivers are drying up at an alarming rate, with devastating consequences for humanity, animals, and the future of the planet, according to the report.

Arctic Orcas Highly Contaminated

Killer whales have become the most contaminated mammals in the Arctic. New Norwegian research has found that killer whales, Orcas, have overtaken polar bears at the head of the toxic table. No other Artic mammals have ingested such a high concentration of hazardous man made chemicals.

"Nature Deficit Disorder"

The President's Council on Physical Fitness and Sports believes that problems of attention deficit disorder and early heart circulation problems in school-aged kids are part of a broader phenomenon. They are the real human costs of less time in Nature, and less Nature in general. In his recent book, **Last Child in the Woods**, Richard Louv claims that alienation from the natural world has given rise to a disorder he has termed "nature deficit disorder."

This disorder is not a verifiable medical condition. Rather, it is the diminished use of the senses, attention difficulties, and higher rates of physical and emotional illness. "Nature is often overlooked as a healing balm for emotional hardships in a child's life." Louv points out several studies that document the restorative power of Nature, and the importance it can play in mental development.

Climate Change Triggers Killer Fungus

Climate change is now believed to be triggering outbreaks of a fungus fatal to amphibians, wiping out entire frog populations, according to a study funded by the National Science Foundation (NSF). The rapid disappearance of amphibians has been raising ecological alarms since the 1980's, and climate change has been a prime suspect. Scientists working in Costa Rica report that chytrid, a skin fungus deadly to harlequin frogs, has found more favorable conditions – cooler days and warmer nights – in mountain cloud forests, where Earth's rising temperatures have led to more clouds. According to the Global Amphibian Assessment, nearly one-third of the world's approximately 6,000 species of frogs, toads, and salamanders face extinction.

People! Amphibians should be considered our canary in the coalmine, and they are dying!

Let's End On Some Good News

The rare good news is that most Americans believe that environmental pollution is a very serious threat to our country. And most scientists agree that the debate is no longer whether global warming is happening, but rather what we are going to do about it. Moreover, key skeptics of global warming among America's Evangelical Christians have made a 180-degree turn around. They now call for immediate action to curb emissions of the heat-trapping carbon dioxide gas that drives climate warming.

Furthermore, over 95% think both public and private sectors should do more about environmental degradation. Almost 90% of Americans support recycling efforts. Products in packaging that help consumers cut down on solid waste, pollution, and degradation of non-renewable resources are growing 30 times faster than all new packaged goods. More than half of Americans believe if a tradeoff were necessary between economic growth and the environment, the environment should be given the nod.

Green-labeling such as West Germany's Blue Angel work to assure that environmentally correct products will become important globally. Companies will be more constrained when using old or new technologies, particularly where wastewater and other environmental issue are concerned. In the European Community, ministers have set a goal of recovering 50% to 65% of the boxes, tins, and crates in which goods are transported and sold. A minimum of 25% and a maximum of 45% of all packaging must, as of the year 2000, be recycled. In seeking to move to a zero waste environment, the Germans are requiring manufacturers to be responsible for their products from cradle to grave.

The more educated, affluent, and politically and socially active will continue to see the environment as a top priority for government spending. More young people will become involved in environmental clean up projects, as well as choosing environmentally related careers. My late colleague, Willis Harmon, believed that there are pockets of indigenous people who can still teach us something about living with the land.

Those of us who can still hear Mother Nature's cries are ready to listen to her voice.

Epilogue
THE AMERICA 2000 PLAN

> They were not prepared for the storm today, so they have all been thrown into great confusion. They do not possess a compass, for ordinarily when the weather is fine; they follow the old tradition and steer by the stars in the sky, without making serious mistakes regarding their direction. This is what we call "depending on heaven for existence."
>
> But now they have run into this bad weather so they have nothing to rely upon. It is not that they don't want to do well, only they do not know the direction and so the further they go the more mistakes they make.

Travels of Lao Can, by Liu E
Beijing, China 1905

I spent years researching this book, and now that I have finished, some thoughts and feelings come up that I would like to share. First, I feel like the Israeli people must have felt in 1948 when Israel became an independent nation. Newsreels showed the people's joy and sense of accomplishment as they danced and sang throughout the night. But while they were partying, they were very aware that the huge armies of seven Arab nations were poised to attack the next day, intending to destroy them and their newly created nation.

Recently, I received a letter from one of the good guys, David Horowitz, president and founder of the Center for the Study of Popular Culture. He was asking for financial help to fight off attacks from a coalition of the radical left including the ACLU, the Modern Language Association, The American Federation of Teachers, the National Education Association, and others you would expect to find at an anti-war rally.

This radical coalition, rather than competing in the world of ideas, has chosen to dedicate their deep pockets to a lawsuit campaign to stop Horowitz from exposing their negative agenda.

The McCarthy-type blacklist they've created continues to kill academic freedom on our campuses and in the media. As the stand-up comedian line goes, "Is their anyone out there I haven't insulted?" I expect that both those on the Left and Right fringes outed in this book will have their fragile egos bruised by the truth.

I'm not afraid of these bullies, because there will always be those who challenge my thoughts. Though the Hindu goddess Kalama wears a necklace of skulls surrounding her neck and is feared for her evil ways, I say, "Come on Kalama, let's see what you've got next!" Eventually, truth wins over lies.

As for the lost generation, until the addict acknowledges he has a problem, recovery can't begin. An addiction to a belief system is as hard to break as one to drugs. The addict remains the prisoner of the drug pusher who supplies him with shit. Let me share a real world lesson that I learned about being willing to challenge closely held belief systems.

When I was in college, I took a course in the Philosophy of Science with a great professor named Lalumia. As he talked about the way science evolved from the dawn of man, I began to think of him as a soul mate. I became so involved in the flow of his logic that I often guessed the next word out of this man's mouth.

By the last day of class, we had reached modern times in the evolution of the Western world's scientific thought. Lalumia then introduced his next brief lecture about Eastern science. When he mentioned levitation in the lecture, I let out a too-audiable "ugh." Surprised, Lalumia asked me to come to his office after class. "Barry, what was that about?" he asked. He knew how much I enjoyed his class, but when he started to talk about irrational beliefs like levitation, I just lost it.

Lalumia then asked me to close the door, which I did. He sat on a table in his office and told me he was going to levitate before me, but under was one condition. I had to assure him that if I saw him levitate I would believe my eyes, and not think it was a trick or some illusion. I told him that knowing the laws of gravity, I believed it would have to be a trick, but I was still eager to see him levitate. Lalumia got off the table, and said something I never forgot.

Barry you have one of the best rational minds I've come in contact with, but you can never close your belief system completely. If you don't leave a small opening for the unexpected, you may miss something very special, something experiential that defies your ingrained beliefs, just as you missed this opportunity to see me levitate.

I tell the story of my closed logic trap in the hopes that you will also learn Lalumia's lesson. Leave an opening in the surety of your beliefs system, in order to allow the light of heartfelt truth – what you can feel at a gut level – begin to dissolve the effects of years of negative conditioning.

For those ready to move on to recovery, my contributors and I have put together a few action steps that will head in the right direction. I wrote this book to bring my ideas to the social marketplace, and I'm looking for buyers who want to trade their ideas about policies to help get the world back on track. I look forward to hearing your thoughts about the following points, as covered in this book.

Lie 1. Diversity Benefits the Us
- Embrace the principle that our society and nation are comprised of individuals, families, and states, not diversity groups. Exclude race / ethnicity, gender, and age (after maturity, as defined by law) as criteria for admission to educational programs, recruiting members for organizations, hiring for employment, or consulting / contracting for products or services.
- Help people move as straightforwardly as possible toward the equality goals implied by the Constitution, as specified in equal-opportunity legislation.
- Implement appropriate programs, non-governmental when possible, governmental when necessary, to assist individuals based on their economic circumstances.
- Re-channel the efforts of the diversity industry and race / ethnicity / advanced-age-based programs in communities, through religious organizations, schools, and scholarship programs.

337

- Work with individuals to encourage pride, so they have the confidence to better themselves. Place allegiance to one or more diversity groups into a context of personal choice rather than societal obligation.
- Work to erase the untoward consequences of inappropriate bias. Reduce the unfair advantage that the diversity stigma has placed on successful people.

Lie 2. The Left Is Right

- Read Professor Stanley Fish's article "Save The World On Your Own Time" at all institutions of higher learning as a nationwide policy. Teachers should teach their subjects. They should not teach peace or war or freedom or diversity or uniformity or nationalism or anti-nationalism or any other agenda that might properly be taught by a political leader or a talk-show host.
- Of course, they should teach subjects, not urge commitments related to history or philosophy or literature or sociology. The only advocacy that should go on in the classroom is the advocacy that James Murphy identified as intellectual virtues – "thoroughness, perseverance, and intellectual honesty" – all components of the cardinal academic virtue of being "conscientious in the pursuit of truth."
- Focus on important philosophy, principles, and goals for the advancement of society and its constituents – national and individual security, freedom and opportunity, within reasonable laws and with appropriate responsibility.
- Optimize the extent to which various elements of society, individuals, communities, businesses, labor unions, religious organizations, government, and so forth can contribute by defining the extent to which each element leads, follows, and gets out of the way.
- Recast the paradigm of discourse to ask to what extent, rather than right or wrong, yes or no.
- Discuss a balanced view. What works and what doesn't? Avoid loaded us / them group labels such as conservative and liberal. Treat people as individuals.

338

- Develop pride in America's vision and accomplishments. Recognize that discussion of problems and opportunities needs such a perspective.
- Encourage individual thinking regarding individual situations / issues. Discourage "you belong to a group that supports us, therefore you support us" thinking, speaking, and acting.
- Channel the supposed passion for social programs into action for practical, non-governmental (when possible), defined goals with finite duration.

Lie 3. The Right Is Right
- Recognize and act on the notion that mixing religion and government in the United States undermines religious endeavors, governmental principles, and actions. Attempt to diffuse threats (to the nation) based on the enemies' characterization of US foreign policy as a threat to the enemies' religions.
- Redirect government from areas where it is not an effective leader to where it will be useful in advancing the country's agenda. Also, simplify government, governance, and the burdens thereof.
- Encourage people to allow room for discussion and improvement. Stop with the "with us or against us" choices.

Lie 4. The Un Is Not Unfair, and Other Arabian Fables
- Develop practical principles and points of view. For example, consider, people, peace, security, and opportunity first. Most people want these, for themselves and for those around them.
- Religions have common themes. The three major religions share much (including early prophets).
- There should be room – in any country – for dissimilar people. Geographic boundaries are impractical and undesirable, and even three-dimensional boundaries cannot work.

- Support groups such as Flame and David Horowitz's Freedom Center.

Lie 5. Economists and Other Pundits: Why the Experts are Missing It
- Develop a new "eco-nomics" to replace today's "e-con-omics."
- Focus on larger eco-systems – environment and energy, freedom and opportunity, societal and national survivability, personal, family, and community wellness, education and talent, business and government, and financial well being for individuals, business, and government.
- Make common sense projections and checkpoints. Where will we be 3, 10, 30, 100, 300, and 1000 years from now if society continues with business as usual? Where do we need to be? How can we close the gap?
- Develop eco-nomics to express and measure problems, provide a basis for debate, progress toward solutions, check that progress, and make corrections in the evolution of eco-nomics itself.
- Encourage consumers of e-con-omic information and projections to focus on the bigger-picture. Include statements regarding error and risk, like those utilized by science and business, so the data is useful in decision making.
- Encourage economists to rethink their focus. Devote more attention to the long-term big picture.
- Design new curriculum for economics and business education to jumpstart the process.

Lie 6. Government Is for the People
- Scrap the sham regulations for private lands that have been written by industry for its own benefits.
- Replace our currently inadequate laws with tough new forest practices laws that truly protect fish, water, wildlife, soil, and natural forest ecosystems. Make tough new laws apply to logging on both private and public lands, so timber

companies that already own lands can't degrade them further.

- Systematically review problems and opportunities for society and our nation. For each, decide to what extent government should take the lead, follow others' leads, or get out of the way. Be realistic. Gain a new sense of effectiveness. Government can be efficient in solving a problem. Perhaps one law and one agency can do it all. Simplify. The law often does not address real issues and opportunities. Agencies cannot carry out the ambiguous and complicated laws crafted with too much special interest input. Add the burden of under-funding and the dire consequences multiply.
- Differentiate between the government's charter to take the lead (e.g., national security) and the private sector's potential effectiveness.
- Tolerate multiple approaches. Think of a "laboratory of democracy" as the best way to achieve the best possible results.
- Rebalance government's vision between principles and goals as stated in the Declaration of Independence and some amendments to the Constitution. Process the law according to the original body of the Constitution, the amendments, and regulations.
- Debate, settle on, and use principles to guide governmental policy and individual expectations regarding Medicare, Social Security, and safety nets. Get beyond approaches based on unsustainable expectations, the "train wreck is coming" scare tactics, and "tweak the formula" experiments.
- Systematically review the laws now on the books. Update or eliminate outdated material. Add, as appropriate, "sunset" provisions that force review of laws and allow expiration if not re-authorized. Do the same for regulations.
- Clarify the role of report language used by Congress to draft laws, as well as "signing memoranda" written in by the Presidents. Currently, branches of the government use

341

them to add to or limit the respective statements that are supposed to stand on their own as law.

- Clarify governmental roles regarding regulation, service, and "bully pulpit." Where regulation is appropriate, provide service so that people and organizations can cope with the regulation.
- Simplify income taxes. Estimates put the preparation of Federal income tax at 6,000,000,000 hours of people's time per year, costs at more than $100,000,000,000 per year, and estimates that this generates more than 1%of GDP. This is an obvious waste for the people who pay the service fees and a tax on the competitiveness of American business.
- Establish, both beyond and in government, effective advocacy goals (e.g., simplicity) that satisfy general needs / wants and have no political constituency.
- Consolidate redundant or overlapping governmental programs in all levels of government.
- Use bold vision and vigorous debate and action to tackle the truly non-sustainable programs, such as Medicare.
- Improve budgeting. Amend the US Constitution to provide for a presidential line-item veto like the veto used by the governors of 40 states.
- Mandate, especially at the state level, but also at the Federal and local levels, control of expenditures so as not to exceed proven revenues unless approved by a super-majority. For example, earn revenue during year X, count that revenue during year X+1, and limit expenditures for year X+2 to that proven revenue figure for year X.
- Attract effective, sensible people to run for and hold office. Explore and perhaps adopt more public financing of political campaigns.
- Stop blaming bureaucrats for things over which they have no control. For example, IRS bureaucrats may do some untoward things, but they have no direct say in tax laws. The key players for setting those laws are in Congress, the Treasury Department, the President's office, the Office of Management and Budget, and lobbyists … not the IRS.

Lie 7. Mass, Not Mess, Immigration
- Cut the numbers of immigrants.
- Allow in only those that provide skills in short supply in America.
- Permit no amnesty or mass guest worker program.
- Protect wages.
- Upgrade Interior Department enforcement and enforce employer penalties.
- Stop special interest abuse.
- Stop the NAFTA superhighway running through the heart of our country from Laredo, Texas to the Canadian border, as it poses a threat to our sovereignty, security, and prosperity.
- Secure the borders and international transportation systems from most illegal migration.
- Implement a plan whereby some current illegal immigrants can earn legal status with amnesty and without fear, based on reasonable criteria such as learning English and paying for back taxes, Social Security, and Medicare.
- Announce an amnesty period for illegal immigrants and deport later illegals. Enact national time limits on benefits for illegal immigrants.
- Have the Federal government implement and fund all of the above.
- Have the Federal government reimburse states, counties, and cities for the cost of education and healthcare for illegal immigrants.
- Develop a consensus program for the long term.
- Aim for assimilation of all immigrants into an evolving American culture.
- Return to using English as a requirement for citizenship, and in government-sponsored education, voting, and other interactions with government. Shift the burdens of facilitating other lingual participation to the communities or charity-sponsored organizations that want to preserve their languages.
- Offer programs to use the talents of multilingual people, immigrants, and non-immigrants, for governmental

functions such as 911 calls, interaction with other governments, to interpret foreign language news, and to broadcast America's message abroad.

- Facilitate legal travel. Check visitor visas to keep their stay within legal limits.
- Encourage private sector "foreign aid" to assist illegal immigrant-generating countries in becoming more attractive to their citizens.
- Tighten the Canadian / US border to prevent human smuggling by biker and Chinese gangs and through the Indian reservations that straddle the border in Ontario and Quebec.
- Get tough with China and Mexico about taking back their citizens caught trying to sneak into the US.
- Support groups like FAIR and the Minute Man Project.

Lie 8. Justice Is Just

- Create remedies to frivolous lawsuits. Enact legislation that requires trial lawyers to obtain permission before suing on a person's "behalf." In other words, no class action suits unless attorneys get written consent from the so-called injured parties.
- Support Alternative Disputes Resolutions, or ADR, which would go a long way to unclogging the courts. Lincoln said, "avoid litigation – negotiate with your neighbor whenever possible." ADR is being written into many contracts in recent years as a huge time and money saver when disagreements arise.
- Consider limiting punitive damages for pain and suffering to something like three times physical damages. All fines and sentences in criminal law are limited in some fashion, aren't they? Punitive damages were originally intended to punish malicious willful intent to harm. Today plaintiff attorneys regularly use it as an instrument of extortion to force settlements whether there is guilt on the part of the defendant or not.
- Limit attorney's fees to a maximum of 15% if a case is settled within 30 or 60 days.

- Do away with the contingency fee system for lawyers all together. Lawyers try to justify these fees by claiming that they draw competent attorneys to risky cases so as to give the common man access to our courts. You would think that these were hollowed lineages dating back to the Magna Carta. Actually, in Europe to this day, contingency fees are considered a corrupting influence precisely because they inflate the costs of litigation and make the lawyer himself a party to the suit. How can justice be the intended goal with the money clouding all issues? "If you sue and lose, you pay," works in the rest of the civilized world, including England, where there were only 200 product liability lawsuits last year, compared to 70,000 in the US.
- Why must a person who is sued lose their entire life's savings, regardless of guilt or innocence, in an effort to defend them self? Often, they never recover from this disruption and distraction in their lives. But they should be due court and legal costs at the very least, if proven not guilty. It's a matter of justice.
- Thomas Jefferson said that the secret to a successful democracy is courage. In the case of seeing justice rather than greed in our civil justice system, he undoubtedly meant the courage to make people whole, not rich by outrageous damage awards in our civil justice courts. We need the courage to work for reasonable tort reform. Contact your legislator and tell him or her that reform is needed.
- On a broader level, a number of public policy measures should be encouraged. Some states are taking steps to tighten enforcement of jury participation laws and to make jury duty less time consuming. According to the American Legislative Exchange Council, 50% of America's courts have now adopted the "One Day, One Trial" system. Under this plan, if a potential juror is not seated on a jury the day they report, they are dismissed. This system makes it easier for all to serve by reducing the number of missed workdays. With that in mind, businesses need to

implement policies to make it easier for their employees to serve on juries when called.

- Thank our president, George W. Bush, for targeting the serious misuse of our civil justice system through meritless lawsuits.
- Enact sensible laws governing judges who excuse themselves or are removed from cases.
- Reconsider the balance between backward-looking justice (punishment) and forward-looking justice (prevention).
- Prevent or prepare to live with the unintended consequences of our current trends toward secondary prosecutions of witnesses, for such actions as misleading an investigation or perjury, and actions of contempt against journalists for refusing to divulge sources. Unintended consequences may include witnesses refusing to cooperate or giving responses in restricted self-protected form, such as "as best I recall at this moment ..." Journalists may withhold stories or refuse to help their superiors make good decisions about running material, etc.
- The 2005 Class Action Fairness Act will stop the venue shopping by plaintiff's attorneys. A case will be tried only in the county where the wrongdoing took place, or the home city of the defendant. Attorneys will not be able to seek out remote venues in small towns where naïve juries may rule against defendants or dispense outlandish sums in punitive damages.
- Another remedy being considered by several state legislators would require that a trial lawyer get permission from the so-called injured party before he or she can sue on their behalf. In other words, no class action suits unless written consent is received from the so-called injured parties.
- Return to the fundamentals.
- Legislators, executives, and the electorate must change the application of laws not working through state remedies, like the initiative processes.
- Install public financing for campaigns for judgeships.
- Prevent the use of slander and libel laws, which are being

346

used to stifle criticism of people and groups that are undermining societal values through lawsuits rather then debating questionable activities.

Lie 9. Media Smear and Malice

Remember the *Elements of Journalism?* Journalism's first obligation is to the truth. Its first loyalty is to citizens. Its essence is a discipline of verification. Its practitioners must maintain an independence from those they cover. It must serve as an independent monitor of power. It must provide a public forum for public criticism and compromise. It must strive to make the significant issues interesting and relevant. It must keep the news comprehensive and proportional.

- Encourage people to develop skills to think, analyze, and then apply these skills to the news. Augment educational curricula to include and emphasize thinking skills and tools.
- Demand or develop provable news services. There should be a substantial market for such a service. Consider launching this service via the Internet.
- Include in factual reporting no statements, adjectives, or adverbs that the journalist cannot substantiate.
- Clearly distinguish editorials, other opinion, entertainment, and calls to action from news.
- State and accept input about policies regarding coverage delivered via the service.
- Institute a new set of awards for news-reporting entities with the awards emphasizing provable accuracy.
- Encourage people to realize that news services are businesses that compete for attention and money, to consider the implications of the same, and to move business elsewhere when appropriate.
- Support media watchdog groups like CAMERA.

Lie 10. Man Is Listening to Mother Nature
- Realize that current science and technology do not provide a solution for long-term sustainability of humanity.
- Promote a slow-down in growth of energy-using activity.

347

Buy time, in hopes that a long-term future can be assured.

- Learn from California, where energy consumption per person has been essentially constant for decades. During the same period, energy consumption per person for the rest of the United States has grown steadily.
- Institute programs that limit human population growth, limit energy consumption, preserve forests, preserve fish populations, etc.
- Accelerate research toward new long-term energy sources, such as ocean waves and controlled fusion.
- Support groups like the Earth Policy Institute, The Nature Conservancy, World Watch Institute, Earth Justice, World Wildlife Fund, The Ocean Conservancy, Sea Turtle Restoration Project, and other quality environmental organizations.

End Notes

Introduction
PBS Nova, "Magnetic Storm", PBS.org, October 2003

Chapter 1 – DIVERSITY BENEFITS THE US
Morano, Marc," Jessie Jackson Accused of "Racketeering " by Top Black Businessman," CNSNews. Com, 22 October 2001

National Association of Scholars, "Is Campus Racial Diversity Correlated with Educational Benefits? " Press Release, 4 April 2001

McWhorter, John, "The Gift of Competition", American Enterprise, 12 December 2000, Vol 11, Issue 8

The Hippie Archives, "A Trip Through the Sixties – The Black Power Movement", www.hippy.com / php/article

Ibid; " Black Panther Party Platform and Program (1966)
Ibid; The Basis of Black Power 27 March 2003

Tapestry: The Institute for Philosophy, Religion, and the Life Sciences, Inc ' Paradigm Shift at the Business Level: Racial Diversity in America, www. Tapestryweb.org/ paradigmbusiness.html, 18 March 2003
Ibid: Minorities and the Television Industry"
Ibid. How Paradigms and Stories Change: Racial Diversity in America

National Center for Policy Analysis, "Some Schools Achieve Dramatic Improvements in Low- Income Students' Test scores Idea House, www.ncpa.org/pi/edu/pd051499g.html

Ibid, " Minorities Will Soon Flock To Campuses, But Will They Succeed?" 18 March 2003

Ibid. " Educators Denounce Double Standards for Schools
Ibid. " NAACP Wants New College Tests"
Ibid; "Trying To Boost Black Students' Performance (July, 1996)

Colombo, Allan B, "Legal Discrimination For Racial Diversity
(Minorities') Sake", www.tpromo.com/gk, 30 March 2001

Miller, John J. et al, " Not Speaking Our Language", National
Review Online, 23 April 2001

Franklin, Stephen, "EEOC seeks to protect undocumented,"
Chicago Tribune, 26 October 1999

Applebome, Peter, "Minorities Falling Behind In Student
Achievement", New York Times, 29 December 1996

Beinart, Peter, "Blind Spot," New Republic, 00286583, 2 March
2003, Vol 228, Issue 4

Ibid; Cottle, Michelle, "Black Power" 17 February 2003, Vol 228
Issue 6

Pell, Terence, "No: "Don't let university illegally engineer racial
mix," Detroit News, December 17,2000

Ryan, Leslie, et al: "Debate on diversity" Electronic Media, 23
March 1998 Vol 17 Issue 13, p1, 2p, 4c

Ash, Philip, " The Implications of the Civil Rights of 1964 For
Psychological Assessment in Industry, " American Psychologist 6
(1966)

Mooney, Chase, Civil Rights Movement." Encyclopedia
Americana, 1996 edition.

The Associated Press, "Ford settles harassment case Chicago,"
9 August 1999

White, Thomas " Courts Confront "Diversity", The Dartmouth

Review, 18 March 2003, Issue 8308

Real People for Real Change, " Al Sharpton's Skeleton Closet "
30 May 2005 supporting sources: Grant, Tracy" Fire & Brimstone"
Black Issues Book Review, and Sep/Oct 2002
"80s Icon Al Sharpton, in the 1980s website, www.80s.com
(ongoing, quoted 2003)

Adversity. Net Case 33: "Boeing Reverse Discrimination, " 23
March 2003 articles and other public documents used in compiling
Case 33: Boeing Press Release 04/15/99
            Ibid 01/22/99
            Topeka Capital Journal 05/24/99
            KOMO TV news story 30/09/99
            Naples Daily News 11/20/99
            Seattle Times 05/24/02

            Ibid; Stanley Holmes 01/22/99
            Ibid; 01/23/99
            Ibid; 05/26/99
            Ibid David Kravets, AP 11/27/02
            Ibid James Grimaldi, 11/19/99
            Ibid 1/17/02
            Ofgang, Kenneth, " Ninth Circuit Throws Out Boeing
Class Action Settlement as Unfair, Metropolitan News-
Enterprise 11/27/02

            Independent Woman's Forum, "The Labor
Department Speaks Softly but Carries a Big Lawsuit", – Fall
2000
            Rainbow/ Push Press Release, 9/11/98
            Claiborne, William, "Jackson's Fundraising Methods
Spur Questions – Washington Post, 3/27/01
            LA Times " When Jackson Presses, Funds Tend to
Follow, -03/13/01
            Chicago Tribune, "PUSH chief scolds firms, accepts
their gifts, 08/07/99
            Detroit News, "Diversity training's new focus changes
the way business is done, -June 2000

Anti- CAIR, "CAIR Libel Suit Against Anti-CAIR's Andrew Whitehead Dismissed" 5/5/2006

Pipes, Daniel, "Moderate' friends of terror " New York Post 22 April 2002

CAIR- NET, " Partial list of CAIR's work with local state and federal law enforcement authorities/6/06

Morel, Lucas " Jessie Jackson Finds Wall Street Bullish on Diversity, The Lima News, 29 January 1998

Metcalf Geoff interviews "Shakedown " author Ken Timmerman "Unmasking Jessie Jackson" WorldNetDaily 21/11/2006

Chapter 2 – THE LEFT IS RIGHT

Betsch, Michael, " Left-Wing Hates America," CNSNEWS.COM, 07 November 2002

The Museum of Left Lunacy," Celebrity / Hollywood Quotes"
    Ben Affleck in a speech to the People for the American Way, in an excerpt shown on MSNBC's Scarborough Country

    Tim Robbins –CBS Late Late Show, 30 October 2005, CBS bleeped the F-word
    Susan Sarandon at an anti-Iraq war protest in Washington DC 26 October, 2005

Horowitz David, " The Left Should Look in the Mirror" News Abroad, 17 May 2002

Ibid; "The Vast Left-Wing Conspiracy'" Salon.com 17, October 2005

Ibid "Ward Churchill quote" letter from David Horowitz, 30 December 2005

Ibid "Attacking the Center's National campaign and me for Academic Freedom," letter from Horowitz dated 5 May 2006

Ibid " The Political Assault On America's Universities

Op-cid Hippyland Archives, " Young Lords Party': 13 – Point Program and Platform
Ibid "Claiming Turf in Berkeley" (1968)
Ibid " Letter From an American Terrorist" (1970)
Ibid " To My Black Brothers in Vietnam " (1970)

National Coalition to Abolish the Death Penalty website " Affiliate Links " 13 April 2006

Roth Hank, "Battleground The Paradox of Left Intolerance," pnews. org, 29, October 2003

Malkin, Michelle, " The party of Maxine Waters", TownHall.com 21 August 2000

Kaplan, Jonathan, "Former Conyers aides press ethics complaints", The Hill, 06 April 2006

Connelly, Ward, Civil Rights Act, Title VI, Sec. 601, letter, 27 August 2004

Kravets, David, "Court Rejects "Friends" Trash Talk Case", Associated Press, 20, April 2006

ADL," End the Hypocrisy'" mailer
Ibid; "American Organizations that Support Terrorist Groups

Kaplan, Joel, "Calling on the Presbyterian Church (USA) to revoke three outrageous declarations, " B'nai B'rith letter
Mariaschin, Daniel, " letter" B'nai B'rith Foundation of the US, 30 June 2005

Bronfman, Edgar, "National Campaign to: Let Our Students Go!"
Hillel: The Foundation for Jewish Campus Life letter

Orland, David, "Writing Us Off", Boundless Webzine, 2001

Bayefsky, Anne, "Human Rights Watch Coverup", Jerusalem Post, 13 April 2004

Lloyd, Rees, "Legion defends Boy Scouts, fights ACLU," The American Legion Magazine

Cadmus, Thomas, " Friends of Terrorists, Foes of Boy Scouts,' The American Legion Guest Editorial, 25 May 2005

Johnson, Ben "Hollywood Hate Group assaults Bush, "(Ed Asner, Danny Glover, Woody Harrelson, Rob Reiner FrontPageMag.Com 12 July 2004

Discoverthenetwork, "History Moveon", 19 April 2006

Oaks, Phil, "The Imaginary "Right" of the Ideological Left," 29 October, 2003

Wheatcroft, Geoffrey, "The Defeat of the Left," The Atlantic Monthly, October 2002.

ACLU website" About Us"

Windschuttle, Keith, "The hypocrisy of Noam Chomsky'" The New Criterion, 21, May 2003

Morse, Chuck, "Communist Sympathies of Amnesty International'" City Metro Enterprises 29 October, 2003
Ibid "Who is Right Wing in America? 13 January 2004

Dissecting Leftist "Exit exams rightly expose grade inflation as a cruel hoax", dissectleft.blogspot.com 30, October 2003
Ibid 'Elsewhere Mike Tremoglie quote" 29, October 2003
Ibid " Arlene Peck quote " 27, October, 2003

May, Clifford, "Our Man in Niger", National Review Online, 12 July 2004

Al-Qioushi, Ahmad, " Dissident Arab Gets the Treatment', FrontPagemagazine.com, 6 January 2005

Michael Smith "letter to Ahmad Al-Qioushi, " Wagon boy's Garage blog 24 April 2005

Metcalf Geoff interviews "Shakedown " author Ken Timmerman "Unmasking Jessie Jackson" WorldNetDaily 21/11/2006

Higgins, Andrew, " Anti Americans on the March", The Wall Street Journal, December 9.2006

Chapter 3 – THE RIGHT IS RIGHT
Fredson, Peter, "Vast Right Wing Conspiracy, " SEB Guest Post, 17 March 2005

People for the American Way, "Right –Wing Religious McCarthyism, 17 October 2005
Ibid; "Right Wing Organizations Cato Institute", 13 January 2004
Ibid; Heritage Foundation
Ibid; Traditional Values Coalition
Ibid; National Right to Life Committee
Ibid; Christian Coalition
Ibid; "Quotes from Louis Sheldon," February 2003

Myers, PZ "Bush endorses Intelligent Design creationism," 2 August
2005

Foxman, Abraham, "ADL Condemns Southern Baptist Leader's Comparison of Judaism to a "Deadly Tumor", ADL 19 June 2003
Ibid " racist skinhead movement", June 2006

Compton, Philip, "Assault Weapons Are Used in attacks On Law Officers", The Ledger, 12 January 2004

LifeWay News, "SBC leaders voice stand on school prayer," September 2000

Stop the NRA.com, One-Dealer Guns, Five Years, and 2,370 Guns Linked to Crimes 13 January 2004
Ibid "Twisted Logic"
Ibid, "Not for Animal Hunters, for People Hunters"
Ibid "See what NRA leaders have to say 12 January 2004
Ibid " NRA Sponsors Water Pollution" 9 January 2004

St. Petersburg Times, "Free ranges" A Times Editorial, 11 January 2004

Main, Frank, Gun –safety group names 4 area stores', Chicago Sun Times 13 January 2004

AARP Bulletin, "Guess Who Are the Big Gun Owners Now?" February 2004

Miller, Steven, "The New Right Wing Agenda", 13 June 2003

Morris, David, "Shock Troops of the Right Wing," AlterNet. Org 7 November 2003

Le Beau, Bryan, " The Political Mobilization of the New Christian Right' Creighton University 25 February 2004

Earth link- Main News, "Air Force Revises Guidelines on Religion" Associated Press, 9 February 2006

NRA, "Barnes given "A" Rating by NRA".
Votebarnes.org/NRA_article.htm 2 /18/04

Virtanen, Timo, "Skinhead Violence" Youth, Racist Violence and anti –racist response in the Nordic countries   20/October 2005

Franken, Al, "Lies And The Lying Liars Who Tell Them: A Fair And Balanced Look At The Right " Dutton September 2003

Chapter 4 – THE UN IS NOT UNFAIR, AND OTHER ARABIAN FABLES

FACTS &LOGIC ABOUT THE MIDDLE EAST (FLAME), "Arabian Fables (1) How the Arabs soften up the world with fanciful myths"

Ibid; "Peace in the Holy Land –Does Israelis "intransigence " stand in the way"
Ibid; "Arabian Fables (11) more fanciful Arab myths to sway world opinion
Ibid ; "Suicide Bombers in Israel-What Do They Really Want"
Ibid; "The Big Lie (1) Are the occupied territories" really occupied territories?
Ibid; "The Myth of "Settlements' are the" root cause" of violence in the Middle East? "
Ibid; "Jerusalem (1) –whose "holy city" –is it?"
Ibid; "The UN and Israel"
Ibid;" Racism in the Islamic World",
Dershowitz, Alan; "Terror Stings its Pal, the UN," Flame, 27 August 2003

Phillips, Howard, Out of the United Nations, letter, The Conservative Caucus

Solomon, Jay, " US Targets Hezbollah Funds", The Wall Street Journal, 24, April 2006

B'nai B'rith, letter, 26 July 2004

Lederer, Edith, "Most Nations back Annan in oil-for-food scandal", 3 December 2004

Sauerbrey, Ellen, "The UN Hates the United States:" Human Events, 17 December 2001

Talon News, "Calls from Hill Get Louder for Annan oust", 9 December 2004

Melloan, George, " The UN Can't Be Reformed, But It Can Be Bypassed,"

Lowellsun.com, " Kofi Must Go", 1 December 2004

Hall, Randy, " Nevada Senator Joins Call For Annan to Reign from UN Post", 3 December 2004

Kincaid, Cliff, " The UN Pushes Global Taxes"

Freerepublic.com/focus/f-news, "Oil –for food probe: UN failures let Saddam pocket $10.2 billion, 10/11/2005.

Darwish, Nonie," The Great Hate", the article originally appeared in The Daily Telegraph

Our Arab "Buddies"... Right, "Arabic /Islamic/States voting records in both the US State Department and United Nations records," e-mail Rock 1V @ aol.com 25 April 2005

Houston Chronicle, "Oil- for- food probe: Un failures let Saddam pocket $10.2 billion 8 September 2005

Chapter 5 – ECONOMISTS AND OTHER PUNDITS: WHY THE EXPERTS ARE MISSING IT

Wallis and Roberts, Statistics: A New Approach, The Free Press of Glencoe, Inc, 1963

Barger, Howard, Money, Banking, and Public Policy, Rand Mc Nally Company, 1962

Commentary, "Economics in Decline," November, 1984

Chapter 6 – GOVERNMENT IS FOR THE PEOPLE

Sharp, Jack et al "Guess What Organization of More Than 500 Employees This Is," Capitol Hill Blue

Christian Coalition of America, "Senate score 2001", www.cc.org/senatesscore2001

Citizens Against Government Waste, "Pig Book", 2003
Ibid, 2005
Ibid, 2006
Ibid, "Porker Of The Month," February 2004
www.outdoorlife, "Where They Stand", Voters guide '02

National Rifle Association, "Project Vote Smart" 1/5/2006

TruthOrFiction.com, "Congressional Criminals?"
www.truthorfiction.com/rumors/c/congressional criminals.htm

Hsu, Spencer, "Waste in Katrina Response is Cited", Washington Post, 4 April 2006

Riedl, Brian, "Top 10 Examples of Government Waste," The Heritage Foundation, 26 April 2006
Ibid, "Examples of Government Waste, 10 March 2004

Shapiro, Michael, " Public Service: A Forgotten Concept?"
www.politicsnj.com

Libertarian Party Press Releases, "The Top Fifteen Stupidest Ways Politicians Are Wasting Our Money," Libertarian Party, 17 April 2001

Kucinich, Dennis," Forests and Logging on Public Lands", Kucinich for President, Inc, 1/15/2004

National Radio Project, "Public Lands Private Profits", Making Contact, 21 June 2000

Seattle Times, "Trading Away the West, " 16 October 1998

Americans for Democratic Action, ADA Ratings, vote-smart.org/issue_rating, 2/19/04

Bandow, Doug, "Shrinking the size of the Federal Government to Prevent Political Corruption, Opposing Viewpoints Resource Center, 10/20/2005

San Jose Mercury, "SJ plan to offer lifetime benefits," 14 November 2006

Chapter 7 – MASS, NOT MESS, IMMIGRATION
Hichens, Greg "Thank you Mexico", e-mail, 4/28/06

Stein, Daniel, letter, Federation For American Immigration Reform, (FAIR), October 2005
Ibid. , Immigration Report, November 2005
Ibid, February 2005
Ibid, December 2005/January 2006
Ibid, February 2004
Ibid, November, 2004
Ibid, December 2004/January 2005
Ibid, "Immigration Skyrocketing since 2000," News Release 25 November 2003
Cohen, D'Vera et al, "Nearly half of all kids in US are minorities, report says, " Washington Post

Terry, Don "Arizona Court Strikes Down Law Requiring English Use'" New York Times, 29 April 1998

Zapler, Mike 'Another Busy Day in Downtown SJ As Crowd Converges for Festivities,' Mercury News

Davis, Aaron et al, "Reconstruction of hurricane areas luring workers from other countries," Mercury News 23 October 2005

Schwartzenegger, Arnold," No immigration reform until borders are secure for years" e-mail 5/52006

Malkin, Michelle "American Flag Comes Second" e-mail 29 March 2006

Garcia, Edwin, "Mexico's fox to sign drug-legalization law", Knight Ridder

Los Angles Times "Thank You Mexico", Greg Hichens e-mail 4/28/2006

Bresnahan, David "e-mail " NewsWithViews.com" April 1,2006

Free Republic, "Myths and Half- Truths about Illegal Immigration," web posted 6/20 /2001

Center for Immigration Studies, 'Illegal Immigration", 2/5/2004

Delaney, Joan "Asian Organized Crime Thriving in Canada", The Epoch Times, December 7-13, 2006

Mujica, Mauro, "Is this the America you want" letter 12/18/06

Chapter 8 – JUSTICE IS JUST
RAND, " RAND STUDY SHOWS "ASBESTOS CLAIMS RISE DRAMATICALLY", RAND News Release, 25 September 2002

Schmitt, Gary, "International Criminal Court", New American Century, 2 January 2001

Alschuler, Albert, "What's good about plea bargaining?" WBGH Frontline, 5/11/2006

Sneider, Jaime, "Statistics Fail Activists", Columbia Daily Spectator, 6 February 2001

Jasper, William, "Judicial Usurpation, " New American 6 January 1997

PR Newswire Association, Inc, " ATRA Cites 13 "Judicial Hellholes in New 2003 Report Identifies courts Where" Equal Justice Under Law " is Elusive," 2/4/2004

Velvel, Lawrence, " A Rebuke of Modern Judicial Practices," Tulane link. Com

Hattiesburgamerican.com, "Our judicial system must be reformed," Opinion 5 January 2003

Roberts, Paul, "Bring back Justice", townhall.com, 7 February 2001

Francis, Samuel, "Judicial Tyranny", New American, 14 April 1997

Daily Policy Digest, " California's Three Strikes Law Works, " National Center For Policy Analysis, 7 October 2002

Victims And Citizens Against Crime, "Victims Need Everyone's Help", 2/4/2004

Chapter 9 – MEDIA SMEAR AND MALICE

Henkin, Yagil, "Urban Warfare and the Lessons of Jenin, Azure, Issue #15, 2/10 /2003

Baker, Brent, " How to Identify Media Bias," fairpress.org, 5/15/2006

UCLA News, " Media Bias is Real, Finds UCLA Political Scientist",

The Truth about Iraq, "Media Bias", thetruthaboutiraq.org,

The Media Research Center, 'Media Bias", www.gargaro.com, CyberAlert, " Tracking Liberal Media Bias", Media Research Center", 12 May 2006
Ibid, 'MSNBC Likens Bush to Nixon, Watergate   20 October 2005
Ibid, " Media Bias Basics', 29 January 2004
Ibid, " "TV's Bad News Brigade," 14 October 2005

Gross, Tom, ' Anti- Semitism at; 'Le Monde' and Beyond, '" The Wall Street Journal Europe, 2 June 2005

Honest Reporting.com, "AP's Circle Dance", Media Critiques 27
September   2005
Ibid, "Israel in the Australian Media, " Special Reports, 10 October
2005
Ibid, 'BBC: Living in a Bubble'' 21 June 2004
Ibid, "Synagogue Desecrations", 20 October 2005

Akdart.com, "Specific examples of biased news coverage,'"
5/15/2006

Dissectingleft.blogspot.com, " Maybe a second Boston Tea Party
is needed, " 28 October 2003

Schrag, Peter,' "Is Doing the Right Thing Wrong", Columbia
Journalism Review 5/5/2006

Mc Chesney et al, The "Left- Wing Media< " Monthly Review,
June 2003

Wikipedia.org, Jayson Blair, 12/8/06

Metro," When First We Practice to Deceive," December 6-12,2006

Horowitz, David, Freedom Center letter, October 31,2006

Chapter 10 – MAN IS LISTENING TO MOTHER NATURE
National Oceanic and Atmospheric Administration, "Co Hits
Record Levels", 3/20/2004

Woodard, Colin, " State of the Oceans," Nature Conservancy, Fall
2004

Inhofe, James, "Evidence is under whelming," USA Today
Editorial /Opinion, 6 /14/2005

Brown, Lester et al, "State of the World", Worldwatch Institute
Reports, 1998-2003

Schmidt et al, "Inhofe and Crichton: Together at Last!" RealClimate.org, 28 September 2005

Earth Justice, "2006 Docket", earthjustice.org, 2006

Radioproject.org, " Public Lands, Private Profits: Logging in US National Forests," 1/15/2004

Kluger, Jeffrey, "The Tipping Point"' Time, 3 April 2006

Roberts, Carter, World Wildlife Fund Letter, 2006

Global Development Briefing, "Invasive Species"' The Development Executive Group, 3/23/2006

Cover Story, " Salmon," Metro Silicon Valley, May 10-16 2006

Seattle Times, "Trading Away the West,"

Earth Policy Institute, Plan B2.0 letter, 2006

Blue Planet, "Will the Class of 2003 Save the Cod"' The Ocean Conservancy, winter/spring 2006

INDEX

367

368

369

370

371

375

Printed in the United States
79136LV00006B/79-249